Kaplan Publishing are constantly fi
ways to make a difference to your s
exciting online resources really do
different to students looking for exam success.

This book comes with free MyKaplan online resources so that
you can study anytime, anywhere. This free online resource is
not sold separately and is included in the price of the book.

Having purchased this book, you have access to the following online study materials:

CONTENT	ACCA (including FFA,FAB,FMA)		FIA (excluding FFA,FAB,FMA)	
	Text	Kit	Text	Kit
iPaper version of the book	✓	✓	✓	✓
Interactive electronic version of the book	✓			
Check Your Understanding Test with instant answers	✓			
Material updates	✓	✓	✓	✓
Latest official ACCA exam questions*		✓		
Extra question assistance using the signpost icon**		✓		
Timed questions with an online tutor debrief using clock icon*		✓		
Interim assessment including questions and answers	✓		✓	
Technical answers	✓	✓	✓	✓

* Excludes F1, F2, F3, F4, FAB, FMA and FFA; for all other papers includes a selection of questions, as released by ACCA
** For ACCA P1-P7 only

How to access your online resources

Kaplan Financial students will already have a MyKaplan account and these extra resources will be available to
you online. You do not need to register again, as this process was completed when you enrolled. If you are having
problems accessing online materials, please ask your course administrator.

If you are already a registered MyKaplan user go to www.MyKaplan.co.uk and log in. Select the 'add a book' feature
and enter the ISBN number of this book and the unique pass key at the bottom of this card. Then click 'finished' or
'add another book'. You may add as many books as you have purchased from this screen.

If you purchased through Kaplan Flexible Learning or via the Kaplan Publishing website you will automatically receive
an e-mail invitation to MyKaplan. Please register your details using this email to gain access to your content. If you do
not receive the e-mail or book content, please contact Kaplan Flexible Learning.

If you are a new MyKaplan user register at www.MyKaplan.co.uk and click on the link contained in the email we sent
you to activate your account. Then select the 'add a book' feature, enter the ISBN number of this book and the unique
pass key at the bottom of this card. Then click 'finished' or 'add another book'.

Your Code and Information

This code can only be used once for the registration of one book online. This registration and your online content will
expire when the final sittings for the examinations covered by this book have taken place. Please allow one hour from
the time you submit your book details for us to process your request.

Please scratch the film to access your MyKaplan code.

Please be aware that this code is case-sensitive and you will need to include the dashes
within the passcode, but not when entering the ISBN. For further technical support,
please visit www.MyKaplan.co.uk

ACCA

Paper F3

and

FIA

Diploma in Accounting and Business

Financial Accounting (FA/FFA)

Complete Text

British library cataloguing-in-publication data

A catalogue record for this book is available from the British Library.

Published by:
Kaplan Publishing UK
Unit 2 The Business Centre
Molly Millars Lane
Wokingham
Berkshire
RG41 2QZ

ISBN 978-1-78415-674-9

© Kaplan Financial Limited, 2016

Printed and bound in Great Britain.

Acknowledgements

We are grateful to the Association of Chartered Certified Accountants and the Chartered Institute of Management Accountants for permission to reproduce past examination questions. The answers have been prepared by Kaplan Publishing.

Contents

Paper Introduction

How to Use the Materials

These Kaplan Publishing learning materials have been carefully designed to make your learning experience as easy as possible and to give you the best chances of success in your examinations.

The product range contains a number of features to help you in the study process. They include:

(1) Detailed study guide and syllabus objectives

(2) Description of the examination

(3) Study skills and revision guidance

(4) Complete text or essential text

(5) Question practice

The sections on the study guide, the syllabus objectives, the examination and study skills should all be read before you commence your studies. They are designed to familiarise you with the nature and content of the examination and give you tips on how to best to approach your learning.

The **complete text or essential text** comprises the main learning materials and gives guidance as to the importance of topics and where other related resources can be found. Each chapter includes:

- The **learning objectives** contained in each chapter, which have been carefully mapped to the examining body's own syllabus learning objectives or outcomes. You should use these to check you have a clear understanding of all the topics on which you might be assessed in the examination.

- The **chapter diagram** provides a visual reference for the content in the chapter, giving an overview of the topics and how they link together.

- The **content** for each topic area commences with a brief explanation or definition to put the topic into context before covering the topic in detail. You should follow your studying of the content with a review of the illustration/s. These are worked examples which will help you to understand better how to apply the content for the topic.

- **Test your understanding** sections provide an opportunity to assess your understanding of the key topics by applying what you have learned to short questions. Answers can be found at the back of each chapter.

- **Summary diagrams** complete each chapter to show the important links between topics and the overall content of the paper. These diagrams should be used to check that you have covered and understood the core topics before moving on.

- **Question practice** is provided at the back of each text.

Quality and accuracy are of the utmost importance to us so if you spot an error in any of our products, please send an email to mykaplanreporting@kaplan.com with full details, or follow the link to the feedback form in MyKaplan.

Our Quality Co-ordinator will work with our technical team to verify the error and take action to ensure it is corrected in future editions.

Icon Explanations

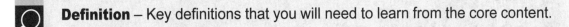 **Definition** – Key definitions that you will need to learn from the core content.

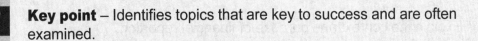 **Key point** – Identifies topics that are key to success and are often examined.

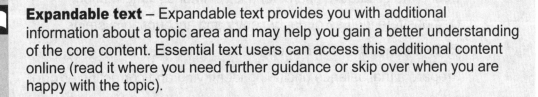 **Expandable text** – Expandable text provides you with additional information about a topic area and may help you gain a better understanding of the core content. Essential text users can access this additional content online (read it where you need further guidance or skip over when you are happy with the topic).

Test your understanding – Exercises for you to complete to ensure that you have understood the topics just learned.

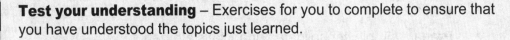 **Illustration** – Worked examples help you understand the core content better.

Tricky topic – When reviewing these areas, care should be taken and all Illustrations and Test your understanding exercises should be completed to ensure that the topic is understood.

On-line subscribers

Our on-line resources are designed to increase the flexibility of your learning materials and provide you with immediate feedback on how your studies are progressing. Ask your local customer services staff if you are not already a subscriber and wish to join.

If you are subscribed to our on-line resources you will find:

(1) On-line reference ware: reproduces your Complete or Essential Text on-line, giving you anytime, anywhere access.

(2) On-line testing: provides you with additional on-line objective testing so you can practice what you have learned further.

(3) On-line performance management: immediate access to your on-line testing results. Review your performance by key topics and chart your achievement through the course relative to your peer group.

Paper introduction

Paper background

The aim of ACCA Paper F3, **Financial Accounting**, FIA Diploma in Accounting and Business, **Financial Accounting**, is to develop knowledge and understanding of the underlying principles and concepts relating to financial accounting and technical proficiency in the use of double-entry accounting techniques including the preparation of basic financial statements.

Objectives of the syllabus

- Explain the context and purpose of financial reporting.
- Define the qualitative characteristics of financial information.
- Demonstrate the use of double entry and accounting systems.
- Record transactions and events.
- Prepare a trial balance (including identifying and correcting errors).
- Prepare basic financial statements for incorporated and unincorporated entities.
- Prepare simple consolidated financial statements
- Interpretation of financial statements

Core areas of the syllabus

- The context and purpose of financial reporting
- The qualitative characteristics of financial information
- The use of double entry and accounting systems
- Recording transactions and events
- Preparing a trial balance
- Preparing basic financial statements
- Preparing simple consolidated statements
- Interpretation of financial statements

Syllabus objectives

We have reproduced the ACCA's syllabus below, showing where the objectives are explored within this book. Within the chapters, we have broken down the extensive information found in the syllabus into easily digestible and relevant sections, called Content Objectives. These correspond to the objectives at the beginning of each chapter.

Syllabus learning objective	Chapter reference
A THE CONTEXT AND PURPOSE OF FINANCIAL REPORTING	
1 The scope and purpose of, financial statements for external reporting	
(a) Define financial reporting – recording, analysing and summarising financial data.[k]	1
(b) Identify and define types of business entity – sole trader, partnership, limited liability company.[k]	1
(c) Recognise the legal differences between a sole trader, partnership and a limited liability company. [k]	1
(d) Identify the advantages and disadvantages of operating as a limited liability company, sole trader or partnership.[k]	1
(e) Understand the nature, principles and scope of financial reporting.[k]	1
2 Users' and stakeholders' needs	
(a) Identify the users of financial statements and state and differentiate between their information needs.[k]	1
3 The main elements of financial reports	
(a) Understand and identify the purpose of each of the main financial statements.[k]	1
(b) Define and identify assets, liabilities, equity, revenue and expenses.[k]	1
4 The regulatory framework	
(a) Understand the role of the regulatory system including the roles of the IFRS Foundation (IFRSF), the International Accounting Standards Board (IASB), the IFRS Advisory Council (IFRS AC) and the IFRS Interpretations Committee (IFRS IC).[k]	2

(b)	Understand the role of International Financial Reporting Standards.[k]	2

5 Duties and responsibilities of those charged with governance — 2

(a) Explain what is meant by governance specifically in the context of the preparation of financial statements.[k]

(b) Describe the duties and responsibilities of directors and other parties covering the preparation of the financial statements.[k]

B THE QUALITATIVE CHARACTERISTICS OF FINANCIAL INFORMATION

1 The qualitative characteristics of financial information

(a) Define, understand and apply qualitative characteristics:[k] — 1

   (i) Relevance

   (ii) Faithful representation

   (iii) Comparability

   (iv) Verifiability

   (v) Timeliness

   (vi) Understandability

(b) Define, understand and apply accounting concepts — 1

   (i) Materiality

   (ii) Substance over form

   (iii) Going concern

   (iv) Business entity concept

   (v) Accruals

   (vi) Fair presentation

   (vii) Consistency

C THE USE OF DOUBLE ENTRY AND ACCOUNTING SYSTEMS

1 Double entry bookkeeping principles including the maintenance of accounting records

(a) Identify and explain the function of the main data sources in an accounting system.[k] — 3

KAPLAN PUBLISHING

3 Inventory

4 Tangible non-current assets

KAPLAN PUBLISHING

7   Accruals and prepayments

(a) Understand how the matching concept applies to accruals and prepayments.[k]   10

(b) Identify and calculate the adjustments needed for accruals and prepayments in preparing financial statements.[s]   10

(c) Illustrate the process of adjusting for accruals and prepayments in preparing financial statements.[s]   10

(d) Prepare the journal entries and ledger entries for the creation of an accrual or prepayment.[s]   10

(e) Understand and identify the impact on profit and net assets of accruals and prepayments.[s]   10

8   Receivables and payables

(a) Explain and identify examples of receivables and payables.[k]   1 & 11 & 12

(b) Identify the benefits and costs of offering credit facilities to customers.[k]   11

(c) Understand the purpose of an aged receivables analysis.[k]   11

(d) Understand the purpose of credit limits.[k]   11

(e) Prepare the bookkeeping entries to write off a irrecoverable debt.[s]   11

(f) Record an irrecoverable debt recovered.[s]   11

(g) Identify the impact of irrecoverable debts on the statement of profit or loss and on the statement of financial position.[s]   11

(h) Prepare the bookkeeping entries to create and adjust an allowance for receivables.[s]   11

(i) Illustrate how to include movements in the allowance for receivables in the statement of profit or loss and how the closing balance of the allowance should appear in the statement of financial position.[s]   11

(j) Account for contras between trade receivables and payables.[s]   14

(k) Prepare, reconcile and understand the purpose of supplier statements.[s]   14

(l) Classify items as current or non-current liabilities in the statement of financial position.[s]   1

E PREPARING A TRIAL BALANCE

KAPLAN PUBLISHING

3 Analysis of financial statements

(a)	Calculate and interpret the relationship between the elements of the financial statements with regard to profitability, liquidity, efficient use of resources and financial position.[s]	20
(b)	Draw valid conclusions from the information contained within the financial statements and present these to the appropriate user of the financial statements. [s]	20

The superscript numbers in square brackets indicate the intellectual depth at which the subject area could be assessed within the examination. Level 1 (knowledge and comprehension) broadly equates with the Knowledge module, Level 2 (application and analysis) with the Skills module and Level 3 (synthesis and evaluation) to the Professional level. However, lower level skills can continue to be assessed as you progress through each module and level.

The examination

Examination format

The syllabus is assessed by either a two-hour paper-based or computer-based examination. Questions will assess all parts of the syllabus and will contain both computational and non-computational elements:

	Number of marks
Thirty five 2-mark objective test questions	70
Two 15-mark multi-task questions	30
Total time allowed: 2 hours	

Examination tips

Spend the first few minutes of the examination reading the paper.

Divide the time you spend on questions in proportion to the marks on offer. One suggestion **for this exam** is to allocate 2 minutes to each mark available.

Objective test questions: Read the questions carefully and work through any calculations required. If you don't know the answer, eliminate those options you know are incorrect and see if the answer becomes more obvious. Guess your final answer rather than leave it blank if necessary.

The longer 15-mark questions will test consolidations and accounts preparation. Make sure you practice preparing full financial statements. There are lots of questions to practice in this text.

Computer-based examination (CBE) – Tips

Be sure you understand how to use the software before you start the exam. If in doubt, ask the assessment centre staff to explain it to you.

Questions are **displayed on the screen** and answers are entered using keyboard and mouse. At the end of the exam, you are given a certificate showing the result you have achieved.

The CBE exam will not only examine multiple choice questions but could include questions that require data entry or a multiple response.

Do not attempt a CBE until you have **completed all study material** relating to it. **Do not skip any of the material** in the syllabus.

Read each question very carefully.

Double-check your answer before committing yourself to it.

Answer every question – if you do not know an answer, you don't lose anything by guessing. Think carefully before you **guess.**

With an objective test question, it may be possible to eliminate first those answers that you know are wrong. Then choose the most appropriate answer from those that are left.

Remember that only **one answer to an objective test question can be right.** After you have eliminated the ones that you know to be wrong, if you are still unsure, guess. But only do so after you have double-checked that you have only eliminated answers that are definitely wrong.

Don't panic if you realise you've answered a question incorrectly. Try to remain calm, continue to apply examination technique and answer all questions required within the time available.

Study skills and revision guidance

This section aims to give guidance on how to study for your ACCA exams and to give ideas on how to improve your existing study techniques.

Preparing to study

Set your objectives

Before starting to study decide what you want to achieve – the type of pass you wish to obtain. This will decide the level of commitment and time you need to dedicate to your studies.

Devise a study plan

Determine which times of the week you will study.

Split these times into sessions of at least one hour for study of new material. Any shorter periods could be used for revision or practice.

Put the times you plan to study onto a study plan for the weeks from now until the exam and set yourself targets for each period of study – in your sessions make sure you cover the course, course assignments and revision.

If you are studying for more than one paper at a time, try to vary your subjects as this can help you to keep interested and see subjects as part of wider knowledge.

When working through your course, compare your progress with your plan and, if necessary, re-plan your work (perhaps including extra sessions) or, if you are ahead, do some extra revision/practice questions.

Effective studying

Active reading

You are not expected to learn the text by rote, rather, you must understand what you are reading and be able to use it to pass the exam and develop good practice. A good technique to use is SQ3Rs – Survey, Question, Read, Recall, Review:

(1) **Survey** the chapter – look at the headings and read the introduction, summary and objectives, so as to get an overview of what the chapter deals with.

(2) **Question** – whilst undertaking the survey, ask yourself the questions that you hope the chapter will answer for you.

(3) **Read** through the chapter thoroughly, answering the questions and making sure you can meet the objectives. Attempt the exercises and activities in the text, and work through all the examples.

(4) **Recall** – at the end of each section and at the end of the chapter, try to recall the main ideas of the section/chapter without referring to the text. This is best done after a short break of a couple of minutes after the reading stage.

(5) **Review** – check that your recall notes are correct.

You may also find it helpful to re-read the chapter to try to see the topic(s) it deals with as a whole.

Note-taking

Taking notes is a useful way of learning, but do not simply copy out the text. The notes must:

- be in your own words
- be concise
- cover the key points
- be well-organised
- be modified as you study further chapters in this text or in related ones.

Trying to summarise a chapter without referring to the text can be a useful way of determining which areas you know and which you don't.

Three ways of taking notes:

Summarise the key points of a chapter.

Make linear notes – a list of headings, divided up with subheadings listing the key points. If you use linear notes, you can use different colours to highlight key points and keep topic areas together. Use plenty of space to make your notes easy to use.

Try a diagrammatic form – the most common of which is a mind-map. To make a mind-map, put the main heading in the centre of the paper and put a circle around it. Then draw short lines radiating from this to the main sub-headings, which again have circles around them. Then continue the process from the sub-headings to sub-sub-headings, advantages, disadvantages, etc.

Highlighting and underlining

You may find it useful to underline or highlight key points in your study text – but do be selective. You may also wish to make notes in the margins.

Revision

The best approach to revision is to revise the course as you work through it. Also try to leave four to six weeks before the exam for final revision. Make sure you cover the whole syllabus and pay special attention to those areas where your knowledge is weak. Here are some recommendations:

Read through the text and your notes again and condense your notes into key phrases. It may help to put key revision points onto index cards to look at when you have a few minutes to spare.

Review any assignments you have completed and look at where you lost marks – put more work into those areas where you were weak.

Practise exam standard questions under timed conditions. If you are short of time, list the points that you would cover in your answer and then read the model answer, but do try to complete at least a few questions under exam conditions.

Also practise producing answer plans and comparing them to the model answer.

If you are stuck on a topic find somebody (a tutor) to explain it to you.

Read good newspapers and professional journals, especially ACCA's Student Accountant – this can give you an advantage in the exam.

Ensure you **know the structure of the exam** – how many questions and of what type you will be expected to answer. During your revision attempt all the different styles of questions you may be asked.

Further reading

You can find further reading and technical articles under the student section of ACCA's website.

A Student's Guide to IFRS by Clare Finch, Kaplan Publishing UK.

Introduction to financial reporting

Chapter learning objectives

Upon completion of this chapter you will be able to:

- define financial reporting
- identify and define types of business entity
- identify users of the financial statements and their information needs
- identify the purpose of the main financial statements
- define the elements of financial statements
- define and explain accounting concepts and characteristics.

1 Overview of accounting

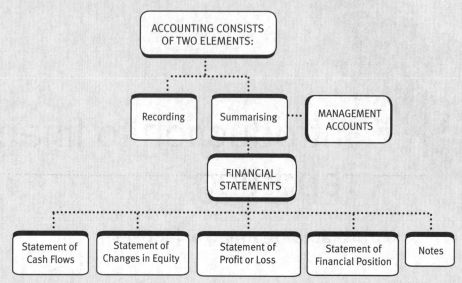

The accounting system of a business records and summarises the financial performance/position of a business over/at a certain period of time. This information is crucial to various stakeholders of the business, who will analyse that information to make significant economic decisions. It is of vital importance that these stakeholders have good quality information to be able to make good quality decisions.

This chapter explores the nature of businesses and their stakeholders and identifies what their information requirements are and how this fits into the process of financial reporting.

Financial accounting and management accounting

Financial accounting

Financial accounting is concerned with the production of financial statements for external users. These are a report on the directors' stewardship of the funds entrusted to them by the shareholders.

Investors need to be able to choose which companies to invest in and compare their investments. In order to facilitate comparison, financial accounts are prepared using accepted accounting conventions and standards. International Accounting Standards (IASs) and International Financial Reporting Standards (IFRSs) help to reduce the differences in the way that companies draw up their financial statements in different countries.

The financial statements are public documents, and therefore they will not reveal details about, for example, individual products' profitability.

Management accounting

Management require much more detailed and up-to-date information in order to control the business and plan for the future. They need to be able to cost-out products and production methods, assess profitability and so on. In order to facilitate this, management accounts present information in any way which may be useful to management, for example by operating unit or product line.

Management accounting is an integral part of management activity concerned with identifying, presenting and interpreting information used for:

- formulating strategy
- planning and controlling activities
- decision making
- optimising the use of resources.

2 Types of business entity

A business can be operated in one of several ways:

A sole trader

This is the simplest form of business where a business is owned and operated by one individual, although they might employ any number of people. With this form of entity there is no legal distinction between the owner and the business. To this end the owner receives all of the profits of the business but has unlimited liability for all the losses and debts of the business.

The capital structure of a sole trader is also relatively simple. There is a capital account which represents the financial interest of the owner in the business. The capital account can be added to by the owner introducing additional capital into the business, or by the business making profits, which the sole trader is entitled to. The capital account can be reduced by the sole trader making withdrawals from the capital account during the year (often referred to a 'drawings') or by the business making losses.

Partnership

Similar to a sole trader the owners of a partnership receive all the profits and have unlimited liability for the losses and debts of the business. The key distinction is that there are at least two owners. The joint owners, or partners, are jointly and severally liable for the losses the business makes (i.e. they are each fully liable in respect of all business liabilities).

Diff'n both sole trader & partnership

The capital structure of a partnership is similar to that of a sole trader. Each partner will have a financial interest in the business and this will be divided between a capital account and current account. The capital account is normally a fixed amount that will only change upon a partner joining or leaving the business. The current account includes the share of profit or loss that each partner is entitled to, less any personal drawings made by that partner.

Limited liability companies

Unlike sole traders and partnerships, limited liability companies are established as separate legal entities to their owners. This is achieved through the process of incorporation. The owners of the company (the shareholders) invest capital in the business in return for a shareholding that entitles them to a share of the residual assets of the business (i.e. what is left when the company is wound up or liquidated). The shareholders are not personally liable for the debts of the company and whilst they may lose their investment if the company becomes insolvent they will not have to pay the outstanding debts of the company if such a circumstance arises. Likewise, the company is not affected by the insolvency (or death) of individual shareholders. Limited liability companies are managed by a board of directors who are elected by the shareholders.

The capital structure of a limited liability company is more formalised than that of a sole trader or partnership and is illustrated within this chapter. Shareholders cannot make withdrawals or 'drawings' from the business in the way that a sole trader or partner is able to do. Instead, they receive a return on their investment in the company referred to as a dividend which is paid from accumulated profits.

Operating as a sole trader, partnership or company

Sole trader

Accounting conventions recognise the business as a separate entity from its owner. However, legally, the business and personal affairs of a sole trader are not distinguished in any way. The most important consequences of this is that a sole trader has complete personal *unlimited liability.* Business debts which cannot be paid from business assets must be met from sale of personal assets, such as a house or a car.

Sole trading organisations are normally small because they have to rely on the financial resources of their owner.

The advantages of operating as a sole trader include flexibility and autonomy. A sole trader can manage the business as he or she likes and can introduce or withdraw capital at any time.

Partnership

Like a sole trader, a partnership is not legally distinguished from its members. Personal assets of the partners may have to be used to pay the debts of the partnership business.

The advantages of trading as a partnership stem mainly from there being many owners rather than one. This means that:

- more resources may be available, including capital, specialist knowledge, skills and ideas;
- administrative expenses may be lower for a partnership than for the equivalent number of sole traders, due to economies of scale; and
- partners can substitute for each other.

Partners can introduce or withdraw capital at any time, provided that all the partners agree.

Comparison of companies to sole traders and partnerships

The fact that a company is a separate legal entity means that it is very different from a sole trader or partnership in a number of ways.

- **Property holding**

  The property of a limited company belongs to the company. A change in the ownership of shares in the company will have no effect on the ownership of the company's property. (In a partnership the firm's property belongs directly to the partners who can take it with them if they leave the partnership.)

- **Transferable shares**

  Shares in a limited company can usually be transferred without the consent of the other shareholders. In the absence of agreement to the contrary, a new partner cannot be introduced into a firm without the consent of all existing partners.

- **Suing and being sued**

  As a separate legal person, a limited company can sue and be sued in its own name. Judgements relating to companies do not affect the members personally.

- **Security for loans**

  A company has greater scope for raising loans and may secure them with floating charges. A floating charge is a mortgage over the constantly fluctuating assets of a company providing security for the lender of money to a company. It does not prevent the company dealing with the assets in the ordinary course of business. Such a charge is useful when a company has no non-current assets such as land, but does have large and valuable inventories.

  Generally, the law does not permit partnerships or individuals to secure loans with a floating charge.

- **Taxation**

  Because a company is legally separated from its shareholders, it is taxed separately from its shareholders. Partners and sole traders are personally liable for income tax on the profits made by their business.

- **Disadvantages of incorporation**

  The disadvantages of being a limited company arise principally from restrictions imposed by relevant company law:

  - When being formed companies have to register and file formal constitution documents with a Registrar. Registration fees and legal costs have to be paid.

  - In addition it is normally a requirement for a company to produce annual financial statements that must be submitted to the Registrar. It is also usually a requirement for those financial statements to be audited (in some countries this is only a requirement for large and medium sized companies). The costs associated with this can be high. Partnerships and sole traders are not subject to this requirement unless their professional bodies require this.

  - A registered company's accounts and certain other documents are open to public inspection. The accounts of sole traders and partnerships are not open to public inspection.

  - Limited companies are subject to strict rules in connection with the introduction and withdrawal of capital and profits.

  - Members of a company may not take part in its management unless they are directors, whereas all partners are entitled to share in management, unless the partnership agreement provides otherwise.

3 The Framework

One of the most important documents underpinning the preparation of financial statements is the Conceptual Framework for Financial Reporting ('the Framework'), which was prepared by the IASB (see Chapter 2 for a discussion of the regulatory bodies).

The framework presents the main ideas, concepts and principles upon which all International Financial Reporting Standards, and therefore financial statements, are based. It includes discussion of:

- the objectives of financial reporting
- the qualitative characteristics of useful financial information
- the definition, recognition and measurement of the elements from which the financial statements are constructed
- the accruals and going concern concepts, and
- the concepts of capital and capital maintenance (not on the syllabus).

The objective of financial reporting

The main objective is to provide financial information about the reporting entity to users of the financial statements that is useful in making decisions about providing resources to the entity, as well as other financial decisions.

Fair presentation

In order to provide useful information to the stakeholders of a business the financial statements must fairly present the position and performance of that business (or show a 'true and fair view'). Whilst this has never been formally defined it embodies the concepts that the financial statements are:

- compliant with relevant laws and regulations
- compliant with the relevant financial reporting framework, and
- they have applied the qualitative characteristics of the Framework as far as possible.

4 Users of the financial statements

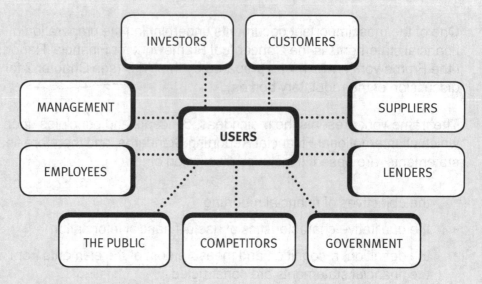

The main users (stakeholders) of financial statements are commonly grouped as follows:

- **Investors** and potential investors are interested in their potential profits and the security of their investment. Future profits may be estimated from the target company's past performance as shown in the statement of profit or loss. The security of their investment will be revealed by the financial strength and solvency of the company as shown in the statement of financial position. The largest and most sophisticated groups of investors are the institutional investors, such as pension funds and unit trusts.

- **Employees** and trade union representatives need to know if an employer can offer secure employment and possible pay rises. They will also have a keen interest in the salaries and benefits enjoyed by senior management. Information about divisional profitability will also be useful if a part of the business is threatened with closure.

- **Lenders** need to know if they will be repaid. This will depend on the solvency of the company, which should be revealed by the statement of financial position. Long-term loans may also be backed by 'security' given by the business over specific assets. The value of these assets will be indicated in the statement of financial position.

- **Government** agencies need to know how the economy is performing in order to plan financial and industrial policies. The tax authorities also use financial statements as a basis for assessing the amount of tax payable by a business.

- **Suppliers** need to know if they will be paid. New suppliers may also require reassurance about the financial health of a business before agreeing to supply goods.

- **Customers** need to know that a company can continue to supply them into the future. This is especially true if the customer is dependent on a company for specialised supplies.

KAPLAN PUBLISHING

- **The public** may wish to assess the effect of the company on the economy, local environment and local community. Companies may contribute to their local economy and community through providing employment and patronising local suppliers. Some companies also run corporate responsibility programmes through which they support the environment, economy and community by, for example supporting recycling schemes.

Management and competitors would also use the financial statements of a business to make economic decisions. Management, however, would predominantly use monthly management accounts as their main source of financial information. It is also unlikely that a business would prepare financial statements for the purpose of aiding competitors!

Test your understanding 1

Which of the following users do you think require the most detailed financial information to be made available to them?

A   Competitors

B   Management of the business

C   Trade unions

D   Investors

5 The elements of the financial statements

In order to appropriately report the financial performance and position of a business the financial statements must summarise five key elements:

(1) **Assets** – An asset is a resource controlled by the entity as a result of past events from which future economic benefits are expected to flow to the entity. For example, a building that is owned and controlled by a business and that is being used to house operations and generate revenues would be classed as an asset.

(2) **Liabilities** – A liability is an obligation to transfer economic benefit as a result of past transactions or events. For example, an unpaid tax obligation is a liability.

(3) **Equity** – This is the 'residual interest' in a business and represents what is left when the business is wound up, all the assets sold and all the outstanding liabilities paid. It is effectively what is paid back to the owners (shareholders) when the business ceases to trade.

(4) **Income** – This is the recognition of the inflow of economic benefit to the entity in the reporting period. This can be achieved, for example, by earning sales revenue or through the increase in value of an asset.

(5) **Expenses** – This is the recognition of the outflow of economic benefit from an entity in the reporting period. This can be achieved, for example, by purchasing goods or services off another entity or through the reduction in value of an asset.

Categorisation of assets, liabilities and equity in the financial statements

There are some additional rules with regard to the classification of assets and liabilities that relate to the length of time they will be employed in the business.

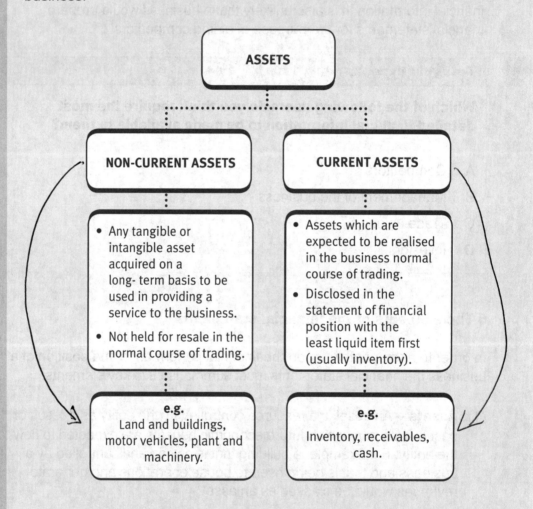

ASSETS

NON-CURRENT ASSETS

- Any tangible or intangible asset acquired on a long- term basis to be used in providing a service to the business.
- Not held for resale in the normal course of trading.

e.g.
Land and buildings, motor vehicles, plant and machinery.

CURRENT ASSETS

- Assets which are expected to be realised in the business normal course of trading.
- Disclosed in the statement of financial position with the least liquid item first (usually inventory).

e.g.
Inventory, receivables, cash.

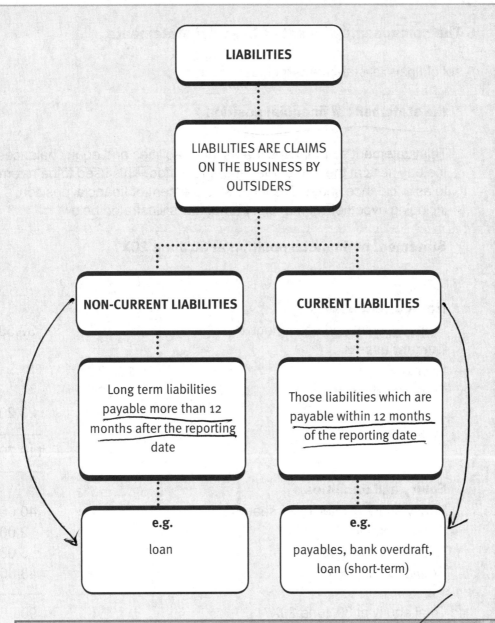

LIABILITIES

LIABILITIES ARE CLAIMS ON THE BUSINESS BY OUTSIDERS

NON-CURRENT LIABILITIES

CURRENT LIABILITIES

Long term liabilities payable more than 12 months after the reporting date

Those liabilities which are payable within 12 months of the reporting date

e.g.

loan

e.g.

payables, bank overdraft, loan (short-term)

Test your understanding 2

Classify the following items into current and non-current assets and liabilities:

- land and buildings
- receivables
- cash
- loan repayable in two years' time
- payables
- delivery van.

6 The components of a set of financial statements

A set of financial statements include:

- **the statement of financial position**

  This statement summarises the assets, liabilities and equity balances of the business at the end of the reporting period. This used to be referred to as a 'balance sheet.' A specimen statement of financial position, including hypothetical monetary amounts is illustrated below.

  Statement of financial position at 30 June 20X7

	$	$
Non-current assets		
Property, plant and equipment		87,500
Current assets		
Inventory	12,000	
Trade receivables	11,200	
		23,200
Total assets		
		110,700
Equity and liabilities		
Equity share capital @ $1 shares		40,000
Share premium		2,000
Revaluation surplus		5,000
Retained earnings		43,650
Total equity at 30 June 20X7		90.650
Non-current liabilities		
6% bank loan (20X9)		10,000
Current liabilities		
Trade payables	5,000	
Bank overdraft	4,150	
Income tax liability	600	
Interest accrual	300	
		10,050
		110,700

Note that there is a standard format to the statement of financial position. Assets and liabilities have each been classified into either 'non-current' or 'current' items. Current assets are those which are expected to be converted into cash within twelve months of the reporting date. Non-current assets are those which are used in the business over a number of years to generate sales revenues and profits.

Non-current liabilities are those which will be settled more than twelve months from the reporting date. Current liabilities are those which will be settled within twelve months of the reporting date.

The capital structure of a limited liability company will be explained in more detail elsewhere in this text. In the case of a sole trader, the items included under the 'Equity' section of the statement would be replaced by a simple capital account.

- **the statement of profit or loss and other comprehensive income**

This statement summarises the revenues earned and expenses incurred by the business throughout the reporting period. This used to be referred to as a 'profit and loss account.' A specimen statement of profit or loss and other comprehensive income, including hypothetical monetary amounts, is illustrated below.

Statement of profit or loss and other comprehensive income for the year ended 30 June 20X7

	$
Sales revenue	120,000
Cost of sales	(72,500)
Gross profit	47,500
Distribution costs	(10,700)
Administrative and selling expenses	(15,650)
Operating profit	21,150
Finance costs	(600)
Profit before tax	20,550
Income tax	(600)
Profit for the year	19.950
Other comprehensive income:	
Revaluation surplus in the year	2,000
Total comprehensive income for the year	21,950

Note that the statement classifies or groups expenses together based upon their function. Cost of sales, for example, may include the cost of raw materials to be converted into finished goods for sale. It may also include wages of employees directly involved in the conversion or production process. Distribution costs will include freight and delivery costs for finished goods, and may also include wages of employees involved in the distribution function. Administrative and selling costs will include the wages costs of those involved with that function, together with other related costs such as telephone and postage expenses.

Items accounted for in arriving at the profit for the year are regarded as having been realised during the accounting period.

In addition, for limited companies. there may be an additional section to the statement to recognise items of other comprehensive income. This will comprise of unrealised gains and losses during the accounting period and are separately disclosed in order to arrive at total comprehensive income for the year. The most common example of other comprehensive income relevant to the F3 syllabus is a revaluation surplus which arises when a company decides to account for an increase in the value of land and buildings. This will be explained in further detail as you progress through your F3 studies.

Both the profit for the year and any items of other comprehensive income are reflected in the statement of financial position and also the statement of changes in equity (see below) at the end of the accounting period.

- **the statement of changes in equity**

This statement summarises the movement in equity balances (share capital, share premium, revaluation surplus and retained earnings - all explained in greater detail later in the text) from the beginning to the end of the reporting period. It applies only to limited liability companies and would not be required for a sole trader or partnership.

Statement of changes in equity for the year ended 30 June 20X7

	Equity share capital $	Share premium $	Reval- uation surplus $	Retained earnings $	Total $
Balance at 1 July 20X6	34,000	1,100	3,000	25,200	63,300
Profit for the year				19,950	19,950
Dividend paid in the year				(1,500)	(1,500)
Revaluation in the year			2,000		2,000
Issue of share capital	6,000	900			6,900
Balance at 30 June 20X7	40,000	2,000	5,000	43,650	90,650

- ## the statement of cash flows

  This statement summarises the cash paid and received throughout the reporting period. Normally, it would be relevant to limited liability companies only, rather than to sole traders and partnerships. It will be explained in greater detail later in the text.

- ## the notes to the financial statements

  The notes to the financial statements comprise a statement of accounting policies and any other disclosures required to enable to the shareholders and other users of the financial statements to make informed judgements about the business. The notes to the financial statements are usually more detailed and extensive for limited liability company financial statements, rather than for the accounts of a sole trader or partnership.

7 Qualitative characteristics

Introduction

Qualitative characteristics are the attributes that make information provided in financial statements useful to others.

The Framework splits qualitative characteristics into two categories:

(i) Fundamental qualitative characteristics

  – Relevance

  – Faithful representation

(ii) Enhancing qualitative characteristics

  – Comparability

  – Verifiability

  – Timeliness

  – Understandability

Fundamental qualitative characteristics

Relevance

Information is relevant if:

- it has the ability to influence the economic decisions of users, and
- is provided in time to influence those decisions.

Materiality has a direct impact on the relevance of information.

Qualities of relevance

Information provided by financial statements needs to be relevant.

Information that is relevant has predictive, or confirmatory, value.

- Predictive value enables users to evaluate or assess past, present or future events.
- Confirmatory value helps users to confirm or correct past evaluations and assessments.

Where choices have to be made between mutually exclusive options, the option selected should be the one that results in the relevance of the information being maximised – in other words, the one that would be of most use in taking economic decisions.

A threshold quality is:

One that needs to be studied before considering the other qualities of that information

- a cut-off point – if any information does not pass the test of the threshold quality, it is not material and does not need to be considered further.
- information is material if its omission or misstatement could influence the economic decisions of users taken on the basis of the financial statements.

Faithful representation

If information is to represent faithfully the transactions and other events that it purports to represent, they must be accounted for and presented in accordance with their substance and economic reality and not merely their legal form. This is known as 'substance over form'.

KAPLAN PUBLISHING

To be a perfectly faithful representation, financial information would possess the following characteristics:

Completeness

To be understandable information must contain all the necessary descriptions and explanations.

Neutrality

Information must be neutral, i.e. free from bias. Financial statements are not neutral if, by the selection or presentation of information, they influence the making of a decision or judgement in order to achieve a predetermined or outcome.

Free from error

Information must be free from error within the bounds of materiality. A material error or an omission can cause the financial statements to be false or misleading and thus unreliable and deficient in terms of their relevance.

Free from error does not mean perfectly accurate in all respects. For example, where an estimate has been used the amount must be described clearly and accurately as being estimate.

Enhancing qualitative characteristics

Comparability, verifiability, timeliness and understandability are qualitative characteristics that enhance the usefulness of information that is relevant and faithfully represented.

Comparability

Users must be able to:

- compare the financial statements of an entity over time to identify trends in its financial and performance
- compare the financial statements of different entities to evaluate their relative financial performance and financial position.

For this to be the case there must be:

- consistency and
- disclosure.

An important implication of comparability is that users are informed of the accounting policies employed in preparation of the financial statements, any changes in those policies and the effects of such changes. Compliance with accounting standards, including the disclosure of the accounting policies used by the entity, helps to achieve comparability.

Because users wish to compare the financial position and the performance and changes in the financial position of an entity over time, it is important that the financial statements show corresponding information for the preceding periods.

Verifiability

Verification can be direct or indirect. Direct verification means verifying an amount or other representation through direct observation i.e. counting cash. Indirect verification means checking the inputs to a model, formula or other technique and recalculation the outputs using the same methodology.

Timeliness

Timeliness means having information available to decision makers in time to be capable of influencing their decisions. Generally, the older the information is the less useful it becomes.

Understandability

Understandability depends on:

- the way in which information is presented
- the capabilities of users.

It is assumed that users:

- have a reasonable knowledge of business and economic activities
- are willing to study the information provided with reasonable diligence.

For information to be understandable users need to be able to perceive its significance.

8 Other important accounting concepts

There are a number of other accounting principles that underpin the preparation of financial statements. The most significant ones include:

Materiality

An item is regarded as material if its omission or misstatement is likely to change the perception or understanding of the user of that information – i.e. they may make inappropriate decisions based upon the misstated information. Note that this is a subjective assessment made by those who prepare the financial statements (usually company directors) and it requires them to consider the reliability of the financial statements for decision-making purposes by users, principally the shareholders.

For example, consider if the bank balance of a major company is mis-stated by $1 in the statement of financial position. This may not be regarded as a material mis-statement which would significantly distort the relevance and reliability of the financial statements. However, if the bank balance was mis-stated by $100,000, this is more likely to be regarded as a material mis-statement as it significantly distorts the information included in the financial statements.

Substance over form

As noted earlier, if information is to be presented faithfully, the economic reality must be accounted for and not just the strict legal form.

An example of substance over form that you will encounter later in the text is the accounting treatment of redeemable preference shares. Although on legal form these are shares, there is an obligation to repay the preference shareholders and so they are accounted for as debt.

The going concern assumption

Financial statements are prepared on the basis that the entity will continue to trade for the foreseeable future (i.e. it has neither the need nor the intention to liquidate or significantly curtail its operations). The normal expectation is that, based upon current knowledge and understanding of the business, it is reasonable to assume that the business will continue to operate for the next twelve months. Note that there is no guarantee that this will always be the case as evidenced by business failures and insolvencies.

The business entity concept

This principle means that the financial accounting information presented in the financial statements relates only to the activities of the business and not to those of the owner. From an accounting perspective the business is treated as being separate from its owners.

The accruals basis of accounting

This means that transactions are recorded when revenues are earned and when expenses are incurred. This pays no regard to the timing of the cash payment or receipt.

For example, if a business enters into a contractual arrangement to sell goods to another entity the sale is recorded when the contractual duty has been satisfied. That is likely to be when the goods have been supplied and accepted by the customer. The payment may not be received for another month but in accounting terms the sale has taken place and should be recognised in the financial statements.

Fair presentation

Fair presentation relates to preparation of the financial statements in accordance with applicable financial reporting standards, together with relevant laws and regulations. Disclosure of compliance with reporting standards should be disclosed in the financial statements. If there is less than full compliance, the extent of non-compliance should be disclosed and explained. As a minimum, IAS 1 Presentation of Financial Statements requires that accounting policies are disclosed and that information is presented in a manner which is relevant, reliable, comparable and understandable.

Consistency

Users of the financial statements need to be able to compare the performance of a company over a number of years. Therefore it is important that the presentation and classification of items in the financial statements is retained from one period to the next, unless there is a change in circumstances or a requirement of a new IFRS. Consistency of accounting treatment and presentation relates not only from one accounting period to the next, but also within an accounting period, so that similar transactions are accounted for in a similar way.

Test your understanding 3

Which of the following statements are correct?

(1) Only tangible assets (i.e. those with physical substance) are recognised in the financial statements.

(2) Faithful representation means that the commercial effect of a transaction must always be shown in the financial statements even if this differs from legal form.

(3) Businesses only report transactions, events and balances that are material to users of the financial statements.

A   All of them

B   1 and 2 only

C   2 only

D   2 and 3 only

Chapter summary

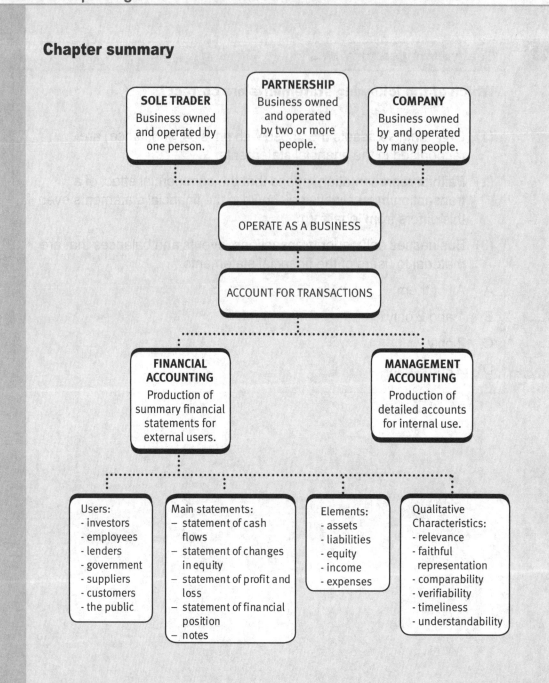

Test your understanding answers

Test your understanding 1

The correct answer is B – Management.

They need detailed information in order to control their business and make informed decisions about the future. Management information must be very up to date and is normally produced on a monthly basis.

Other parties will need far less detail:

- Competitors will be monitoring what the competition are currently planning and working on, but they will not be making the key decisions themselves.

- Trade unions will only require information which relates to their job role. They will only be particularly interested in disputes.

- Investors are interested in profitability and the security of their investment.

Test your understanding 2

- Land and buildings – **non-current asset**.
- Receivables – **current asset**.
- Cash – **current asset**.
- Loan repayable in two years' time – **non-current liability**.
- Payables – **current liability**.
- Delivery van – **non-current asset**.

Test your understanding 3

The correct answer is C.

Both tangible and intangible assets may be recognised as long as they meet the definition of an asset as described earlier.

Faithful representation includes the concept that transactions should reflect their economic substance, rather than the legal form of the transaction.

Businesses should report all transactions, events and balances in their financial statements. Materiality is simply a measure for determining how significant that information is to users.

The regulatory framework

Chapter learning objectives

Upon completion of this chapter you will be able to:

- understand the role of the financial reporting regulatory system

- understand the role of International Financial Reporting Standards (IFRS)

- explain what is meant by corporate governance, and

- describe the duties and responsibilities of company directors.

1 Overview

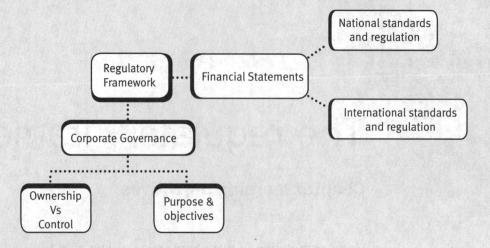

2 The regulatory framework

Why a regulatory framework is necessary

A regulatory framework for the preparation of financial statements is necessary for a number of reasons:

- To ensure that the needs of the users of financial statements are met with at least a basic minimum of information.

- To ensure that all the information provided in the relevant economic arena is both comparable and consistent. Given the growth in multinational companies and global investment this arena is an increasing international one.

- To increase users' confidence in the financial reporting process.

- To regulate the behaviour of companies and directors towards their investors.

Accounting standards on their own would not be sufficient to achieve these aims. In addition there must be some legal and market-based regulation.

National regulatory frameworks for financial reporting

There are many elements to the regulatory environment of accounting. A typical regulatory structure includes:

- National financial reporting standards

- National law

- Market regulations

- Security exchange rules.

For example the UK has the Financial Reporting Council that issues financial reporting standards in the UK. The main piece of legislation affecting businesses in the UK is the Companies Act 2006. However, there are also many other pieces of UK, EU and even US legislation (the Sarbanes Oxley Act) that affect accountability in the UK. There are also numerous industry specific regulatory systems that affect accounting in the UK, for example, the Financial Services Authority, whose aim is to achieve public accountability of the financial services industry. Finally, there are regulations provided by the London Stock Exchange for companies whose shares are quoted on this market.

3 International Financial Reporting Standards (IFRS)

Due to the increasingly global nature of investment and business operation there has been a move towards the 'internationalisation' of financial reporting. This 'harmonisation' was considered necessary to provide consistent and comparable information to an increasingly global audience.

If companies use different methods of accounting then before any decisions can be made about different entities the accounts would have to be re-written so that the accounting concepts and principles applied are the same; only then relevant comparisons be made.

Harmonisation illustration

To try and illustrate the importance of harmonisation do some research on the internet about words that have totally different meanings in different countries. Once you have done this you will undoubtedly have a much better appreciation of the benefits of a harmonised approach to information that will be available in an international arena.

Your research may also help you avoid some very embarrassing predicaments in the future!

IFRS are not enforceable in any country. As we will see shortly, they are developed by an international organisation that has no international authority. To become enforceable they must be adopted by a country's national financial reporting standard setter.

Within the European Union, IFRS were adopted for all listed entities in 2005. Other countries to have adopted IFRS include: Argentina, Australia, Brazil, Canada, Russia, Mexico, Saudi Arabia and South Africa. The US, China and India are going through a process of 'convergence,' whereby they are updating their national standards over time so that they are consistent with IFRS.

4 Structure of the IFRS regulatory system

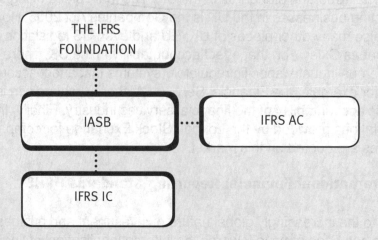

International Financial Reporting Standards (IFRS) Foundation

The IFRS Foundation (formerly known as the International Accounting Standards Committee Foundation (IASC)) is the supervisory body for the IASB and is responsible for governance issues and ensuring each member body is properly funded.

The principal objectives of the IFRS Foundation are to:

- develop a set of high quality, understandable, enforceable and globally accepted financial reporting standards

- promote the use and rigorous application of those standards

- to take account of the financial reporting needs of emerging economies and small and medium sized entities

- bring about the convergence of national and international financial reporting standards.

International Accounting Standards Board (IASB)

The IASB is the independent standard setting body of the IFRS foundation. Its members are responsible for the development and publication of IFRSs and interpretations developed by the IFRS IC. Upon its creation the IASB also adopted all existing International Accounting Standards.

All of the most important national standard setters are represented on the IASB and their views are taken into account so that a consensus can be reached. All national standard setters can issue IASB discussion papers and exposure drafts for comment in their own countries, so that the views of all preparers and users of financial statements can be represented. Each major national standard setter 'leads' certain international standard-setting projects.

The IFRS Interpretations Committee (IFRS IC)

The IFRS IC reviews widespread accounting issues (in the context of IFRS) on a timely basis and provides authoritative guidance on these issues (IFRICs). Their meetings are open to the public and, similar to the IASB, they work closely with national standard setters.

The IFRS Advisory Council (IFRS AC)

The IFRS AC is the formal advisory body to the IASB and the IFRS Foundation. It is comprised of a wide range of members who are affected by the IASB's work. Their objectives include:

- advising the IASB on agenda decisions and priorities in the their work,

- informing the IASB of the views of the Council with regard to major standard-setting projects, and

- giving other advice to the IASB or to the Trustees.

Development of an IFRS

The procedure for the development of an IFRS is as follows:

- The IASB identifies a subject and appoints an advisory committee to advise on the issues.

- The IASB publishes an exposure draft for public comment, being a draft version of the intended standard.

- Following the consideration of comments received on the draft, the IASB publishes the final text of the IFRS.

- At any stage the IASB may issue a discussion paper to encourage comment.

- The publication of an IFRS, exposure draft or IFRIC interpretation requires the votes of at least eight of the 15 IASB members.

5 Company ownership and control

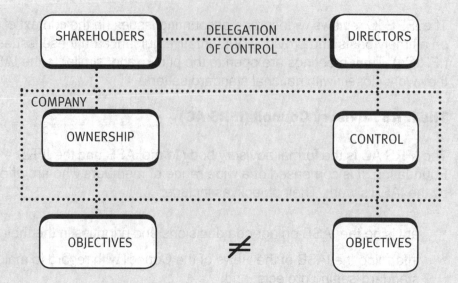

 A company is a corporate body that has registered in accordance with the requirements of relevant national company law (e.g. the Companies Act 2006), thus becoming its own legal entity. Ownership of the company is evidenced by the issuing of shares to the owners (i.e. the shareholders).

For some smaller and medium sized companies the owners may also be the directors/managers of the company. It is also possible for directors of large, publically listed companies to own shares in the companies they work for. However, of the largest 100 UK companies, directors typically own less than 1% of the shares of the company they work for.

Typically large, listed companies are owned by a wide range of individuals and organisations, such as pension funds, trusts and investment banks. These individuals and entities will not have any involvement in the day-to-day running of the business. Imagine if you had to organise a meeting of all shareholders every time the business needed to make a decision such as the hiring of a new member of staff or which leasing company to rent cars from; it would take far too long to make these decisions and consensus amongst such a large group might be difficult to achieve.

Instead, directors are appointed to manage the business on behalf of the owners. This leads to the separation of ownership and control within the company. Unfortunately the objectives of owners and directors often conflict; whilst they might both have the objective of increasing their own personal wealth, if the directors increase their own salaries and bonuses this reduces the profit available to the shareholders. Also, the directors will be rewarded for the financial success of the business, which leads towards bias in the preparation of the financial statements. This could ultimately result in a reduction in reliability/credibility of the financial statements.

The current financial reporting environment

Recent history has been dogged with examples of unreliable, and often fraudulent, financial reporting, where directors have put their own personal interests above those of the shareholders. Enron and WorldCom are just a couple of examples, albeit very high profile ones, where directors have been convicted of manipulating published results and therefore misleading shareholders, often at very significant personal gain.

These cases only serve to exacerbate the problem of shareholder confidence, creating a culture of mistrust in the directors (and auditors) of large companies. This has sadly lead to a loss of credibility in published financial reports. Whilst the various regulators around the world have responded, not least with the move to harmonise both financial reporting and auditing, there is still a long way to go in the fight to restore credibility to financial statements.

6 What is 'corporate governance'?

The **Cadbury Report 1992** provides a useful definition:

- 'the system by which companies are directed and controlled'.

An appropriate expansion to this definition might include:

- 'in the interests of shareholders and in relation to those stakeholders beyond the company boundaries' or

The use of the term stakeholders suggests that companies (and therefore their management team) have a much broader responsibility to the economy and society at large. This includes concepts such as public duty and corporate social responsibility.

If directors of a company have a responsibility to these groups then they must also be held accountable to them.

7 Purpose and objectives of corporate governance

The basic purpose of corporate governance is to monitor those parties within a company who control the resources and assets of the owners.

The primary objective of sound corporate governance is to contribute to improved corporate performance and accountability in creating long-term shareholder value.

```
CORPORATE GOVERNANCE
```

PURPOSES

Primary:
Monitor those parties within a company who control the resources owned by investors.

Supporting:
- Ensure there is a suitable balance of power on the board of directors.
- Ensure executive directors are remunerated fairly.
- Make the board of directors responsible for monitoring and managing risk.
- Ensure the external auditors remain independent and free from the influence of the company.
- Address other issues, e.g. business ethics, corporate social responsibility (CSR), and protection of 'whistleblowers'.

OBJECTIVES

Primary:
Contribute to improved corporate performance and accountability in creating long-term shareholder value.

Supporting:
- Control the controllers by increasing the amount of reporting and disclosure to all stakeholders.
- Increase level of confidence and transparency in company activities for all investors (existing and potential) and thus promote growth .
- Ensure that the company is run in a legal and ethical manner.
- Build in control at the top that will 'cascade' down the organisation.

The need for corporate governance

Simply put, if the stock market mechanism is to succeed then there needs to be a system that ensures publically owned companies are run in the interests of the shareholders and that provides adequate accountability of the people managing those companies.

The basic elements of sound corporate governance include:

- effective management

- effective systems of internal control

- oversight of management by non-executive directors

- fair appraisal of director performance

- fair remuneration of directors
- fair financial reporting, and
- constructive relationships with shareholders.

In order to be accountable to the stakeholders of the business the directors of a company are responsible for preparing various documents and reports. One of the most important reports is the financial statements. These provide a summary of the financial performance and position of the business. This information is crucial for the shareholders in particular, who need to be able to assess the success of the business during the financial period and the affect this has had on their own personal wealth.

The directors of a company are responsible for ensuring that the company has an effective system in place for adequately identifying, recording, and summarising all the transactions and events that take place during the year. They must ensure that the controls that exist within that system are sufficient to both prevent and detect fraud and error within the system. They are also responsible for monitoring that system to ensure that the controls and procedures are being rigorously applied.

Examples of corporate governance

The UK Corporate Governance Code (2010)

The UK adopts what is commonly referred to as a 'comply or explain' approach to corporate governance. All listed companies in the UK have to submit a report stating how they have complied with the provisions of the code and a statement of compliance with the code. If they have not been compliant they have to explain why they have not complied and what alternative action they have taken.

The code provides guidance on five areas of governance:

(i)   leadership of the company

(ii) effectiveness of the board

(iii) accountability of the board

(iv) remuneration of the board

(v)   board relations with shareholders.

The US Sarbanes Oxley Act

In the US corporate governance is enshrined in law, meaning compliance is compulsory and failure to comply could lead to criminal conviction. The Act enforces:

- sound systems of internal control

- clear documentation of financial processes, risks and controls

- evidence that management have evaluated the adequacy and design of systems and controls

- evidence that the auditor has evaluated the adequacy and design of systems and controls

The fundamental aim of the Act is 'to provide the company, its management, its board and audit committee, and its owners and other stakeholders with a reasonable basis to rely on the company's financial statements.'

Test your understanding 1

Briefly describe the role of corporate governance.

8 Chapter summary

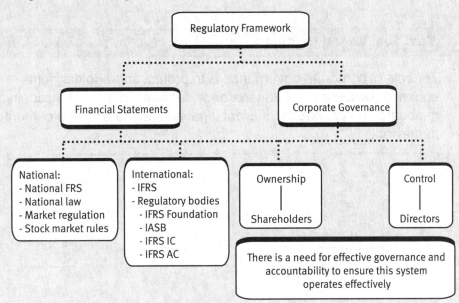

Test your understanding answers

Test your understanding 1

The role of corporate governance is to protect shareholder rights, enhance disclosure and transparency, facilitate effective functioning of the board and provide an efficient legal and regulatory enforcement framework.

KAPLAN PUBLISHING

Double entry bookkeeping

Chapter learning objectives

Upon completion of this chapter you will be able to:

- explain the main forms of business transaction and documentation
- identify, explain and understand the main forms of accounting record, including:
  - day books
  - the cash book
  - the journal
  - the general ledger
- understand and apply the concepts of duality, double-entry and the accounting equation.

1 Overview

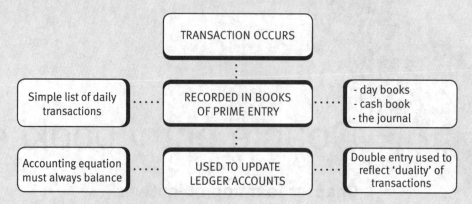

2 Business transactions and documentation

In every business a number of transactions and events will take place every day. The role of financial reporting is to effectively measure the effects of those transactions and events, record the effects on the business and summarise those transactions and their consequences in a format that is useful to the users of the financial statements.

The main transactions that take place include sales, purchases (of goods and of services) and payroll related transactions. Others include rental costs, raising finance, repayment of finance, and taxation related costs to name but a few. All of these transactions must be adequately captured by the financial reporting system.

With most transactions a supporting document will be created to confirm the transaction has taken place, when the transaction took place and the associated value of the transaction. This documentation is vital to the financial accountant, who uses the information on the documents as a data source to initiate the measurement and recording of the transactions.

The table below summarises the main types of business documentation and sources of data for an accounting system, together with their content and purpose.

	Contents	Purpose
Quotation	Quantity/description/details of goods required.	To establish price from various suppliers and cross refer to purchase requisition.
Purchase order	Details of supplier, e.g. name, address. Quantity/ description/details of goods required and price. Terms and conditions of delivery, payment, etc.	Sent to supplier as request for supply. To check to the quotation and delivery note.

Sales order	Quantity/description/details of goods required and price.	Cross checked with the order placed by customer. Sent to the stores/ warehouse department for processing of the order.
Despatch note (goods despatched note – GDN)	Details of supplier, e.g. name and address. Quantity and description of goods	Provided by supplier. Checked with goods received and purchase order.
Goods received note (GRN)	Quantity and description of goods.	Produced by company receiving the goods as proof of receipt. Matched with delivery note and purchase order.
Invoice	Name and address of supplier and customer; details of goods, e.g. quantity, price, value, sales tax, terms of credit, etc.	Issued by supplier of goods as a request for payment. For the supplier selling the goods/services this will be treated as a sales invoice. For the customer this will be treated as a purchase invoice.
Statement	Details of supplier, e.g. name and address. Has details of date, invoice numbers and values, payments made, refunds, amount owing.	Issued by the supplier. Checked with other documents to ensure that the amount owing is correct.
Credit note	Details of supplier, e.g. name and address. Contains details of goods returned, e.g. quantity, price, value, sales tax, terms of credit, etc.	Issued by the supplier. Checked with documents regarding goods returned.
Debit note	Details of the supplier. Contains details of goods returned, e.g. quantity, price, value, sales tax, terms of credit, etc.	Issued by the company receiving the goods. Cross referred to the credit note issued by the supplier.
Remittance advice	Method of payment, invoice number, account number, date, etc.	Sent to supplier with, or as notification of, payment.
Receipt	Details of payment received.	Issued by the selling company indicating the payment received.

The above list is based upon the documents created by a traditional manufacturing company. Not all companies will produce all of these documents. In the same manner some companies may produce alternative forms of documentation, particularly if they operate in the services industry or overseas.

3 Accounting records

Once the relevant document/data source has been received by the financial accountant they have to make a record of it in an appropriate place in the accounting system. However, transactions cannot simply be entered into the financial statements for the shareholders; there is a complex accounting process that has to take place before the results for the year can be summarised. Many controls have to be performed to prevent and detect fraud and error before the final results can be prepared.

The accounting system is also used to monitor the effectiveness of the business and to help conclude relevant transactions (for example, many goods/services are sold on credit, giving the customer a number of days/months to settle their debt. Credit control requires information from the accounting system with regard to who has not settled their debts and, for that reason, who needs to be chased for payment).

The flow of information from the initial transaction to the financial statements is illustrated as follows:

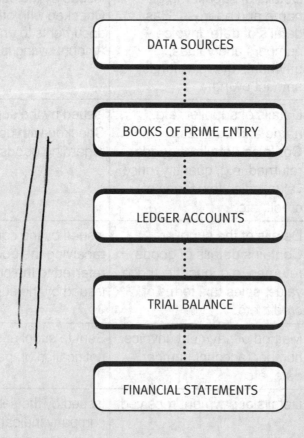

Books of prime entry

The ledger accounts of a business are the main source of information used to prepare the financial statements. However, if a business were to update their ledgers each time a transaction occurred, the ledger accounts would quickly become cluttered and errors might be made. This would also be a very time consuming process.

Example – Ford Motor Company

According to their 2011 annual report Ford sold 5.695 million vehicles in 2011 (2.686 million in the US alone). Ford would need to record 15,603 transactions per day for a full 365 days per year if they were to record every single sale in their accounting ledgers! That does not even take into account their associated purchases and payroll transactions! That is an awful lot of transactions to record in one set of company accounts.

To avoid this complication, all transactions are initially recorded in a book of prime entry. This is a simple note of the transaction, the relevant customer/supplier and the amount of the transaction. It is, in essence, a long list of daily transactions.

Several books of prime entry exist, each recording a different type of transaction:

Book of prime entry	Transaction type
Sales day book	Credit sales
Purchases day book	Credit purchases
Sales returns day book	Returns of goods sold on credit
Purchases returns day book	Returns of goods bought on credit
Cash book	All bank transactions
Petty cash book	All small cash transactions
The journal	All transactions not recorded elsewhere

The sum total of the day's transactions is recorded in the accounting ledgers of the company. This is done in a 'double entry' format. This important concept will be explored in greater depth later in this chapter.

4 Sales and purchases day books

Sales day book

The sales book summarises the daily sales made on credit terms (i.e. the goods are sold and payment is collected at a later date). Cash sales are recorded in the cash book.

Date	Invoice	Customer	Ledger Ref	$
4.1.X6	1	Jake	RL3	4,500
4.1.X6	2	Bella	RL18	3,000
4.1.X6	3	Fizz	RL6	2,200
4.1.X6	4	Milo	RL1	10,000
4.1.X6	5	Max	RL12	500
Total for 4.1.X6				20,200

The total sales for the day of $20,200 will be entered into the accounting ledgers in double entry format.

Purchases day book

The purchase day book summarises the daily purchases made on credit terms (i.e. the goods are purchased and payment is made at a later date). Cash purchases are recorded in the cash book.

Date	Invoice	Supplier	Ledger Ref	$
4.1.X6	34	Harry	PL2	2,700
4.1.X6	11	Ron	PL37	145
4.1.X6	5609	Hermione	PL12	4,675
4.1.X6	2	Neville	PL9	750
4.1.X6	577	Draco	PL1	345
Total for 4.1.X6				8,615

The total purchases for the day of $8,615 will be entered into the accounting ledgers in double entry format.

Sales and purchase returns day books

Format of the sales returns day book

Date	Invoice	Customer	Ledger Ref	$
4.1.X6	1	Max	RL12	50
4.1.X6	2	Ernie	RL2	450
4.1.X6	3	Pat	RL20	390
4.1.X6	4	Sam	RL27	670
4.1.X6	5	Milo	RL1	2,300
Total for 4.1.X6				3,860

Format of the purchases returns day book

Date	Invoice	Supplier	Ledger Ref	$
4.1.X6	112	Harry	PL3	600
4.1.X6	56	Cho	PL16	75
4.1.X6	7	Fleur	PL2	800
4.1.X6	890	Neville	PL1	50
4.1.X6	12	Draco	PL12	100
Total for 4.1.X6				1,625

Illustration 1

Mr Kipper-Ling runs a business providing equipment for bakeries. He always makes a note of sales and purchases on credit and associated returns, but he is not sure how they should be recorded for the purposes of his accounts.

Write up the following credit transactions arising in the first two weeks of August 20X6 into the relevant day books.

1 August   Mrs Bakewell buys $500 worth of cake tins.   S

1 August   Mr Kipper-Ling purchases $2,000 worth of equipment from wholesalers TinPot Ltd.   P

2 August   Mr Kipper-Ling returns goods costing $150 to another supplier, I Cook.   PR

3 August   Jack Flap buys $1,200 worth of equipment.   S

3 August   Mrs Bakewell returns $100 worth of the goods supplied to her.   SR

4 August   Victoria Sand-Witch buys a new oven for $4,000.   S

5 August	Mr Kipper-Ling purchases $600 worth of baking trays from regular supplier TinTin Ltd.
8 August	Mr Kipper-Ling purchases ovens costing $10,000 from Hot Stuff Ltd.
8 August	Mr Kipper-Ling returns equipment costing $300 to TinPot Ltd.
9 August	Pavel Ova purchases goods costing $2,200.
11 August	Mrs Bakewell buys some oven-proof dishes costing $600.

Solution to Illustration 1

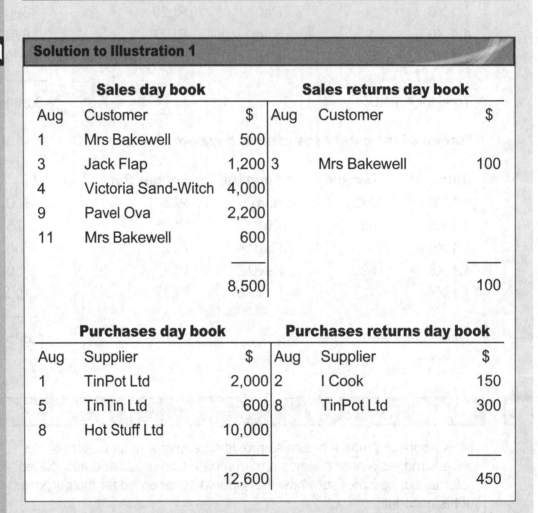

Sales day book

Aug	Customer	$
1	Mrs Bakewell	500
3	Jack Flap	1,200
4	Victoria Sand-Witch	4,000
9	Pavel Ova	2,200
11	Mrs Bakewell	600
		8,500

Sales returns day book

Aug	Customer	$
3	Mrs Bakewell	100
		100

Purchases day book

Aug	Supplier	$
1	TinPot Ltd	2,000
5	TinTin Ltd	600
8	Hot Stuff Ltd	10,000
		12,600

Purchases returns day book

Aug	Supplier	$
2	I Cook	150
8	TinPot Ltd	300
		450

5 The cash book

- All transactions involving cash at bank are recorded in the cash book.

- Many businesses have two distinct cash books – a **cash payments book** and a **cash receipts book.**

- A note of cash discounts given and received is also recorded in the cash book. This is to facilitate the recording of discounts in both the general and accounts payable/receivable ledgers.

- It is common for businesses to use a columnar format cash book in order to analyse types of cash payment and receipt.

Illustration 2 – The cash book

The cash payments book

The following is the cash payments book of a small print business.

Date	Detail	Bank $	Discount $	Payables $	Rent $
18.7.X6	Mr A	1,400	100	1,400	
18.7.X6	Office	3,000			3,000
18.7.X6	Mr B	210		210	
18.7.X6	Mr C	1,600	80	1,600	
18.7.X6	Shop	400			400
		6,610	180	3,210	3,400

What are the accounting entries arising from the totals in the cash book at the end of the day, assuming control accounts are kept?

Solution to Illustration 2

The cash transactions are recorded in total as follows:

Dr Payables ledger control account $3,210

Dr Rent expense $3,400

Cr Bank $6,610

The discount is recorded as follows:

Dr Payables ledger control account $180

Cr Discounts received $180

Entries must also be made to Mr A, Mr B and Mr C's individual accounts in the accounts payable ledger in order to reflect the payments made and discounts received.

Test your understanding 1

The following is the cash receipts book of the SM Art Gallery.

Date	Detail	Bank received	Discount	Receiv-ables	Bank interest
		$	$	$	$
18.7.X6	C Monet	10,000	500	10,000	
18.7.X6	Interest Acc # 1	20			20
18.7.X6	V V Gogh	25,000		25,000	
18.7.X6	Interest Acc # 2	100			100
18.7.X6	P Picasso	13,700	300	13,700	
		48,820	800	48,700	120

What are the accounting entries arising from the totals in the cash book at the end of the day, assuming that individual accounts for each customer and supplier are maintained?

Petty cash

Controls over petty cash

The following controls and security over petty cash should be found in a business:

- The petty cash must be kept in a petty cash box.

- The petty cash box must be secured in a safe.

- The person responsible for petty cash must be reliable and know what he/she is doing.

- All petty cash must be supported by invoices.

- Petty cash vouchers must be signed by the claimant and the person responsible for running the petty cash.

- Regular spot checks must be carried out to ensure that the petty cash is accurate.

Petty cash book

In this book the business will record small cash transactions. The cash receipts will be recorded together with the payments which will be analysed in the same way as a cash book.

An imprest system will be adopted for the petty cash book. An amount is withdrawn from the bank account which is referred as a 'petty cash float'. This 'float' will be used to pay for the various sundry expenses. The petty cash book cashier will record any payments.

Any expenditure must be evidenced by an expense receipt and the petty cashier will attach a petty cash voucher to each expense.

At any point in time the cash together with the expense vouchers should agree to the total float. At the end of the period the petty cash float is 'topped up' by withdrawing an amount from the bank totalling the petty cash payment made during the period.

6 The journal

The journal is a book of prime entry which records transactions which are not routine (and not recorded in any other book of prime entry), for example:

- year-end adjustments
  - depreciation charge for the year
  - irrecoverable debt write-off
  - record the movement in the allowance for receivables
  - accruals and prepayments
  - closing inventory

- acquisitions and disposals of non-current assets
- opening balances for statement of financial position items
- correction of errors.

The journal is a clear and comprehensible way of setting out a bookkeeping double entry that is to be made.

Presentation of a journal

A journal should be laid out in the following way:

Dr Non-current asset	X
Cr Payables	X

to record the purchase of a new non-current asset on credit.

A brief narrative should be given to explain the entry.

Test your understanding 2

Igor Romanov runs a Russian restaurant. He is a very good chef but not quite so good at accounting and needs help to record the following transactions:

(1) Closing inventory of 250 bottles of vodka at a cost of $2,750 has not been recorded.

(2) Igor needs to charge depreciation on his restaurant. He holds a 25-year lease which cost him $150,000 ten years ago.

(3) A regular customer, V Shady, keeps a tab behind the bar. He currently owes $350 but was last seen buying a one-way ticket to Moscow. Igor has given up hope of payment and intends to write the debt off.

(4) On the last day of the year Igor bought two new sofas for cash for the bar area of the restaurant. They cost $600 each but the purchase has not been reflected in the accounts.

What journals should Igor post?

7 Ledger accounts and the division of the ledger

In most companies each class of transaction and their associated assets and liabilities are given their own account. For example, there will be separate accounts for sales, purchases, rent, insurance costs, cash assets, inventory assets, liabilities to pay suppliers (payables), amounts due from customers (receivables) etc. There is no rule as to how many accounts a business should have but the system should facilitate effective and efficient accounting and control. Each account in the system is referred to as a 'ledger.'

KAPLAN PUBLISHING

Ledger accounts – A definition

In simple terms the ledger accounts are where the double entry records of all transactions and events are made. They are the principal books or files for recording and totalling monetary transactions by account. A company's financial statements are generated from summary totals in the ledgers.

The term 'general ledger' is used to refer to the overall system of ledger accounts within a business. It houses all the separate ledgers required to produce a complete trial balance and, consequently, set of financial statements.

As stated above, each class of transaction, asset, liability and item of equity will have its own ledger account. The summary of these ledger balances will eventually be transferred into the corresponding caption in the primary financial statements. For a summary of the main classifications please refer to the later chapter on preparing basic financial statements, where example illustrations have been reproduced.

Books of prime entry are covered in more detail in a later chapter. In this chapter we will focus on the entries made in the ledger accounts. In particular we will look at the nature of 'double entry' bookkeeping.

8 Duality, double entry and the accounting equation

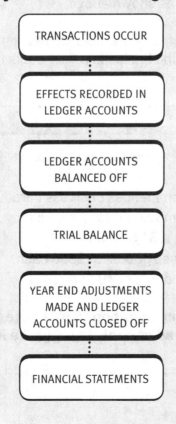

Each transaction that a business enters into affects the financial statements in two ways.

For example, a business buys a vehicle for cash. The two effects on the business are:

(1) It has increased the vehicle assets it has at its disposal for generating income, and

(2) There is a decrease in cash available to the business.

To follow the rules of double entry bookkeeping, each time a transaction is recorded, both effects must be taken into account. These two effects are equal and opposite and, as such, the accounting equation will always be maintained.

The accounting equation

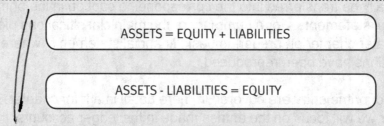

ASSETS = EQUITY + LIABILITIES

ASSETS - LIABILITIES = EQUITY

The statement of financial position shows the position of a business at one point in time. A statement of financial position will always satisfy the accounting equation as shown above.

The accounting equation is a simple expression of the fact that at any point in time the assets of the business will be equal to its liabilities plus the equity of the business.

Illustration 3 – The accounting equation

The transactions of a new business in its first five days are as follows:

Day 1   Avon commences business introducing $1,000 cash.
Day 2   Buys a motor car for $400 cash.
Day 3   Obtains a $1,000 loan.
Day 4   Purchases goods for $300 cash.
Day 5   Sells goods for $400 on credit.

Use the accounting equation to illustrate the position of the business at the end of each day. (Ignore inventory for this example).

Solution to Illustration 3

Day 1: Avon commences business introducing $1,000 cash

The dual effect of this transaction is:

(a) the business has $1,000 of cash

(b) the business owes the owner $1,000 – this is capital/equity.

Assets	=	Equity	+	Liabilities
1,000		1,000		0

Day 2: Buys a motor car for $400 cash

The dual effect of this transaction is:

(a) the business has an asset of $400

(b) the business has spent $400 in cash

This transaction changes the form in which the assets are held.

Assets	=	Equity	+	Liabilities
1,000		1,000		0
400 – 400		0		0
———		———		———
1,000		1,000		0

Note that the acquiring of an asset must lead to one of the following:

*   reducing another asset by a corresponding amount (as above)

*   incurring a corresponding liability

*   increasing the equity of the owner (either capital invested or profits made and owed to the owners).

Day 3: Obtains a $1,000 loan

The dual effect of this transaction is:

(a) the business has $1,000 of cash

(b) the business owes $1,000 to the bank.

Assets	=	Equity	+	Liabilities
1,000		1,000		0
1,000		0		1,000
2,000		1,000		1,000

Day 4: Purchases goods for $300 cash

The purchase represents a cost (or an expense) to the business. This cost will reduce the profits of the business, which will in turn reduce the equity in the business.

The dual effect of is:

(a) The business has an expense of $300 (expenses reduce the amount due to the owners, i.e. they reduce equity)

(b) The business has reduced cash by $300.

Assets	=	Equity	+	Liabilities
2,000		1,000		1,000
(300)		(300)		0
1,700		700		1,000

Day 5: Sells goods for $400 on credit

The dual effect of this transaction is:

(a) The business has earned sales revenue of $400.

(b) The business has a new asset to receive payment of $400 from their customer.

The sales revenue will increase profits and will therefore increase equity in the business.

Assets	=	Equity	+	Liabilities
1,700		700		1,000
400		400		0
_____		_____		_____
2,100		1,100		1,000

9 Ledger accounts, debits and credits

- Transactions and events are eventually recorded in the relevant ledger accounts using a double entry to reflect the duality concept explained previously. There is a ledger account for each asset, liability, equity, income and expense item.

- Traditionally each account was drawn as an enlarged 'T' that has two sides – a debit and a credit side:

Debit   **Credit**
(Dr)   **(Cr)**

Name of account e.g. cash, sales

Date Narrative $	Date Narrative $

- The duality concept means that each transaction will affect at least two ledger accounts.

- One account will be debited and the other credited.

- Whether an entry is to the debit or credit side of an account depends on the type of account and the transaction:

Debit	**Credit**
Increase in:	Increase in:
Purchases	**R**evenues
Expenses	**L**iabilities
Assets	**S**hareholder's equity

You can use the mnemonic 'PEARLS' to help you remember this vitally important double entry rule.

It is important to note that the opposite is also true; for example, a reduction in assets would constitute a credit entry into the ledgers.

Summary of steps to record a transaction

(1) Identify the items that are affected.

(2) Consider whether they are being increased or decreased.

(3) Decide whether each account should be debited or credited.

(4) Check that a debit entry and a credit entry have been made and they are both for the same amount.

Chapter summary

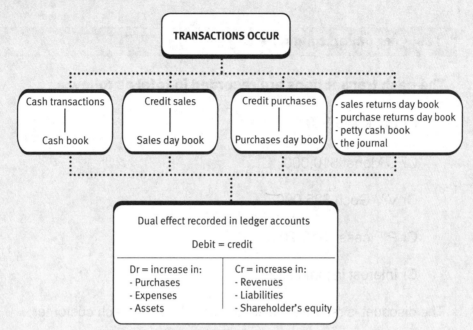

TRANSACTIONS OCCUR

Cash transactions	Credit sales	Credit purchases	- sales returns day book
Cash book	Sales day book	Purchases day book	- purchase returns day book
			- petty cash book
			- the journal

Dual effect recorded in ledger accounts

Debit = credit

Dr = increase in:	Cr = increase in:
- Purchases	- Revenues
- Expenses	- Liabilities
- Assets	- Shareholder's equity

Test your understanding answers

Test your understanding 1

The cash transactions are recorded in total as follows:

Dr Bank $48,820

Cr C Monet $10,000

Cr V V Goch $25,000

Cr P Picasso $13,700

Cr Interest income $120

The discount is recorded as follows in relation to each customer:

Dr Discounts allowed $800 (an expense in the statement of profit or loss)

Cr C Monet $500

Cr P Picasso $300

Test your understanding 2

(1) Dr Closing inventory (statement of financial position) $2,750

Cr Closing inventory (cost of sales) $2,750

To record the closing inventory of vodka.

(2) Dr Depreciation expense $6,000 ($150,000/25 yrs)

Cr Accumulated depreciation $6,000

To record depreciation on the restaurant lease.

(3) Dr Irrecoverable debt expense $350

Cr Receivables – V Shady $350

To record the write-off of a debt outstanding from V Shady.

(4) Dr Fixtures and Fittings cost $1,200

Cr Cash $1,200

To record the purchase of two sofas for the bar.

Recording basic transactions and balancing the ledgers

Chapter learning objectives

Upon completion of this chapter you will be able to:

- understand and illustrate the use of journals and the posting of journals into ledger accounts

- illustrate how to balance and close a ledger account

- record sales, purchase and cash transactions in ledger accounts.

1 Overview

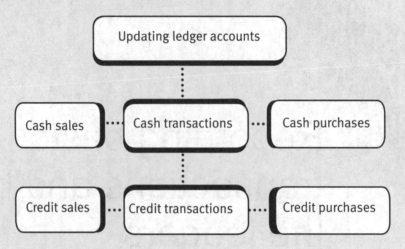

2 Recording cash transactions

Cash transactions are those where payment is made or received immediately (i.e. when cash is exchanged at the point of sale/purchase). Sales and purchases made by cheque, however, are classed as cash transactions. The main reason for this is that traditionally such transactions would be processed using a cash register or cash till. The cheques and cash in the till would be counted at the end of the day and then transferred to the bank account.

Credit transactions, on the other hand, where goods are sold and purchased and paid for at a later date are more commonly paid using electronic payments methods (i.e. they are paid online) and are commonly referred to as bank transactions.

For the sake of simplicity the following illustrations all refer to payments and receipts of cash being made out of the 'cash' account, rather than distinguishing between 'bank ledgers' and 'cash ledgers'.

When cash is received (i.e. receipt of an asset) the entry in the cash ledger is a debit. When cash is paid out (i.e. a reduction in an asset) the entry in the cash ledger is a credit.

Illustration 1

Show the following transactions in ledger accounts: (Tip: The ledger accounts you need are Cash, Rent, Purchases and Sales.)

(1) Kamran pays $80 for rent by cheque.

(2) Kamran sells goods for $230 cash which he banks.

(3) He then purchases $70 of goods for resale using cash.

(4) Kamran sells more goods for cash, receiving $3,400.

Solution to Illustration 1

The double entry journals for these transactions are as follows:

(1) Dr rental expenses $80

    Cr cash $80

(2) Dr cash $230

    Cr sales revenue $230

(3) Dr purchases $70

    Cr cash $70

(4) Dr cash $3,400

    Cr sales revenue $3,400

Cash

	$		$
Sales (2)	230	Rent (1)	80
Sales (4)	3,400	Purchases (3)	70

Sales

	$		$
		Cash (2)	230
		Cash (4)	3,400

Rent

	$		$
Cash (1)	80		

Purchases

	$		$
Cash (3)	70		

Test your understanding 1

Yusuf enters into the following transactions in his first month of trading:

(1) Buys goods for cash for $380.

(2) Pays $20 in sundry expenses.

(3) Makes $1,000 in sales.

(4) Receives a bank loan of $5,000.

(5) Pays $2,600 for fixtures and fittings.

What is the total entry to the credit side of the cash T-account?

A $6,000

B $6,380

C $3,000

D $2,620

3 Recording credit transactions

Credit sales and purchases are transactions where goods or services change hands immediately, but payment is not made or received until some time in the future.

Money that a business is owed is accounted for in the receivables ledger.

Money that a business owes is accounted for in the payables ledger.

Test your understanding 2

Norris notes down the following transactions that happened in June.

(1) Sell goods for cash for $60.
(2) Pay insurance premium by cheque – $400.
(3) Sell goods for $250 – the customer will pay in a month.
(4) Pay $50 petrol for the delivery van.
(5) Buy $170 goods for resale on credit.
(6) Buys $57 of goods for resale, paying by cheque.
(7) Buy another $40 goods for resale, paying cash.
(8) Buy a new computer for the business for $800, paying cash.

Record these transactions using ledger accounts.

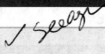

Test your understanding 3

For each of the following individual transactions state the two ledger accounts affected, and whether the ledger account should be debited or credited:

(1) Ole purchases goods for $5,000, and pays by cheque.

(2) Ole makes a sale to a customer for $500. The customer pays in 30 days' time.

(3) Ole pays a telephone bill amounting to $40, and pays by cheque.

(4) Ole receives bank interest income of $150.

(5) Ole purchases stationery for $12 and pays cash.

(6) Ole makes a sale to a customer for $400. The customer pays cash.

4 Balancing off a ledger account

Once the transactions for a period have been recorded, it will be necessary to find the balance on the ledger account:

(1) Total both sides of the T-account and find the larger total.

(2) Put the larger total in the total box on the debit and credit side.

(3) Insert a balancing figure to the side of the T-account which does not currently add up to the amount in the total box. Call this balancing figure 'balance c/f' (carried forward) or 'balance c/d' (carried down).

(4) Carry the balance down diagonally and call it 'balance b/f' (brought forward) or 'balance b/d' (brought down).

Illustration 2

Balance off the following account:

Cash

	$		$
Capital	10,000	Purchases	200
Sales	250	Rent	150
		Electricity	75

Solution to Illustration 2

Cash

	$		$
Capital	10,000	Purchases	200
Sales	250	Rent	150
		Electricity	75
		Balance c/f	9,825
	10,250		10,250
Balance b/f	9,825		

Test your understanding 4

Balance off the following account:

Cash

	$		$
Capital	10,000	Purchases	1,000
Sales	300	Rent	2,500
		Electricity	750
		New van	15,000

£950

5 Closing off the ledger accounts

At the year end, the ledger accounts must be closed off in preparation for the recording of transactions in the next accounting period.

Statement of financial position ledger accounts

- Assets/liabilities at the end of a period = Assets/liabilities at start of the next period, e.g. the cash at bank at the end of one day will be the cash at bank at the start of the following day.

- Balancing the account will result in:
  - a balance c/f (being the asset/liability at the end of the accounting period)
  - a balance b/f (being the asset/liability at the start of the next accounting period).

Profit or loss ledger accounts

- At the end of a period any amounts that relate to that period are transferred out of the income and expenditure accounts into another ledger account called profit or loss.

- This is done by closing the account.

- Do not show a balance c/f or balance b/f but instead put the balancing figure on the smallest side and label it 'profit or loss'.

Test your understanding 5

Johnny had receivables of $4,500 at the start of 20X5. During the year to 31 December 20X5 he makes credit sales of $45,000 and receives cash of $46,500 from credit customers.

What is the balance on the receivables account at 31 December 20X5?

A $6,000Dr

B $6,000Cr

C $3,000Dr

D $3,000Cr

Test your understanding 6

Matthew set up a company and in the first nine days of trading the following transactions occurred:

1 January   Matthew buys $10,000 of share capital in the newly formed company, paying by cheque.

2 January   Matthew buys supplies worth $4,000 and pays by cheque.

3 January   Matthew buys a delivery van for $2,000 and pays by cheque.

4 January   Matthew buys $1,000 of purchases on credit.

5 January   Matthew sells goods for $1,500 and receives a cheque of that amount.

6 January   Matthew sells all his remaining goods for $5,000 on credit.

7 January   Matthew pays $800 to his supplier by cheque.

8 January   Matthew pays rent of $200 by cheque.

Complete the relevant ledger accounts.

Chapter summary

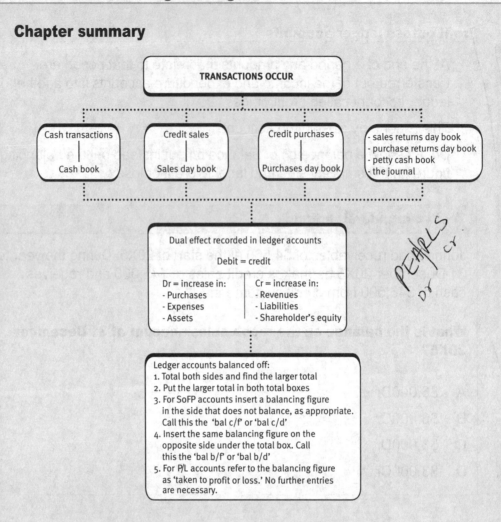

TRANSACTIONS OCCUR

Cash transactions	Credit sales	Credit purchases	- sales returns day book
			- purchase returns day book
			- petty cash book
Cash book	Sales day book	Purchases day book	- the journal

Dual effect recorded in ledger accounts

Debit = credit

Dr = increase in:	Cr = increase in:
- Purchases	- Revenues
- Expenses	- Liabilities
- Assets	- Shareholder's equity

PEARLS
Dr   Cr

Ledger accounts balanced off:
1. Total both sides and find the larger total
2. Put the larger total in both total boxes
3. For SoFP accounts insert a balancing figure in the side that does not balance, as appropriate. Call this the 'bal c/f' or 'bal c/d'
4. Insert the same balancing figure on the opposite side under the total box. Call this the 'bal b/f' or 'bal b/d'
5. For P/L accounts refer to the balancing figure as 'taken to profit or loss.' No further entries are necessary.

Test your understanding answers

Test your understanding 1

The correct answer is C.

Cash

	$		$
Sales	1,000	Purchases	380
Loan	5,000	Sundry expenses	20
		Fixtures and fittings	2,600

Test your understanding 2

Cash

	$		$
Sales (1)	60	Insurance (2)	400
		Motor expenses (4)	50
		Purchases (6)	57
		Purchases (7)	40
		Non-current assets (8)	800

Sales

	$		$
		Bank (1)	60
		Receivables (3)	250

Insurance (expense)

	$		$
Bank (2)	400		

Receivables

	$		$
Sales (3)	250		

Motor expenses

	$		$
Bank (4)	50		

Purchases

	$		$
Payables (5)	170		
Cash (6)	57		
Cash (7)	40		

Payables

	$		$
		Purchases (5)	170

Non-current asset (computer)

	$		$
Bank (8)	800		

Test your understanding 3

			$	$
1	Dr	Purchases	5,000	
	Cr	Cash		5,000
2	Dr	Receivables	500	
	Cr	Sales		500
3	Dr	Telephone expense	40	
	Cr	Cash		40
4	Dr	Cash	150	
	Cr	Interest income		150
5	Dr	Stationery expense	12	
	Cr	Cash		12
6	Dr	Cash	400	
	Cr	Sales		400

Test your understanding 4

Cash

	$		$
Capital	10,000	Purchases	1,000
Sales	300	Rent	2,500
		Electricity	750
Balance c/f	8,950	New van	15,000
	———		———
	19,250		19,250
	———		———
		Balance b/f	8,950

Test your understanding 5

The correct answer is C.

Receivables

	$		$
Balance b/f	4,500		
Sales	45,000	Cash received	46,500
		Balance c/f	3,000
	———		———
	49,500		49,500
	———		———
Balance b/f	3,000		

Test your understanding 6

Cash

		$			$
1 Jan	Capital	10,000	2 Jan	Purchases	4,000
5 Jan	Sales	1,500	3 Jan	Delivery van	2,000
			7 Jan	Payables	800
			8 Jan	Rent	200
				Balance c/f	4,500
		11,500			11,500
	Balance b/f	4,500			

Share capital

		$			$
	Balance c/f	10,000	1 Jan	Cash	10,000
		10,000			10,000
				Bal b/f	10,000

Purchases

		$			$
2 Jan	Cash	4,000		To P/L	5,000
4 Jan	Payables	1,000			
		5,000			5,000

Delivery van

		$			$
3 Jan	Cash	2,000	Balance c/f		2,000
		2,000			2,000
	Balance b/f	2,000			

Payables

		$			$
7 Jan	Cash	800	4 Jan	Purchases	1,000
	Balance c/f	200			
		1,000			1,000
				Balance b/f	200

Sales

		$			$
To P/L		6,500	5 Jan	Cash	1,500
			6 Jan	Receivables	5,000
		6,500			6,500

Receivables

		$		$
7 Jan	Sales	5,000	Balance c/f	5,000
		5,000		5,000
	Balance b/f	5,000		

Rent

		$		$
8 Jan	Cash	200	To P/L	200
		200		200

5

Returns, discounts and sales tax

Chapter learning objectives

Upon completion of this chapter you will be able to:

- record sales and purchase returns
- record discounts allowed and received
- understand and record sales tax on transactions.

1 Overview

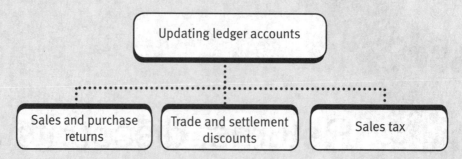

2 Recording sales and purchases returns

- It is normal for customers to return unwanted goods to a business; equally the business will occasionally have cause to return unwanted goods to their supplier.

- The double entries arising will depend upon whether the returned goods were initially purchased on credit:

	Originally a credit transaction	Originally a cash transaction
Sales returns (returns inwards)	Dr Sales returns Cr Receivables	Dr Sales returns Cr Cash
Purchases returns (returns outwards)	Dr Payables Cr Purchases returns	Dr Cash Cr Purchases returns

Test your understanding 1

For each of the following, state the double entry required to record the transaction in the accounts:

(1) Alfie transfers $10,000 of his own personal life savings into his business bank account.

(2) He then buys goods from Isabel, a supplier for $1,000 and pays by cheque.

(3) A sale is made for $400 – the customer pays by cheque.

(4) Alfie makes a sale for $600 and the customer promises to pay in the future.

(5) Alfie then buys goods from his supplier, Kamen, for $500 on credit.

(6) Alfie pays a telephone bill of $150 by cheque.

(7) The credit customer pays the balance on her account.

(8) Alfie pays Kamen $340.

(9) Bank interest of $30 is received.

(10) A cash customer returned $20 goods to Alfie for a refund.

(11) Alfie sent goods of $100 back to Kamen.

3 Discounts

Trade discounts

Trade discounts are given to try and increase the volume of sales being made by the supplier. By reducing the selling price, buying items in bulk then becomes more attractive. If you are able to source your products cheaper, you can then also sell them on to the consumer cheaper too. For example, if we were to buy over 1000 items, the supplier might be able to drop the price of those items by 5%.

Accounting for trade discounts

From an accounting perspective, trade discounts are deducted at the point of sale. When accounting for a sale that is subject to a trade discount - it is the net amount that should be recorded i.e. the trade discount does not get recorded separately.

Test your understanding 2

Oliver sells goods with a book value of $1,000 to Sam on a cash basis and allows her a trade discount of 10%.

Show how the above should be recorded in both the books of Oliver and Sam.

Early settlement discounts

This type of discount encourages people to pay for items much quicker. If you pay for the goods within a set time limit, then you will receive a % discount. These are often referred to as 'cash discounts.' For example, a cash discount of 3% is offered to any customers who pay within 14 days.

Whilst offering this discount makes the cash flow in quicker, it is still a 'lost cost' to the business who offers such a discount.

Accounting for settlement discounts

Discounts may be given in the case of credit transactions for prompt payment:

- A business may give its customer a discount – known as **Discount allowed**.

- A business may receive a discount from a supplier – known as **Discount received**.

The correct double entries are:

Discount allowed

Dr Discount allowed (expense)   X

Cr Receivables   X

The expense is shown beneath gross profit in the statement of profit or loss, alongside other expenses of the business.

Discount received

Dr Payables   X

Cr Discount received (income)   X

The income is shown beneath gross profit in the statement of profit or loss.

> ### Test your understanding 3
>
> George owes a supplier, Herbie, $2,000 and is owed $3,400 by a customer, Iris. George offers a cash discount to his customers of 2.5% if they pay within 14 days and Herbie has offered George a cash discount of 3% for payment within ten days.
>
> George pays Herbie within ten days and Iris takes advantage of the cash discount offered to her.

What ledger entries are required to record these discounts?

A	Dr	Payables	60	Dr	Discount allowed	85
	Cr	Discount received	60	Cr	Receivables	85
B	Dr	Discount allowed	60	Dr	Payables	85
	Cr	Receivables	60	Cr	Discount received	85
C	Dr	Payables	50	Dr	Discount allowed	102
	Cr	Discount received	50	Cr	Receivables	102
D	Dr	Discount allowed	50	Dr	Payables	102
	Cr	Receivables	50	Cr	Discount received	102

4 Sales tax

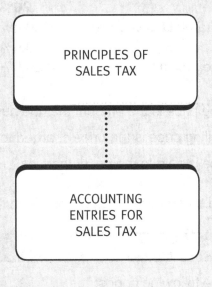

PRINCIPLES OF SALES TAX

ACCOUNTING ENTRIES FOR SALES TAX

PI   SO

SO > PI business pays The excess tax

5 Principles of sales tax

Sales tax is levied on the final consumer of a product. Unless they are the final consumer of the product or service then a business that is registered for sales tax is essentially the collection agent for the relevant authority.

Sales tax is charged on purchases (input tax) and sales (output tax). A business registered for sales tax will effectively pay over the sales tax it has added to its sales and recover the sales tax it has paid on its purchases. To this end the business incurs no sales tax expenses and earns no sales tax income. Therefore sales tax is excluded from the reported sales and purchases of the business.

Periodically the business calculates the total amount of sales tax added to sales and the total sales tax added to purchases. If output tax (on sales) exceeds input tax (on purchases), the business pays the excess to the tax authorities. If input tax exceeds output tax, the business is repaid the excess by the tax authorities.

Sales tax is sometimes referred to as value added tax or goods and services tax. Sales tax is charged on most goods and services.

6 Calculation of sales tax

Sales tax is charged at a variety of rates around the world. It is also subject to different rates for different products within national boundaries. To reflect this ACCA will examine a variety of rates in the F3 exam. The rate will always be given to you in the question.

Commonly examinable rates include 20% (the current standard rate in the UK), 17.5% (the previous standard rate in the UK), 15% and 10%. For these rates the following price structures are relevant:

Proforma

	20%	17.5%	15%	10%
Net selling price (tax exclusive price)	100.0%	100.0%	100.0%	100.0%
Sales tax	20.0%	17.5%	15%	10%
Gross selling price (tax inclusive price)	120.0%	117.5%	115%	110%

- The net selling price is the amount that the business wishes to achieve.
- The gross selling price is the price charged to customers.
- The difference is paid to the tax authorities.

Note: You should be prepared to apply any % to the proforma above.

Illustration 1 – Calculation of sales tax

Orlando sells the following goods:

(1) to Bruno at a tax inclusive price of $470.

(2) to Cosmo at a tax exclusive price of $700.

How much sales tax is Orlando collecting on behalf of the government if the rate of sales tax is 17.5%?

Solution to Illustration 1

Sales tax can be calculated using the relevant percentage depending on whether the price is tax inclusive or exclusive.

Sales to Bruno (sales price tax inclusive) (17.5%/117.5%) × $470 = $70

Sales to Cosmo (sales price tax exclusive) (17.5%/100%) × $700 = $122.50

Total sales tax collected: $70 + $122.50 = $192.50

Test your understanding 4

Lorenzo purchases goods for $174,240 (including sales tax) and sells goods for $230,400 (including sales tax).

What amount of sales tax is ultimately payable to the tax authorities?

A $9,360

B $14,926

C $4,471

D $11,232

The sales tax rate is 20%.

7 Accounting entries for sales tax

The usual bookkeeping entries for purchases and sales are only slightly amended by sales tax, the main addition being the introduction of a sales tax account, which is a receivable or payable account with the tax authorities.

Sales tax paid on purchases (input tax)

Dr Purchases – excluding sales tax (net cost)

Dr Sales tax (sales tax)

Cr Payables/cash – including sales tax (gross cost)

- The purchases account does not include sales tax because it is not an expense – it will be recovered.
- The payables account does include sales tax, as the supplier must be paid the full amount due.

Sales tax charged on sales (output tax)

Dr Receivables/cash – sales price including sales tax (gross selling price)

Cr Sales – sales price excluding sales tax (net selling price)

Cr Sales tax (sales tax)

- The sales account does not include sales tax because it is not income – it will have to be paid to the tax authorities.
- The receivables account does include sales tax, as the customer must pay the full amount due.

Payment of sales (output) tax

Dr Sales tax (amount paid)

Cr Cash (amount paid)

- If output tax exceeds input tax, a payment must be made to the tax authorities.

Receipt of sales (output) tax

Dr Cash (amount received)

Cr Sales tax (amount received)

- If input tax exceeds output tax, there will be a receipt from the tax authorities.

Test your understanding 5

		Net	Sales tax	Total
		$	$	$
Purchases	(all on credit)	180,000	18,000	198,000
Sales	(all on credit)	260,000	26,000	286,000

Record these transactions in the ledger accounts.

Test your understanding 6

Valerie's business is registered for sales tax purposes. During the quarter ending 31 March 20X6, she made the following sales, all of which were subject to sales tax at 17.5%:

$10,000 excluding sales tax

$7,402 including sales tax

$6,745 excluding sales tax

$11,632 including sales tax.

She also made the following purchases all of which were subject to sales tax at 17.5%:

$15,000 excluding sales tax

$12,455 including sales tax

$11,338 including sales tax

$9,870 including sales tax.

What is the balance on the sales tax account on 31 March 20X6?

A $7,639 Dr

B $1,875 Dr

C $7,639 Cr

D $1,875 Cr

8 Sales tax in day books

If a business is registered for sales tax, the sales and purchases day books must include entries to record the tax.

Illustration 2 – Sales tax in day books

Sales day book

Date	Invoice	Customer	Ledger Ref	Gross	Sales tax	Net
				$	$	$
8.7.X6	1	Spencer	J1	587.50	87.50	500.00
10.7.X6	2	Archie	S5	705.00	105.00	600.00
				1,292.50	192.50	1,100.00

Purchases day book

Date	Supplier	Ledger Ref	Gross	Sales tax	Net
			$	$	$
8.7.X6	Peggy	Y1	1,762.50	262.50	1,500
10.7.X6	Zena	Z8	352.50	52.50	300
			2,115.00	315.00	1,800

What double entry arises from the day books?

Solution to Illustration 2

The double entry for the above transactions will be:

Sales

Dr Receivables $1,292.50

Cr Sales tax $192.50

Cr Sales $1,100.00

Purchases

Dr Sales tax $315

Dr Purchases $1,800

Cr Payables $2,115

Test your understanding 7

The following sales invoices have been issued by Quincy in July:

Date	Customer	Inv No	Ledger ref.	Sales
8 July	Simpson	1100	A8	$ 411.25 (including sales tax)
10 July	Burns	1101	B5	$ 1,300 (excluding sales tax)

Quincy is registered for sales tax, applied at a rate of 17.5%

What accounting entries are required to record the transactions on the assumption that Quincy maintains one receivables account for all amounts due from credit sales customers?

		Dr		Cr
A	Receivables	$1,711.25	Sales	$2,010.72
	Sales tax	$299.47		
B	Receivables	$2,010.72	Sales	$1,711.25
			Sales tax	$299.47
C	Receivables	$1,650.00	Sales	$1,938.75
	Sales tax	$288.75		
D	Receivables	$1,938.75	Sales	$1,650.00
			Sales tax	$288.75

Chapter summary

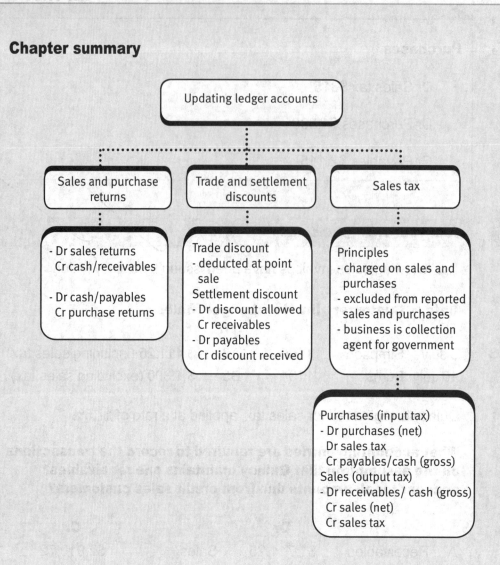

Test your understanding answers

Test your understanding 1

			$	$
1	Dr	Cash	10,000	
	Cr	Capital		10,000
2	Dr	Purchases	1,000	
	Cr	Cash		1,000
3	Dr	Cash	400	
	Cr	Sales		400
4	Dr	Receivables	600	
	Cr	Sales		600
5	Dr	Purchases	500	
	Cr	Payables		500
6	Dr	Telephone expense	150	
	Cr	Cash		150
7	Dr	Cash	600	
	Cr	Receivables		600
8	Dr	Payables	340	
	Cr	Cash		340
9	Dr	Cash	30	
	Cr	Interest income		30
10	Dr	Sales returns	20	
	Cr	Cash		20
11	Dr	Payables	100	
	Cr	Purchases returns		100

Test your understanding 2

Oliver's books:

Dr Cash	900
Cr Sales	900

(Net sale = $1,000 – 10%)

Sam's books:

Dr Purchases	900
Cr Cash	900

(Net purchase = $1,000 – 10%)

Test your understanding 3

The correct answer is A.

Payables

	$		$
Cash (97% × 2,000)	1,940	Balance b/f	2,000
Discount received	60		
	2,000		2,000

Receivables

	$		$
Balance b/f	3,400	Cash (97.5% × 3,400)	3,315
		Discount allowed	85
	3,400		3,400

Discount received

	$		$
		Payables	60

Discount allowed

	$		$
Receivables	85		

Test your understanding 4

The correct answer is A

	$
Output tax:	
Sales (including sales tax)	230,400
Sales tax (230,400 × 20/120)	38,400
	———
Input tax:	
Purchases (including sales tax)	174,240
Sales tax (174,240 × 20/120)	29,040
	———
Payable to tax authorities:	
Output tax – Input tax (38,400 – 29,040)	9,360
	———

Test your understanding 5

Sales

	$		$
		Receivables	260,000

Note that sales are recorded excluding sales tax, as this is not income for the business.

Purchases

	$		$
Payables	180,000		

Note that purchases are recorded net of sales tax, as this is not a cost to the business.

Receivables

	$		$
Sales/Sales tax	286,000		

Receivables are recorded including sales tax (the gross amount) as the customer must pay to the business the cost of the goods plus the sales tax.

Payables

	$		$
		Purchases/Sales tax	198,000

As with receivables, the payables must be recorded inclusive of sales tax, as the business needs to pay its suppliers the gross amount.

Sales tax account (a personal account with tax authorities)

	$		$
Payables	18,000	Receivables	26,000
Balance c/f	8,000		

Note: As the balance on the sales tax account represents a normal trade liability it is included in accounts payable on the statement of financial position.

Test your understanding 6

The correct answer is B.

Sales tax

	$		$
Purchases:		Sales	
15,000 × 17.5%	2,625	10,000 × 17.5%	1,750
12,455 × 17.5/117.5	1,855	7,402 × 17.5/117.5	1,102
11,338 × 17.5/117.5	1,689	6,745 × 17.5%	1,180
9,870 × 17.5/117.5	1,470	11,632 × 17.5/117.5	1,732
		Balance c/f	1,875
	7,639		7,639
Balance b/f	1,875		

Test your understanding 7

The correct answer is D.

Sales day book

Date	Customer	Invoice	Ledger ref.	Gross	Sales tax	Net
				$	$	$
8 July	Simpson	1100	A8	411.25	61.25	350.00
10 July	Burns	1101	B5	1,527.50	227.50	1,300.00
				1,938.75	288.75	1,650.00

The double entry for the above transaction will be:

Dr	Receivables	$1,938.75
Cr	Sales tax	$288.75
Cr	Sales	$1,650.00

6

Inventory

Chapter learning objectives

Upon completion of this chapter you will be able to:

- record the adjustments for opening and closing inventory
- apply the principles of inventory valuation in accordance with IAS 2
- recognise the costs that should be included in inventory
- calculate inventory cost using the FIFO and AVCO methods
- understand and identify the impact of inventory valuation on reported profits and assets.

1 Overview

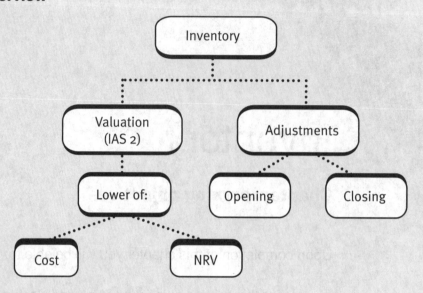

2 Inventory in the financial statements

Inventory is only recorded in the ledger accounts at the end of the accounting period. During the year the relevant sales and purchases are recorded but the increase and decrease in inventory assets is ignored. The movement in inventory is only considered on an annual basis. In this way a business can calculate exactly how much inventory they have used in the year to calculate cost of sales.

The standard proforma for calculating sales, cost of sales and gross profit is illustrated below:

	$	$
Revenue		X
Opening inventory	X	
Purchases	X	
Less: Closing inventory	(X)	
Cost of sales		(X)
Gross profit		X

Imagine a business that has some inventory left over from the previous year. They then add to this by purchasing more inventories for the year ahead. They then use this pool of inventory to manufacture their products, which they will sell to generate sales revenue. At the end of the year there is likely to be some inventory left over to sustain the business in the future.

When calculating gross profit we match the revenue generated from the sales of goods in the year with the costs of manufacturing those goods. You should be able to appreciate that the costs of the unused inventories should not be included in this figure. These are carried forward into the next accounting period where they will be used to manufacture goods that are sold in that period.

The goods carried forward are classified as assets on the statement of financial position.

Further explanation of inventory matching

The carrying forward of unused inventory is the application of the matching concept. This is an extension of the accruals concept. Inventory costs are matched to the revenues they help generate.

Illustration 1 – Gross profit calculation

At the beginning of the financial year a business has $1,500 of inventory left over from the preceding accounting period. During the year they purchase additional goods costing $21,000 and make sales totalling $25,000. At the end of the year there are $3,000 of goods left that have not been sold

What is the gross profit for the year?

Solution to Illustration 1

The unsold goods are referred to as closing inventory. This inventory is deducted from purchases in the statement of profit or loss.

Gross profit is thus:

	$	$
Sales revenue		25,000
Opening inventory	1,500	
Purchases	21,000	
Less: Closing inventory	(3,000)	
Cost of sales		(19,500)
Gross profit		5,500

Closing inventory of $3,000 will appear on the statement of financial position as an asset.

Test your understanding 1

Peter buys and sells washing machines. He has been trading for many years. On 1 January 20X7, his opening inventory is 30 washing machines which cost $9,500. He purchased 65 machines in the year amounting to $150,000 and on 31 December 20X7 he has 25 washing machines left in inventory with a cost of $7,500. Peter has sold 70 machines with a sales value of $215,000 in the year.

Calculate the gross profit for the year ended 31 December 20X7.

3 Year-end inventory adjustments

At the end of the year two basic adjustments are required to recognise opening and closing inventories in the correct place:

(1) Inventory brought forward from the previous year is assumed to have been used to generate assets for sale. It must be removed from inventory assets and recognised as an expense in the year

> Dr opening inventory in cost of sales
>
> Cr inventory assets

(2) The unused inventory at the end of the year is removed from purchase costs and carried forward as an asset into the next year:

> Dr inventory assets
>
> Cr closing inventory in cost of sales

Once these entries have been completed, the cost of sales account contains both opening and closing inventory and the inventory ledger account shows the closing inventory for the asset remaining at the end of the year.

Illustration 2 – Recording inventory in the ledger accounts

In TYU 1 Peter has opening inventory of $9,500 at the beginning of the year-ended 31 December 20X7. Peter's opening inventory ledger account would be presented as follows:

Inventory

20X7	$		$
1 Jan Balance b/f	9,500		

As inventory is an asset this is currently shown as a debit balance.

At the end of the year the opening inventory must be removed from assets and the expense recognised, as follows:

Dr cost of sales 9,500

Cr inventory assets 9,500

To provide a simple illustration of the effect of this adjustment a cost of sales T-account has been set up. This already includes the $150,000 of purchases Peter has incurred during the year.

Inventory

20X7	$		$
1 Jan bal b/f	9,500	Cost of sales	9,500

Cost of sales

20X7	$		$
Various purchases	150,000		
Inventory	9,500		

Next, the closing inventory for the year of $7,500 must be recognised using the following adjustment:

Dr inventory assets 7,500

Cr cost of sales 7,500

Inventory

20X7	$		$
1 Jan bal b/f	9,500	Cost of sales	9,500
31 Dec cost of sales	7,500		

Cost of sales

20X7	$		$
Various purchases	150,000		
Inventory	9,500	31 Dec inventory	7,500

Finally, the ledger accounts can be closed off for the year.

Inventory

20X7	$		$
1 Jan bal b/f	9,500	Cost of sales	9,500
31 Dec cost of sales	7,500	31 Dec bal c/f	7,500
	17,000		17,000
1 Jan X8 bal b/f	7,500		

Cost of sales

20X7	$		$
Various purchases	150,000		
Inventory	9,500	31 Dec inventory	7,500
		Taken to profit or loss	152,000
	159,500		159,500

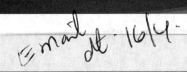

Test your understanding 2

The trading position of a simple cash-based business for its first week of trading was as follows:

	$
Capital introduced by the owner	1,000
Purchases for cash	800
Sales for cash	900

At the end of the week there were goods which had cost $300 left in inventory.

Write up the ledger accounts for the first week and then prepare a vertical statement of profit or loss (i.e. sales revenue, costs of sales and gross profit).

Clearly show the closing inventory asset that would be shown on the statement of financial position at the end of the first week.

You will need to set up two inventory T-accounts: one for inventory assets and one for inventory within cost of sales.

Test your understanding 3

The business described in Test your understanding 2 now continues into its second week. Its transactions are as follows:

	$
Sales for cash	1,000
Purchases for cash	1,100

The goods left in inventory at the end of this second week originally cost $500.

Write up the ledger accounts and the vertical statement of profit or loss for week two.

Clearly identify the closing inventory asset that would appear on the statement of financial position at the end of the second week.

4 Valuation of inventory

Inventory consists of:

- goods purchased for resale
- consumable stores (such as oil)
- raw materials and components (used in the production process)
- partly-finished goods (usually called **work in progress – WIP**)
- finished goods (which have been manufactured by the business).

IAS 2 Inventories

Inventory is included in the statement of financial position at:

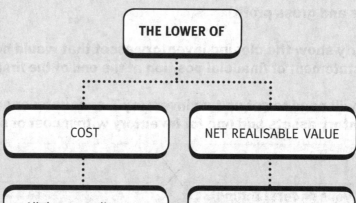

THE LOWER OF

COST	NET REALISABLE VALUE
• All the expenditure incurred in bringing the product or service to its present location and condition. • This includes cost of **purchase** – material costs, import duties, freight and cost of **conversion** – this includes **direct costs** and **production overheads**.	• Revenue expected to be earned in the future when the goods are sold, less any selling costs.

Cost

Cost includes all the expenditure incurred in bringing the product or service to its present location and condition.

This includes:

- Cost of purchase – material costs, import duties, freight.
- Cost of conversion – this includes direct costs and production overheads (depreciation of productive machinery/buildings is included here – see later chapter).

Costs which must be **excluded** from the cost of inventory are:

- selling costs
- storage costs
- abnormal waste of materials, labour or other costs
- administrative overheads.

Net realisable value (also referred to as 'fair value less further costs to sell')

Net realisable value is the net amount that would be realised after incurring any further costs required to make the sale. In effect, it is the fair value of the item, less any further costs that must be incurred in order to sell that item. This may include, for example, further work and costs required in order to make items of work in progress into finished goods before they could be sold. When items of inventory are old or obsolete, they are likely to be valued at net realisable value, rather than cost, in accordance with the requirements of IAS 2.

IAS 2 disclosure requirements

IAS 1 Presentation of Financial Statements requires that companies disclose the accounting policies adopted in preparing the financial statements, including those used to account for inventories. IAS 2 also requires that the total carrying amount of inventories are broken down into appropriate sub-headings or classifications and that the total amount of inventory carried at net realisable value is disclosed.

An example of a specimen disclosure note is as follows:

Inventories are valued at the lower of cost and net realisable value for each separate product or item. Cost is determined by recognising all costs required to get inventory to its location and condition at the reporting date and is applied on a 'first in, first out' basis. Net realisable value is the expected selling price of inventory, less any further costs expected to be incurred to achieve the sale.

	$000
Raw materials	200
Work in progress	600
Finished goods	350
	1,050

Within the carrying amount of inventories, the amount carried at net realisable value is $150,000.

Cost vs Fair value less further costs to sell (NRV)

Example

Gordano is a small furniture manufacturing company. All of its timber is imported from Scandinavia and there are only three basic products - bookcases, dining tables and cupboards. The company has 200 completed bookcases in inventory at the end of the year. For final accounts purposes, these will be stated at the lower of cost and net realisable value. How is 'cost' arrived at?

Solution

'Cost' will include several elements:

- Cost of purchase. First of all we must identify the timber used in the manufacture of bookcases (as opposed to dining tables and cupboards). The relevant costs will include the cost of the timber, the import duty and all the insurance and freight expenses associated with transporting the timber from Scandinavia to the factory.

- Cost of conversion. This will include costs which can be directly linked to the bookcases produced during the year. This includes labour costs 'booked' and sundry material costs (e.g. hinges and screws). Production overheads present particular problems. Costs such as factory heating and light, salaries of supervisors and depreciation of equipment are likely to relate to the three product ranges. These costs must be allocated to these product ranges on a reasonable basis. In particular, any percentage additions to cover overheads must be based on the normal level of production. If this provision was not made, the inventory could be overvalued at the end of a period of low production, because there would be a smaller number of items over which to spread the overhead cost.

These groups of cost must relate to either:

- bookcases sold during the year, or
- bookcases in inventory at the year-end (i.e. 200 bookcases).

Fair value less further costs to sell (NRV)

The comparison between cost and fair value less further costs to sell must be made item by item, not on the total inventory value. It may be acceptable to consider groups of items together if all are worth less than cost.

Test your understanding 4

Cole's business sells three products X, Y and Z. The following information was available at the year-end:

	X	Y	Z
	$	$	$
Cost	7	10	19
Fair value less further costs to sell (NRV)	10	8	15
Units	100	200	300

What was the value of the closing inventory?

A $8,400

B $6,800

C $7,100

D $7,200

Test your understanding 5

In what circumstances might the fair value less further costs to sell of inventory be lower than its cost?

Test your understanding 6

Storm, an entity, had 500 units of product X at 30 June 20X5. The product had been purchased at a cost of $18 per unit and normally sells for $24 per unit. Recently, product X started to deteriorate but can still be sold for $24 per unit, provided that some rectification work is undertaken at a cost of $3 per unit.

What was the value of closing inventory at 30 June 20X5?

Test your understanding 7

Hurricane, an entity, had 1,500 units of product Y at 30 June 20X8. The product had been purchased at a cost of $30 per unit and normally sells for $40 per unit. Recently, product Y started to deteriorate and can now be sold for only $38 per unit, provided that some rectification work is undertaken at a cost of $10 per unit.

What was the value of inventory at 30 June 20X8?

Test your understanding 8

IAS 2 Inventories defines the items that may be included in computing the value of an inventory of finished goods manufactured by a business.

Which one of the following lists consists only of items which may be included in the statement of financial position value of such inventories according to IAS 2?

A   Foreman's wages, carriage inwards, carriage outwards, raw materials.

B   Raw materials, carriage inwards, costs of storage of finished goods, plant and machinery costs.

C   Plant and machinery costs, carriage inwards, raw materials, foreman's wages.

D   Carriage outwards, raw materials, foreman's wages, plant and machinery costs.

5 Methods of calculating the cost of inventory

Method	Key points	
Unit cost	This is the actual cost of purchasing identifiable units of inventory.	Only used when items of inventory are individually distinguishable and of high value
FIFO – first in first out	For costing purposes, the first items of inventory received are assumed to be the first ones sold.	The cost of closing inventory is the cost of the most recent purchases of inventory.
AVCO – Average cost	The cost of an item of inventory is calculated by taking the average of all inventory held.	The average cost can be calculated periodically or continuously.

Periodic weighted average cost

With this inventory valuation method, an average cost per unit is calculated based upon the cost of opening inventory plus the cost of all purchases made during the accounting period. This method of inventory valuation is calculated at the end of an accounting period when the total quantity and cost of purchases for the period is known.

Continuous weighted average cost

With this inventory valuation method, an updated average cost per unit is calculated following a purchase of goods. The cost of any subsequent sales are then accounted for at that weighted average cost per unit. This procedure is repeated whenever a further purchase of goods is made during the accounting period.

Note: When using either of the two methods of weighted average cost to determine inventory valuation, it is possible that small rounding differences may arise. They do not affect the validity of the approach used and can normally be ignored.

Illustration 3

Invicta has closing inventory of 5 units at a cost of $3.50 per unit at 31 December 20X5. During the first week of January 20X6, Invicta entered into the following transactions:

Purchases

- 2nd January – 5 units at $4.00 per unit
- 4th January – 5 units at $5.00 per unit
- 6th January – 5 units at $5.50 per unit

Invicta sold 7 units for $10.00 per unit on 5th January.

Required:

(a) **Calculate the value of the closing inventory at the end of the first week of trading using the following inventory valuation methods:**

    (1) **FIFO**

    (2) **periodic weighted average cost**

    (3) **continuous weighted average cost.**

(b) **Prepare the statement of profit or loss (sales revenue, cost of sales, gross profit) for the first week of trading using each method of inventory valuation.**

Solution to Illustration 3

(a)

    (1) **Inventory valuation – FIFO**

        With this method of inventory valuation it is assumed that the oldest items of inventory are sold first, thereby leaving the business with the most recently purchased items. This provides an up-to-date valuation method for remaining items of inventory as it uses a recent purchase price to value the majority of goods.

When Invicta sells the 7 units on 5 January we assume it sells the oldest items first. Therefore Invicta will sell all of the 5 units within opening inventory on 1st January and 2 of the items purchased on 2nd January. This leaves Invicta with the following items:

3 units × $4.00 =	$12.00
5 units × $5.00 =	$25.00
5 units × $5.50 =	$27.50
Closing inventory cost	**$64.50**

(2) Inventory valuation – periodic AVCO

With this inventory valuation method, we work out an average cost per unit based upon the cost of opening inventory plus the cost of all purchases made during the accounting period as follows:

Average cost per unit: $((5 × \$3.50) + (5 × \$4.00) + (5 × \$5.00) + (5 × \$5.50)) / 20$ units = $4.50 per unit

Closing inventory cost = 13 units × $4.50 = **$58.50**

Cost of sales = 7 units × $4.50 = $31.50

(3) Inventory valuation – continuous AVCO

With this inventory valuation method we work out an updated average cost per unit each time a purchase of inventory is made. Any subsequent sales are accounted for at that average cost per unit until the next purchase is made and a new average cost per unit is calculated.

The best way to deal with this is to prepare a schedule dealing with transactions in date order as follows:

Date	Transaction	Units	Cost	Total cost
			$	$
1 Jan X6	Op inventory	5	3.50	17.50
2 Jan X6	Purchase	5	4.00	20.00
		10	(37.50/ 10) = 3.75	37.50
4 Jan X6	Purchase	5	5.00	25.00
		15	(62.50/ 15) = 4.17	62.50
5 Jan X6	**Sale at cost**	**(7)**	**4.17**	**(29.19)**
		8		33.31
6 Jan X6	Purchase	5	$5.50	27.50
7 Jan X6	Closing inventory	13	(60.81/ 13) = 4.68	60.81

(b) **Statements of profit or loss**

Statement of profit or loss using the FIFO method

	$	$
Sales (7 × $10.00)		70.00
Cost of sales		
Opening inventory (5 × $3.50)	17.50	
Purchases (5 × $4.00) + (5 × $5.00) + (5 × $5.50)	72.50	
Less: Closing inventory (see part a)	(64.50)	
		(25.50)
Gross profit		**44.50**

Statement of profit or loss using the periodic AVCO method

	$	$
Sales (7 × $10.00)		70.00
Cost of sales		
Opening inventory (5 × $3.50)	17.50	
Purchases (5 × $4.00) + (5 × $5.00) + (5 × $5.50)	72.50	
Less: Closing inventory (see part a)	(58.50)	
		(31.50)
Gross profit		**38.50**

Statement of profit or loss using the continuous AVCO method

	$	$
Sales (7 × $10.00)		70.00
Cost of sales		
Opening inventory (5 × $3.50)	17.50	
Purchases (5 × $4.00) + (5 × $5) + (5 × $5.50)	72.50	
Less: Closing inventory (see part a)	(60.81)	
		(29.19)
Gross profit		**40.81**

Test your understanding 9

A business commenced on 1 January and purchases are made as follows:

Month	No of units	Unit price	Value
		$	$
Jan	380	2.00	760
Feb	400	2.50	1,000
Mar	350	2.50	875
Apr	420	2.75	1,155
May	430	3.00	1,290
Jun	440	3.25	1,430
	2,420		6,510

In June, 1,420 articles were sold for $7,000.

What is the cost of closing inventory and gross profit for the period using the FIFO method:

	Closing inventory $	Gross profit $
A	2,690	3,180
B	2,310	2,800
C	3,077	3,567

Test your understanding 10

On 1 July 20X6 an entity, Pinto, had 10 items of inventory at a unit cost of $8.50. Pinto then made the following purchases and sales during a six-month period to 31 December 20X6:

Purchases:

Date	Quantity	Unit cost $	Total cost $
14 Oct X6	15	9.00	135.00
22 Nov X6	25	9.20	230.00
13 Dec X6	20	9.50	190.00
	60		555.00

Sales:

Date	Quantity	Unit selling price $	Total cost $
23 Aug X6	7	12.00	84.00
20 Oct X6	10	12.25	122.50
30 Nov X6	15	12.50	187.50
24 Dec X6	18	13.00	234.00
	50		628.00

Required:

Based upon the available information, calculate the closing inventory valuation at 31 December 20X6 using:

(a) **periodic weighted average cost**

(b) **continuous weighted average cost.**

Profit and statement of financial position

The impact of valuation methods on profit and the statement of financial position.

Different valuation methods will result in different closing inventory values. This impacts both profit and statement of financial position asset value. For this reason it is important that once a method has been selected it is applied consistently. It is not appropriate to keep switching between methods to manipulate reported profits.

Similarly any incorrect valuation of inventory will impact the financial statements.

If inventory is overvalued then:

- assets are overstated in the statement of financial position
- profit is overstated in the statement of profit or loss (as cost of sales is too low)

If inventory is undervalued then:

- assets are understated in the statement of financial position
- profit is understated in the statement of profit or loss (as cost of sales is too high).

Period-end vs continuous inventory records

Keeping inventory records

When preparing the financial statements, quantifying closing inventory can be a major exercise for a business. Traditionally inventory is counted and compared to inventory records at the year-end. This is referred to as the 'period-end' or 'periodic' method of inventory counting.

Alternatively a business could count a sample of inventory items at each week or month end and compare the results of those counts with the inventory records at that time. Throughout the accounting period the idea would be to count all lines of inventory at least once. This is referred to as 'continuous' inventory counting.

The merits of continuous inventory records are as follows:

- There is better information for inventory control.
- Excessive build-up of certain lines of inventory whilst having insufficient inventory of other lines is avoided.
- Less work is needed to calculate inventory at the end of the accounting period.

The merits of period-end inventory records are as follows:

- They are cheaper in most situations than the costs of maintaining continuous inventory records.
- Even if there is a continuous inventory record, there will still be a need to check the accuracy of the information recorded by having a physical check of some of the inventory lines.

6 Chapter summary

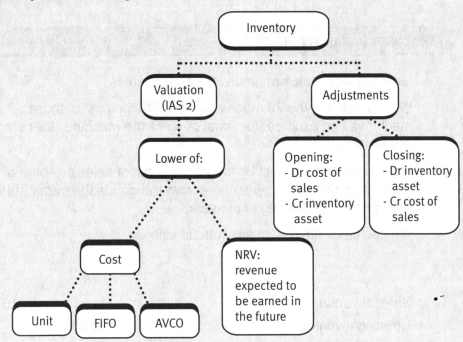

Test your understanding answers

Test your understanding 1

- Gross profit is sales revenue less cost of sales.

- We must match the 70 machines sold with the cost of those machines and exclude from cost of sales the machines that are left in inventory.

- Opening inventory must be included in cost of sales as some of the goods sold during the year come from the goods the trader started off with at the beginning of the year.

- We can calculate the gross profit as follows:

	$	$
Sales revenue		215,000
Opening inventory	9,500	
Purchases	150,000	
	–––––––	
	159,500	
Less: Closing inventory	(7,500)	
	–––––––	
Cost of sales		(152,000)
		–––––––
Gross profit		63,000
		–––––––

Test your understanding 2

First, the transactions are entered into the ledger accounts, and the accounts are balanced. Revenue and purchases are then transferred to the statement of profit or loss.

Capital

	$		$
Bal c/f	1,000	Cash	1,000
	1,000		1,000
		Bal b/f	1,000

Cash

	$		$
Capital	1,000	Purchases	800
Sales revenue	900	Balance c/f	1,100
	1,900		1,900
Balance b/f	1,100		

Sales revenue

	$		$
Taken to profit or loss	900	Cash	900

Purchases

	$		$
Cash	800	Taken to profit or loss	800

Next, the closing inventory must be accounted for in the inventory asset account and the profit or loss account. There is no opening inventory as this is the first week of trading for the business.

Inventory assets

	$		$
Profit or loss	300	Bal c/f	300
	300		300
Bal b/f	300		

Inventory (cost of sales)

	$		$
Taken to profit or loss	300	Closing inventory	300
	300		300

Statement of profit or loss for Week 1

	$	$
Sales Revenue		900
Cost of goods sold:		
Purchases	800	
Less: Closing inventory	(300)	
		(500)
Gross Profit		400

The closing inventory asset in the statement of financial position would be £300.

Test your understanding 3

First, the ledger accounts must be written up. You must remember that there are opening balances on the statement of financial position accounts (cash and capital) but the profit or loss accounts have no opening balances as they were transferred to the statement of profit or loss in Week 1.

Capital

	$		$
Bal c/f	1,000	Bal b/f	1,000
	1,000		1,000
		Bal b/f	1,000

Cash

	$		$
Balance b/f	1,100	Purchases	1,100
Sales Revenue	1,000	Balance c/f	1,000
	2,100		2,100
Balance b/f	1,000		

Sales revenue

	$		$
Taken to profit or loss	1,000	Cash	1,000

Purchases

	$		$
Cash	1,100	Taken to profit or loss	1,100

The opening inventory must be transferred to the statement of profit or loss, and the closing inventory entered into the ledger accounts (inventory and profit or loss) leaving the balance carried forward which will be included in the statement of financial position.

Inventory

	$		$
Balance b/f	300	Cost of sales	300
Cost of sales	500	Bal c/f	500
	800		800
Bal b/f	500		

Inventory (cost of sales)

	$		$
Opening inventory	300	Closing inventory	500
Taken to profit or loss	200		
	500		500

Statement of profit or loss for week 2

	$	$
Sales revenue		1,000
Cost of goods sold:		
Opening inventory	300	
Purchases	1,100	
	1,400	
Less: Closing inventory	(500)	
		(900)
Gross profit		100

The inventory asset on the statement of financial position at the end of week two will be $500.

Test your understanding 4

The correct answer is B.

X	$7	(cost) × 100	=		$700
Y	$8	(NRV) × 200	=		$1,600
Z	$15	(NRV) × 300	=		$4,500
					—————
Total					$6,800

Test your understanding 5

Fair value less further costs to sell may be relevant in special cases, such as where goods are slow-moving, damaged or obsolete. However, items of inventory will normally be stated at cost if they can be sold at a price greater than their cost of purchase.

Test your understanding 6

$9,000

IAS 2 requires that inventory is valued at the lower of either cost ($18 per unit) or fair value less further costs to sell ($24 - $3 = $21 per unit). Inventory is therefore valued at $18 per unit, giving a valuation for 500 units of $9,000.

Test your understanding 7

$42,000

IAS 2 requires that inventory is valued at the lower of either cost ($30 per unit) or fair value less further costs to sell ($38 - $10 = $28 per unit). Inventory is therefore valued at fair value less further costs to sell of $28 per unit, giving a valuation for 1,500 units of $42,000.

Test your understanding 8

The correct answer is C.

The other three answers contain items which cannot be included in inventory according to IAS 2.

Test your understanding 9

The correct answer is C.

- Inventory valuation (inventory in hand 2,420 – 1,420 = 1,000 units)
- FIFO – inventory valued at latest purchase prices

		$
440	articles at $3.25	1,430
430	articles at $3.00	1,290
130	articles at $2.75	357
1,000		3,077

Calculation of gross profit:

	$	$
Sales revenue		7,000
Purchases	6,510	
Less:		
Closing inventory	(3,077)	
Cost of goods sold		(3,433)
Gross profit		3,567

Test your understanding 10

(a) Periodic weighted average cost per unit

Date	Quantity	Unit cost $	Total cost $
1 Jul X6 – op inventory	10	8.50	85.00
14 Oct X6	15	9.00	135.00
22 Nov X6	25	9.20	230.00
13 Dec X6	20	9.50	190.00
	70		640.00

Therefore, periodic weighted average cost per unit = $640.00 / 70 units = $9.14

Closing inventory = 70 units − 50 sold = 20 units × $9.14 = $182.80

(b) **Continuous weighted average cost per unit**

Date	Quantity	Unit cost $	Total cost $
1 Jul X6 – op inventory	10	8.50	85.00
23 Aug X6 – sales	(7)	8.50	(59.50)
	3		25.50
14 Oct X6 – purchases	15	9.00	135.00
	18	(160.50 / 18) = 8.92	160.50
20 Oct X6 – sales	(10)	8.92	(89.20)
	8		71.30
22 Nov X6 – purchases	25	9.20	230.00
	33	(301.30 / 33) = 9.13	301.30
30 Nov X6 – sales	(15)	9.13	(136.95)
	18		164.35
13 Dec X6 – purchases	20	9.50	190.00
	38	(354.35 / 38) = 9.32	354.35
24 Dec X6 – sales	(18)	9.32	(167.76)
Closing inventory	**20**	**9.32**	**186.40**
		Rounding – ignore	0.19

Non-current assets: acquisition and depreciation

Chapter learning objectives

Upon completion of this chapter you will be able to:

- define non-current assets
- explain the difference between capital and revenue expenditure
- explain the purpose of an asset register
- prepare ledger entries to record the acquisition of non-current assets
- define, calculate and record the depreciation charge on non-current assets.

1 Overview

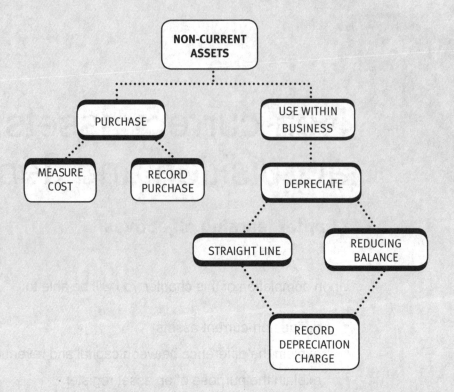

2 Non-current assets

Non-current assets are distinguished from current assets because they:

- are long-term in nature

- are not normally acquired for resale

- could be tangible or intangible

- are used to generate income directly or indirectly for a business

- are not normally liquid assets (i.e. not easily and quickly converted into cash without a significant loss in value).

3 Capital and revenue expenditure

It follows that a business' expenditure may be classified as one of two types:

CAPITAL EXPENDITURE
- Expenditure on the acquisition of non-current assets required for use in the business, not for resale.
- Expenditure on existing non-current assets aimed at increasing their earning capacity.

REVENUE EXPENDITURE
- Expenditure on current assets.
- Expenditure relating to running the business (such as administration costs).
- Expenditure on maintaining the earning capacity of non-current assets e.g. repairs and renewals.

Capital expenditure is long-term in nature as the business intends to receive the benefits of the expenditure over a long period of time.

Revenue expenditure relates to the current accounting period and is used to generate revenue in the business.

4 Non-current asset registers

Non-current asset registers are, as the name suggests, a record of the non-current assets held by a business. These form part of the internal control system of an organisation.

Non-current asset register

Details held on such a register may include:
- cost
- date of purchase
- description of asset
- serial/reference number
- location of asset
- depreciation method
- expected useful life
- carrying amount (net book value).

5 Acquisition of a non-current asset

A non-current asset register is maintained in order to control non-current assets and keep track of what is owned and where it is kept.

It is periodically reconciled to the non-current asset accounts maintained in the general ledger.

- The cost of a non-current asset is any amount incurred to acquire the asset and bring it into working condition

Includes	Excludes
Capital expenditure such as • purchase price • delivery costs • legal fees • subsequent expenditure which enhances the asset • trials and tests	Revenue expenditure such as: • repairs • renewals • repainting • administration • general overheads • training costs • wastage

- The correct double entry to record the purchase is:

Dr Non-current asset X

Cr Bank/Cash/Payables X

- A separate cost account should be kept for each category of non-current asset, e.g. motor vehicles, fixtures and fittings.

Subsequent expenditure

Subsequent expenditure on the non-current asset can only be recorded as part of the cost (or capitalised), if it enhances the benefits of the asset, i.e. increases the revenues capable of being generated by the asset.

An example of subsequent expenditure which meets this criterion, and so can be capitalised, is an extension to a shop building which provides extra selling space.

An example of subsequent expenditure which does not meet this criterion is repair work. Any repair costs must be debited to the statement of profit or loss, i.e. expensed.

Test your understanding 1

Acquisition of a non-current asset

Bilbo Baggins started a business providing limousine taxi services on 1 January 20X5. In the year to 31 December he incurred the following costs:

	$
Office premises	250,000
Legal fees associated with purchase of office	10,000
Cost of materials and labour to paint office in Bilbo's favourite colour, purple	300
Mercedes E series estate cars	116,000
Number plates for cars	210
Delivery charge for cars	180
Road licence fee for cars	480
Drivers' wages for first year of operation	60,000
Blank taxi receipts printed with Bilbo Baggins' business name and number	450

What amounts should be capitalised as 'Land and buildings' and 'Motor vehicles'?

	Land and buildings	Motor vehicles
A	260,000	116,390
B	250,000	116,870
C	250,300	116,390
D	260,300	116,870

6 Depreciation

- **IAS 16 Property, Plant and Equipment**, defines depreciation as 'the measure of the cost or revalued amount of the economic benefits of the tangible non-current asset that has been consumed during the period'.

- In simple terms, depreciation spreads the cost of the asset over the period in which it will be used.

- Depreciation matches the cost of using a non-current asset to the revenues generated by that asset over its useful life.

- Depreciation must also be matched to the pattern of use of the asset. This must be regularly reviewed and may be changed if the method no longer matches the usage of the asset.

- This is achieved by recording a depreciation charge each year, the effect of which is twofold ('the dual effect'):
  - Reduce the statement of financial position value of the non-current asset by accumulated depreciation to reflect the wearing out.
  - Record the depreciation charge as an expense in the statement of profit or loss to match to the revenue generated by the non-current asset.

Further discussion of depreciation

Depreciation may arise from:

- use
- physical wear and tear
- passing of time, e.g. a ten-year lease on a property
- obsolescence through technology and market changes, e.g. plant and machinery of a specialised nature
- depletion, e.g. the extraction of a mineral from a quarry.

The purpose of depreciation is not to show the asset at its current value in the statement of financial position, nor is it intended to provide a fund for the replacement of the asset. It is simply a method of allocating the cost of the asset over the periods estimated to benefit from its use (the useful life).

Land normally has an unlimited life and so **does not require depreciation**, but buildings should be depreciated.

Depreciation of an asset begins when it is available for use.

7 Methods of calculating depreciation

```
          STRAIGHT LINE          REDUCING BALANCE

    Depreciation charge          A reducing amount
    is the same each             of depreciation is
    year and so assumes          charged each year
    that the benefit is          and so assumes
    consumed evenly.             that more benefit is
                                 consumed in earlier
                                 years.

    Useful for assets            Useful for assets
    which provide equal          which provide more
    benefit each year,           benefit in earlier
    e.g. machinery.              years, e.g. cars, IT
                                 equipment.
```

Straight-line method

Depreciation charge = (Cost – Residual value)/Useful life

Alternatively it can simply be given as a simple percentage of cost.

Residual value: the estimated disposal value of the asset at the end of its useful life.

Useful life: the estimated number of years during which the business will use the asset.

The straight line method results in the same charge every year and is used wherever the pattern of usage of an asset is consistent throughout its life. Buildings are commonly depreciated using this method because businesses will commonly get the same usage out of a building every year.

Useful life

The useful life does not necessarily equal the physical life of the asset. For example many businesses use a three-year useful life for computers. This does not mean that a computer can no longer be used after three years; it means that the business is likely to replace the computer after three years due to technological advancement.

Reducing balance method

Depreciation charge = X % × carrying amount

CV: original cost of the non-current asset less accumulated depreciation on the asset to date.

The reducing balance method results in a constantly reducing depreciation charge throughout the life of the asset. This is used to reflect the expectation that the asset will be used less and less as it ages. This is a common method of depreciation for vehicles, where it is expected that they will provide less service to the business as they age because of the increased need to service/repair them as their mileage increases.

Assets bought/sold in the period

If a non-current asset is bought or sold in the period, there are two ways in which the depreciation could be accounted for:

*   provide a full year's depreciation in the year of acquisition and none in the year of disposal

*   monthly or pro-rata depreciation, based on the exact number of months that the asset has been owned.

Illustration 1 – Reducing balance method

Dev, a trader, purchased an item of plant for $1,000 on 1 August 20X1 which he depreciates on the reducing balance at 20% pa.

What is the depreciation charge for each of the first five years if the accounting year end is 31 July?

Solution to Illustration 1

Year	Depreciation charge % × CV	Depreciation charge $	Accumulated depreciation $
1	20% × $1,000	200	200
2	20% × $(1,000 – 200)	160	360
3	20% × $(1,000 – 360)	128	488
4	20% × $(1,000 – 488)	102	590
5	20% × $(1,000 – 590)	82	672

Test your understanding 2

Karen has been running a successful nursery school 'Little Monkeys' since 20X1. She bought the following assets as the nursery grew:

- a new oven for the nursery kitchen at a cost of $2,000 (purchased 1 December 20X4).

- a minibus to take the children on trips for $18,000 (purchased 1 June 20X4).

She depreciates the oven at 10% straight line and the minibus at 25% reducing balance. A full year's depreciation is charged in the year of purchase and none in the year of disposal.

What is the total depreciation charge for the year ended 31 October 20X6?

A $2,531

B $2,700

C $4,231

D $2,731

Test your understanding 3

The following information relates to Bangers & Smash, a car repair business:

	Machine 1	**Machine 2**
Cost	$12,000	$8,000
Purchase date	1 August 20X5	1 October 20X6
Depreciation method	20% straight line pro rata	10% reducing balance pro rata

What is the total depreciation charge for the years ended 31 December 20X5 and 20X6?

	20X5	**20X6**
	$	$
A	2,400	2,600
B	1,000	2,600
C	2,400	3,200
D	1,000	3,200

8 Accounting for depreciation

Whichever method is used to calculate depreciation, the accounting remains the same:

Dr Depreciation expense (IS) X

Cr Accumulated depreciation (SFP) X

- The depreciation expense account is a profit or loss account and therefore is not accumulated.

- The accumulated depreciation account is a statement of financial position account and as the name suggests is accumulated, i.e. reflects all depreciation to date.

- On the statement of financial position it is shown as a reduction against the cost of non-current assets:

	$
Cost	X
Accumulated depreciation	(X)
CV	X

"]

Illustration 2 – Accounting for depreciation

Santa runs a large toy shop in Windsor. In the year ended 31 August 20X5, she bought the following non-current assets:

- A new cash register for $5,000. This was purchased on 1 December 20X4, in time for the Christmas rush, and was to be depreciated at 10% straight line.

- A new delivery van, purchased on 31 March 20X5, at a cost of $22,000. The van is to be depreciated at 15% reducing balance.

Santa charges depreciation on a monthly basis.

- **What is the depreciation charge for the year ended 31st August 20X5?**

- **Show the relevant ledger accounts and statement of financial position presentation at that date.**

Solution to Illustration 2

Cash register Depreciation charge: 10% × $5,000 × 9/12

= $375

Delivery van Depreciation charge: 15% × $22,000 × 5/12

= $1,375

Cost (cash register)

	$		$
Cost	5,000	Balance c/f	5,000
	─────		─────
	5,000		5,000
	─────		─────
Balance b/f	5,000		

Cost (delivery van)

	$		$
Cost	22,000	Balance c/f	22,000
	22,000		22,000
Balance b/f	22,000		

Accumulated depreciation (cash register)

	$		$
Balance c/f	375	Depreciation expense 20X5	375
	375		375
		Balance b/f	375

Accumulated depreciation (delivery van)

	$		$
Balance c/f	1,375	Depreciation expense 20X5	1,375
	1,375		1,375
		Balance b/f	1,375

Depreciation expense

	$		$
Accumulated depreciation (cash register)	375		
Accumulated depreciation delivery van)	1,375	Profit or loss	1,750
	1,750		1,750

Statement of financial position extract at 31 August 20X5

Non-current assets	Cost	Accumulated depreciation	CV
	$	$	$
Cash register	5,000	(375)	4,625
Delivery van	22,000	(1,375)	20,625
Total	27,000	(1,750)	25,250

Test your understanding 4   X cash

Coco acquired two non-current assets for cash on 1 August 20X5 for use in her party organising business:

- a 25-year lease on a shop for $200,000
- a chocolate fountain for $4,000.

The fountain is to be depreciated at 25% pa using the reducing balance method.

A full year of depreciation is charged in the year of acquisition and none in the year of disposal.

Show the ledger account entries for these assets for the years ending 31 October 20X5, 20X6 and 20X7.

9 Changing estimates

Businesses should apply the same rates and methods of depreciation consistently throughout the life of their business. However, if they believe that their estimates of useful life and/or residual value are inappropriate they are permitted to change them with no further recourse. In order to do this you simply work out the new depreciation charge of the asset based on the revised estimate of useful life or residual value.

Illustration 3 – Changes to estimates

Alfie purchased a non-current asset for $100,000 on 1 January 20X2 and started depreciating it over five years. Residual value was taken as $10,000.

At 1 January 20X3 a review of asset lives was undertaken and the remaining useful life of the asset was estimated at eight years. Residual value was estimated to be nil.

Calculate the depreciation charge for the year ended 31 December 20X3 and subsequent years.

Solution to Illustration 3

Initial depreciation charge
= ($100,000 – $10,000) / 5 years = $18,000 pa.

At 1 Jan 20X3 the asset would have accumulated one year's worth of depreciation. Its carrying amount would therefore be $100,000 – $18,000 = $82,000.

At this point the asset is estimated to have a remaining useful life of 8 years and $nil residual value. From now on the depreciation charge will be $82,000 / 8 years = **$10,250 pa.**

Test your understanding 5

Alberto bought a wood-burning oven for his pizza restaurant for $30,000 on 1 January 20X0. At that time he believed that the oven's useful life would be 20 years after which it would have no value.

On 1 January 20X3, Alberto revises his estimations: he now believes that he will use the oven in the business for another 12 years after which he will be able to sell it second-hand for $1,500.

What is the depreciation charge for the year ended 31 December 20X3?

A $2,000

B $2,125

C $1,875

D $2,375

Chapter summary

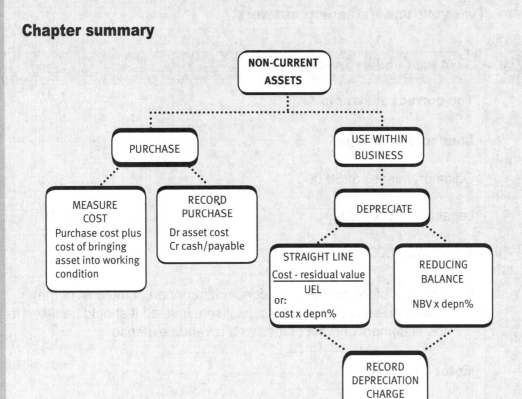

Test your understanding answers

Test your understanding 1

The correct answer is A.

Land and buildings

Office premises: $250,000

Legal fees: $10,000

Total: $260,000

- The cost of the purple paint does not form part of the cost of the office and so should not be capitalised. Instead it should be taken to the statement of profit or loss as a revenue expense.

Motor vehicles

3 Mercedes E series: $116,000

Number plates: $210

Delivery charges: $180

Total: $116,390

- The number plates are one-off charges which form part of the purchase price of any car.
- The road licence fee, drivers' wages and receipts are ongoing expenses, incurred every year. They cannot be capitalised, but should be taken to the statement of profit or loss as expenses.

Test your understanding 2

The correct answer is D.

Oven	20X6
	$
£2,000 × 10%	200
Minibus	
20X4 : 25% × $18,000 = $4,500	
20X5: 25% × $(18,000 – 4,500) = $3,375	
20X6: 25% × $(18,000 – 7,875) = $2,531	2,531
	———
Total depreciation charge	2,731

Test your understanding 3

The correct answer is B.

Machine 1

20X5: 20% × $12,000 × 5/12 = 1,000

20X6: 20% × $12,000 = 2,400

Machine 2

20X6: 10% × $8,000 × 3/12 = 200

Total depreciation charge

20X5: 1,000

20X6: $2,400 + $200 2,600

Lease (cost)

	$		$
1.8.X5 Cash	200,000	Balance c/f	200,000
	200,000		200,000
Balance b/f	200,000		

Fountain (cost)

	$		$
1.8.X5 Cash	4,000	Balance c/f	4,000
	4,000		4,000
Balance b/f	4,000		

Depreciation charge – Lease & Fountain

	$		$
X5 accumulated depreciation	9,000	Profit or loss	9,000
X6 accumulated depreciation	8,750	Profit or loss	8,750
X7 accumulated depreciation	8,563	Profit or loss	8,563

Accumulated depreciation – Lease

	$		$
		X5 depreciation charge	8,000
Balance c/f	8,000		
	8,000		8,000
		Balance b/f	8,000
		X6 depreciation charge	8,000
Balance c/f	16,000		
	16,000		16,000
		Balance b/f	16,000
		X7 depreciation charge	8,000
Balance c/f	24,000		
	24,000		24,000
		Balance b/f	24,000

Accumulated depreciation – Fountain			
	$		$
		X5 depreciation charge	1,000
Balance c/f	1,000		
	1,000		1,000
		Balance b/f	1,000
		X6 depreciation charge	750
Balance c/f	1,750		
	1,750		1,750
		Balance b/f	1,750
		X7 depreciation charge	563
Balance c/f	2,313		
	2,313		2,313
		Balance b/f	2,313

KAPLAN PUBLISHING

Annual depreciation workings:

Note, details of the depreciation method and rate for the lease are not given in the question. We are however told that the lease term is 25 years. This suggests that it would be appropriate to use the straight-line method with a useful life of 25 years.

20X5
Lease: $200,000/25 years = 8,000
Fountain: $4,000 × 25% = 1,000

Total: 9,000

20X6
Lease: $200,000/25 years = 8,000
Fountain: $3,000 × 25% = 750

Total: 8,750

20X7
Lease: $200,000/25 years = 8,000
Fountain: $2,250 × 25% = 563

Total: 8,563

Test your understanding 5

The correct answer is A.

Initial depreciation charge = $30,000 /20 years = $1,500

CV at date of change = $30,000 – ($1,500 × 3 years)

    = $25,500

New depreciation charge = $25,500 – $1,500 / 12 years

    = $2,000 pa

Non-current assets: disposal and revaluation

Chapter learning objectives

Upon completion of this chapter you will be able to:

- prepare ledger entries to record the disposal of non-current assets, including part exchange transactions

- calculate profits or losses on disposal

- record the revaluation of a non-current asset

- calculate the profit or loss on the disposal of a revalued asset

- illustrate how non-current assets are disclosed in the financial statements.

1 Overview

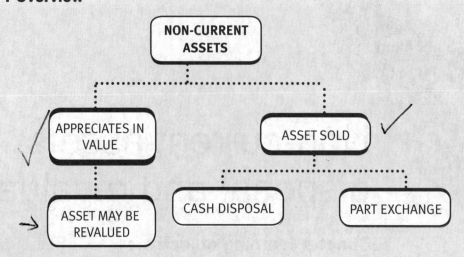

2 Disposal of non-current assets

When a tangible non-current asset is disposed of there are a number of adjustments required to remove the asset and associated accumulated depreciation from the statement of financial position and to record a profit or loss on the disposal.

Profit/loss on disposal

Proceeds > CV at disposal date   = Profit
Proceeds < CV at disposal date   = Loss
Proceeds = CV at disposal date   = Neither profit or loss

Note: A disposals T-account is required when recording the disposal of a non-current asset. This is a profit or loss account.

Disposal for cash consideration

This is a three-step process:

(1) Remove the **original cost** of the non-current asset from the 'non-current asset' account.

    Dr Disposals account

    Cr NC assets cost account

(2) Remove **accumulated depreciation** on the non-current asset from the 'accumulated depreciation' account.

    Dr Accumulated depreciation account

    Cr Disposals account

(3) Record the **proceeds**.

Dr Cash account

Cr Disposals account

The balance on the disposals T-account is the profit or loss on disposal:

Disposal

Original cost	X	Accumulated depreciation	X
		Proceeds	X
Profit on disposal	ß	Loss on disposal	ß
	X		X

The profit or loss on disposal can also be calculated as proceeds less CV of asset at disposal.

Test your understanding 1

Percy Throwerp runs a landscape gardening business. On 1 February 20X2, he purchased a sit-on lawnmower costing $3,000. He depreciates it at 10% straight line on a monthly basis. A few years later he decides to replace it with one which has an enclosed cabin for when it rains. He sells the lawnmower to an old friend, Alan Titchmuck, for $2,000 on 31 July 20X5.

How much is charged to Percy's statement of profit or loss in respect of the asset for the year ended 31 December 20X5?

Disposal through a part exchange agreement (PEA)

A part exchange agreement arises where an old asset is provided in part payment for a new one, the balance of the new asset being paid in cash.

The procedure to record the transaction is very similar to the three-step process seen for a cash disposal.

The first two steps are identical; however steps 3 and 4 are as follows:

(3) Record the **part exchange allowance** (PEA) as proceeds.

Dr NC assets cost account (= part of cost of new asset)

Cr Disposals account (= sale proceeds of old asset)

(4) Record the **cash paid** for the new asset.

Dr NC assets cost account

Cr Cash account

Again, the balance on the disposals T-account is the profit or loss on disposal:

Disposal

Original cost	X	Accumulated depreciation		X
		Proceeds		X
Profit on disposal	ß	Loss on disposal		ß
	___			___
	X			X
	___			___

Test your understanding 2

Bindi Bobbin runs a business altering and repairing clothes. When she started business on 1 January 20X2, she bought a Soopastitch II sewing machine for $2,500. She depreciates sewing machines using the straight-line method at a rate of 20% pa, and she charges a full year of depreciation in the year of acquisition and none in the year of disposal.

The business has now grown such that she needs a faster machine, and she will upgrade to the Soopastitch V during December 20X5. The Soopastitch salesman has offered her a part exchange deal as follows:

Part exchange allowance for Soopastitch II $750

Balance to be paid in cash for Soopastitch V $4,850

Show the ledger entries for the year ended 31 December 20X5 to reflect this transaction.

3 Revaluation of non-current assets

Some non-current assets, such as land and buildings may rise in value over time. Companies (rather than sole traders and partnerships) may choose to reflect the current value of the asset in their statement of financial position. This is known as revaluing the asset.

The difference between the CV of the asset and the revalued amount (normally a gain) is recorded in a revaluation surplus account in the equity or capital section of the statement of financial position. This will be covered later in the text.

This gain is not recorded in the statement of profit or loss because it is unrealised. Think about owning a house; the value of the house may appreciate in value over time. You can't go out and spend that increase in value on a new car though because it is not a real gain to you; it only becomes real when you sell the house and receive the benefit from that sale. Until that point it is a hypothetical gain (i.e. how much you would gain if you sold it at that point in time). Don't forget, the house could fall in value again by the time you sell it leaving you to find other ways to fund that car you just agreed to buy!

As this increase in value represents an unrealised gain we cannot record it as part of the profit earned during the year. IAS 1 requires that revaluation gains are disclosed separately from profit in 'other comprehensive income'. (This is covered in a later chapter.)

Illustration 1 – Revaluation of non-current assets

Vanguard owns land which originally cost $250,000. No depreciation has been charged on the land in accordance with IAS 16. Vanguard wishes to revalue the land to reflect its current market value, which it has been advised is $350,000.

How is this reflected in the financial statements?

Solution to Illustration 1

The land is currently held at cost of $250,000. This needs to be increased by $100,000 to reflect the new valuation of $350,000. Therefore the following is required:

Statement of profit or loss and other comprehensive income:

Other comprehensive income – item that will not be reclassified in subsequent accounting periods:

Revaluation surplus in the year $100,000

Statement of financial position:

Dr Non-current asset – land $100,000

Cr Revaluation surplus (within equity) $100,000

Illustration 2 – Revaluation of non-current assets

Hamstrung runs a kilt-making business in Scotland. It has run the business for many years from a building which originally cost $300,000 and on which $100,000 accumulated depreciation has been charged to date. Hamstrung wishes to revalue the building to $750,000.

How is this reflected in the financial statements?

Solution to Illustration 2

The current balances in the accounts are:

Building cost $300,000

Accumulated depreciation $100,000

- The building asset account needs to be raised by $450,000 to $750,000.
- On revaluation, the accumulated depreciation account is cleared out.

Therefore the double entry required is:

Dr Non-current asset – building $450,000

Dr Accumulated depreciation $100,000

Cr Revaluation surplus $550,000

The gain of $550,000 reflects the difference between the CV pre-revaluation of $200,000 and the revalued amount of $750,000.

Extract from the statement of profit or loss and other comprehensive income: (covered in more detail later in the text).

Other comprehensive income: Item that will not be reclassified in subsequent accounting periods:

Gain on property revaluation in year $550,000

Asset (building)

	$		$
Balance b/f	300,000		
Revaluation surplus	450,000	Balance c/f	750,000
	750,000		750,000
Balance b/f	750,000		

Accumulated depreciation (building)

	$		$
Revaluation surplus	100,000	Balance b/f	100,000
	100,000		100,000

Revaluation surplus			
	$		$
		Non-current asset (building)	450,000
Balance c/f	550,000	Accumulated depreciation (building)	100,000
	550,000		550,000
		Balance b/f	550,000

In summary

Revaluation surplus = Revalued amount – CV

For a non-depreciated asset:

Dr Non-current asset	revaluation surplus
Cr Revaluation surplus	revaluation surplus

Note that the revaluation surplus within equity is an accumulated revaluation surplus. The amount recognised within other comprehensive income is the revaluation surplus accounted for in that year.

For a depreciated asset:

Dr Accumulated depreciation	depreciation to date
Dr Non-current asset – cost	ß
Cr Revaluation surplus	revaluation gain

The revaluation gain for the year is disclosed on the face of the statement of profit or loss and other comprehensive income as an item of 'other comprehensive income'. This amount is added to any earlier revaluation from a previous accounting period to arrive at a cumulative revaluation surplus in the statement of changes in equity (SOCIE) and statement of financial position.

Test your understanding 3

Max owns a fish finger factory. The premises were purchased on 1 January 20X1 for $450,000 and depreciation charged at 2% pa on a straight- line basis.

Max now wishes to revalue the factory premises to $800,000 on 1 January 20X7 to reflect the market value.

What is the balance on the revaluation surplus after accounting for this transaction?

A $350,000

B $395,000

C $404,000

D $413,000

4 Depreciation and disposal of a revalued asset

Depreciation of a revalued asset

- When a non-current asset has been revalued, the charge for depreciation should be based on the revalued amount and the remaining useful life of the asset.

- This charge will be higher than depreciation prior to the revaluation and will be charged to profit or loss as normal.

- The excess of the new annual depreciation charge over the old depreciation charge may be the subject of an annual transfer from revaluation surplus to retained earnings (within the equity section of the statement of financial position) as follows:

Dr Revaluation surplus X

Cr Retained earnings X

In exam questions, you should review the question content carefully to determine whether this annual transfer is required. IAS 16 states that the annual transfer of excess depreciation is an optional policy decided upon by each company that revalues its non-current assets. If the policy is adopted, then the transfer should be made every year. It is not permitted to make the transfer in some years and not others.

Note: Retained earnings are where the accumulated profits and losses of a company are reflected on the statement of financial position. This will be described in more detail later when the text considers company accounts.

Illustration 3 – Depreciation of a revalued asset

Esoteric owns a retail unit in central Springfield. It bought the property 25 years ago for $100,000, depreciating it over 50 years on a straight-line basis. At the start of 20X6 the company decides to revalue the unit to $800,000. The unit has a remaining useful life of 25 years at the date of the revaluation. It is company policy to make the annual transfer of excess depreciation between revaluation surplus and retained earnings within equity.

What accounting entries should be made in the financial statements for 20X6?

Solution to Illustration 3

Statement of profit or loss and other comprehensive income:

Other comprehensive income: items that will not be reclassified to profit or loss in future periods:

Revaluation surplus on property in the year $750,000

Statement of financial position:

On revaluation at start of 20X6

    Dr Non-current asset – retail unit $700,000

    Dr Accumulated depreciation $50,000

    Cr Revaluation surplus $750,000

Depreciation for 20X6

    Dr Depreciation expense ($800,000/25 yrs) $32,000

    Cr Accumulated depreciation $32,000

Transfer of excess depreciation within equity for 20X6

    Dr Revaluation surplus ($32,000 – $2,000) $30,000

    Cr Retained earnings $30,000

(handwritten margin note) 100,000 × 0.5 = 50,000

Disposal of a revalued asset

The disposal of a revalued asset is recorded as normal, with the asset and accumulated depreciation accounts cleared to a disposal account so that a gain or loss on disposal can be calculated. However, with a revalued asset, there is an additional step required to clear any balance on the revaluation surplus account. This is achieved by taking the balance on the revaluation surplus account and transferring it to retained earnings which contains only realised gains and losses. If the company no longer owns the asset because it has been disposed of, it is inappropriate to maintain a revaluation surplus account for that asset. Any balance on revaluation surplus at the disposal date has now been realised and should be transferred to retained earnings. The double entry within equity is as follows:

Dr Revaluation surplus

Cr Retained earnings

Retained earnings are the sum total of all the profits and losses earned to date and is included within equity on the statement of financial position.

Test your understanding 4

Tiger Trees owns and runs a golf club. Some years ago the company purchased land next to the existing course with the intention of creating a smaller nine-hole course. The cost of the land was $260,000. Over time the company had the land revalued to $600,000. It has now decided that building the new course is uneconomical and has sold the land for $695,000.

What accounting entries are required to reflect the disposal?

5 IAS 16 disclosure requirements

Statement of financial position	Statement of profit or loss	Notes to the accounts
Aggregate CV of non-current assets disclosed on the face of the statement of financial position	Depreciation charge included within relevant expense categories.	• Disclosure of depreciation methods and rates used. • Non-current assets disclosure. • Details of revaluations.

IAS 16 Property Plant and Equipment contains a number of disclosure requirements relating to non-current assets. The principal disclosure requirements include:

(1) The measurement bases used for arriving at the carrying amount of the asset (e.g. cost or valuation). If more than one basis has been used, the amounts for each basis must be disclosed.

(2) Depreciation methods used, with details of useful lives or the depreciation rates used.

(3) The gross amount of each asset heading and its related accumulated depreciation (aggregated with accumulated impairment losses) at the beginning and end of the period.

(4) A reconciliation of the carrying amount at the beginning and end of the period, showing:

 – additions

 – assets classified as held for sale

 – disposals

 – revaluations

 – depreciation.

(5) Any commitments for future acquisition of property, plant and equipment.

(6) If assets are stated at revalued amounts, the following should be disclosed:

 – the effective date of the revaluation

 – whether an independent valuer performed the valuation

 – the methods and assumptions applied in estimating the items' fair value

 – the carrying amount that would have been recognised had the assets been carried at cost

 – the revaluation surplus, indicating the change for the period.

Note: Items (3) and (4) are often referred to as preparation of the movements schedule or grid for the year.

If there has been a revaluation of property, plant and equipment in the year, this may be performed by either an employee or director of the company, or by an independent third party. Who performed the valuation is regarded as relevant or useful information to those who make investment decisions based upon the content of the financial statements. If the valuation was performed by an employee or director of the company, although it is permitted by IAS 16, there is potential for objectivity to be compromised, and therefore details of the valuer should be disclosed in the notes to the financial statements.

The movements schedule or grid is illustrated as follows:

	Land & bldgs	Plant & equip't	Motor vehicles	Fixtures	Total
Cost or valuation:	$000	$000	$000	$000	$000
Balance b/fwd	X	X	X	X	X
Additions	X	X	X	X	X
Revaluation in year	X	X	X	X	X
Disposals	(X)	(X)	(X)	(X)	(X)
Balance c/fd	X	X	X	X	X
Accumulated depreciation:					
Balance b/fwd	X	X	X	X	X
Charge for the year	X	X	X	X	X
Revaluation in year	(X)	(X)	(X)	(X)	(X)
Disposals	(X)	(X)	(X)	(X)	(X)
Balance c/fwd	X	X	X	X	X
Carrying amount 31 Dec 20X4	**X**	**X**	**X**	**X**	**X**
Carrying amount 31 Dec 20X3	**X**	**X**	**X**	**X**	**X**

Chapter summary

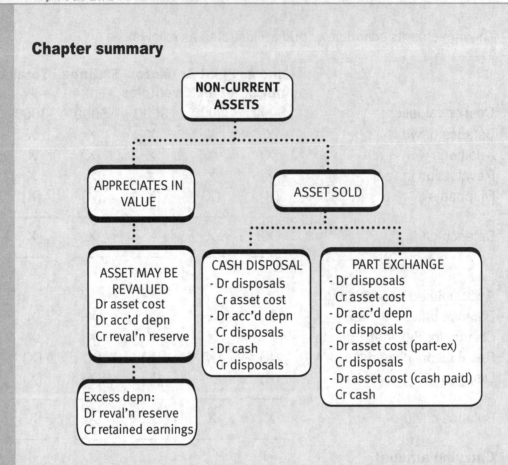

Test your understanding answers

Test your understanding 1

(1) Dr Disposals $3,000

Cr Fixtures and fittings cost $3,000

(2) Dr Accumulated depreciation $1,050

Cr Disposals $1,050

Depreciation working:

X2 10% × 3,000 × 11/12 = 275

X3 10% × 3,000 = 300

X4 10% × 3,000 = 300

X5 10% × 3,000 × 7/12 = 175

Total: 1050

(3) Dr Cash $2,000

Cr Disposals $2,000

Disposals

	$		$
31.7.X5 fixtures and fittings cost	3,000	Accumulated depreciation	1,050
Profit on disposal (ß)	50	Cash proceeds	2,000
	3,050		3,050

The charge to the statement of profit or loss for the year ended 31 December 20X5 is:

Depreciation charge for the year $175

Profit/loss on disposal $(50)

Note: As depreciation is charged monthly, it is necessary to charge an amount to the statement of profit or loss for the period 1 January 20X5 to the disposal date 31 July 20X5.

Test your understanding 2

Sewing machine

	$		$
Balance b/f	2,500	Disposal	2,500
New asset PEA	750		
Cash	4,850	Balance c/f	5,600
	8,100		8,100
Balance b/f	5,600		

Accumulated depreciation (sewing machine)

	$		$
Disposal	1,500	Balance b/f	1,500
Balance c/f	1,120	Depreciation charge X5	1,120
	2,620		2,620
		Balance b/f	1,120

Depreciation b/f working:

$2,500 × 20% × 3 years = $1,500

Disposals

	$		$
Sewing machine cost	2,500	Sewing machine accumulated depreciation	1,500
		PEA	750
		Loss on disposal (ß)	250
	2,500		2,500

Depreciation charge

	$		$
Sewing machine accumulated depreciation	1,120	Profit or loss	1,120

Depreciation charge working:

$5,600 × 20% = $1,120

Test your understanding 3

The correct answer is C.

Non-current asset – factory

	$		$
Balance b/f	450,000		
Revaluation	350,000	Balance c/f	800,000
	800,000		800,000
Balance b/f	800,000		

Accumulated depreciation (factory)

	$		$
Revaluation	54,000	Balance b/f	54,000
(2% × $450,000			
× 6 years)			
	54,000		54,000

Revaluation surplus

	$		$
		Factory asset	350,000
Balance c/f	404,000	Accumulated depreciation	54,000
	404,000		404,000
		Balance b/f	404,000

Test your understanding 4

Land (valuation)

	$		$
Original cost	260,000		
Revaluation surplus	340,000	Bal c/f	600,000
	600,000		600,000
Bal b/f	600,000	Disposals	600,000

Revaluation surplus

	$		$
Retained earnings	340,000	Land	340,000

Cash

	$		$
Disposals	695,000		

Disposal

	$		$
Land	600,000	Cash	695,000
Gain on disposal	95,000		

Note that the gain on disposal is included in the statement of profit or loss in arriving at the profit for the year.

Retained earnings

	$		$
		Revaluation surplus	340,000

Intangible non-current assets

Chapter learning objectives

Upon completion of this chapter you will be able to:

- recognise the difference between tangible and intangible non-current assets

- define and explain the treatment of research costs and development costs in accordance with IAS 38

- calculate the amounts to be capitalised or expensed with regard to R&D

- explain the purpose of, calculate and account for amortisation of intangible assets.

1 Overview

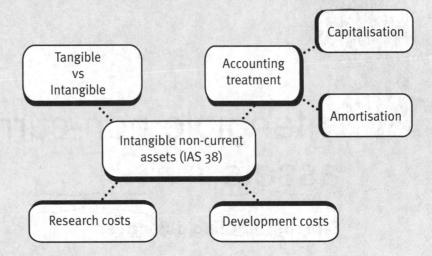

2 Intangible non-current assets (IAS 38)

Non-current assets are assets used within the business on an ongoing basis in order to generate revenue.

IAS 38 defines an intangible asset as 'an identifiable non-monetary asset without physical substance'. In particular, the key characteristics of an intangible non-current asset are as follows:

- it is a resource controlled by the entity from which the entity expects to derive future economic benefits,

- it lacks physical substance, and

- it is identifiable and separately distinguishable from goodwill.

The basic principle of recognition of an intangible asset in the financial statements is that:

- it should meet the definition of an intangible asset,

- the cost of the asset can be reliably measured, and

- that it is probable that future economic benefits will be received by the entity from the asset.

Examples of intangible assets include the following:

- licences

- patents

- brands

- trademarks

- copyrights
- franchises.

Development costs are internally generated intangible assets which are capitalised provided that specified criteria have been complied with. They are considered elsewhere within this chapter.

Tangible non-current assets

Normally have physical substance, e.g land and buildings.

Normally involve expenditure being incurred.

Cost of the tangible non-current asset is capitalised.

Depreciation is a reflection of the wearing out of the asset.

Intangible non-current assets

Do not normally have physical substance, e.g. copyright.

Can be purchased or may be created within a business without any expenditure being incurred, i.e. internally generated, e.g. brands.

Purchased intangible non-current assets are capitalised. Generally, internally generated assets may not be capitalised.

Amortisation is a reflection of the wearing out of the (capitalised) asset.

Examples:
- Development costs
- Goodwill
- Trade marks
- Licences
- Patents
- Copyrights
- Franchises

Amortisation = wearing out of capitalised assets

Test your understanding 1

Willis Ltd purchased a patent, with a useful life of ten years for $20,000 on 1 January 20X9.

Prepare extracts of the financial statements for the year ended 31 December 20X9?

3 Research and development

IAS 38 contains specific requirements relating to accounting for research and development activities. First, it is necessary to understand the definition of research expenditure and development costs before their respective accounting treatment is considered.

Research can be defined as original and planned investigation undertaken with the prospect of gaining new scientific or technical knowledge and understanding.

Development can be defined as the application of research findings or other knowledge to a plan or design for the production of new or substantially improved materials, devices, products, processes, systems or services before the start of commercial production or use.

Accounting treatment of research and development

When a company undertakes research and development activity, expenditure is incurred with the intention of producing future economic benefits i.e. increased sales revenues and profits.

The accounting issue is therefore whether these costs should be expensed to the statement of profit or loss or capitalised as an intangible asset on the statement of financial position to match against future benefits arising.

Research

- All research expenditure should be written off to the statement of profit or loss as it is incurred. This is in compliance with the prudence concept.

- Research expenditure does not directly lead to future benefits and therefore it is not possible to follow the matching concept.

- Any capital expenditure on research equipment (property, plant and equipment) should be capitalised and depreciated as normal in accordance with IAS 16.

Development costs

- IAS 38 requires that development costs must be capitalised as an intangible asset provided that all of the following criteria are met:
  - Technical feasibility to complete the intangible asset, so that it is available for sale or for use
  - Intention to complete and use or sell the intangible asset
  - Ability to use or sell the intangible asset
  - Existence of a market to sell either the asset itself or its output, or the usefulness of the asset can be demonstrated if it is to be used by the business
  - Adequate technical, financial and other resources to complete the project so that the intangible asset can be subsequently used or sold
  - Ability to reliably measure the expenditure incurred during the development of the intangible asset.

- If the above criteria are not met, development expenditure must be written off to the statement of profit or loss as it is incurred.

- If research expenditure has been treated as an expense, it cannot subsequently be reinstated as an asset.

Subsequent treatment of capitalised development expenditure

- The asset should be amortised over the period that is expected to benefit. This ensures that costs are matched to the revenue in the statement of profit or loss.

- Amortisation should commence with commercial production and charged over the period over which the business expects to generate economic benefits.

- Each project should be reviewed at the year end to ensure that the 'SECTOR' criteria are still met. If they are no longer met, the previously capitalised expenditure must be written off to the statement of profit or loss immediately.

If a policy of capitalisation is adopted, it should be applied to all projects that meet the criteria.

IAS 38 Intangible Assets

Development

An intangible asset arising from development (or from the development phase of an internal project) should be recognised if, and only if, an enterprise can demonstrate all of the following:

- the technical feasibility of completing the intangible asset so that it will be available for use or sale

- its intention to complete the intangible asset and use or sell it

- its ability to use or sell the intangible asset

- how the intangible asset will generate probable future economic benefits. Among other things, the enterprise should demonstrate the existence of a market for the output of the intangible asset or the intangible asset itself or, if it is to be used internally, the usefulness of the intangible asset.

- the availability of adequate technical, financial and other resources to complete the development and to use or sell the intangible asset

- its ability to measure reliably the expenditure attributable to the intangible asset during its development.

The amount to be included is the cost of the development. Note that expenditure, having been accounted for as an expense, cannot be reinstated as an asset.

Amortisation

If the useful life of an intangible asset is finite, the capitalised development costs must be amortised once commercial exploitation begins.

The amortisation method used should reflect the pattern in which the asset's economic benefits are consumed by the enterprise. If that pattern cannot be determined reliably, the straight-line method should be used.

An intangible asset with an indefinite useful life should not be amortised. An asset has an indefinite useful life if there is no foreseeable limit to the period over which the asset is expected to generate net cash inflows for the business. Instead, it should be subject to an annual impairment review.

Illustration 1 – Accounting for development costs

Brightspark Ltd is developing a new product, the widget. This is expected to be sold over a three-year period starting in 20X6. The forecast data is as follows:

	20X5 $000	20X6 $000	20X7 $000	20X8 $000
Net revenue from other activities	400	500	450	400
Net revenue from widgets	–	450	600	400
Development costs	(900)	–	–	–

Show how the development costs should be treated if:

(a) **the costs do not qualify for capitalisation**

(b) **the costs do qualify for capitalisation and are amortised on a straight-line basis.**

Solution to Illustration 1

(a) **Profit treating development costs as expenses when incurred**

	20X5 $000	20X6 $000	20X7 $000	20X8 $000
Net revenue from other activities	400	500	450	400
Net revenue from widgets	–	450	600	400
Development costs	(900)	–	–	–
Net profit/(loss)	(500)	950	1,050	800

(b) **Net profit amortising development costs over life of widgets**

	20X5 $000	20X6 $000	20X7 $000	20X8 $000
Net revenue from other activities	400	500	450	400
Net revenue from widgets	–	450	600	400
Development costs amortised	–	(300)	(300)	(300)
Net profit	400	650	750	500

Note that amortisation is spread over the period over which economic benefits are expected to be received.

Test your understanding 2

Which of the following should be classified as development?

(1) Braynee Ltd has spent $300,000 investigating whether a particular substance, flubber, found in the Amazon rainforest is resistant to heat.

(2) Cleverclogs Ltd has incurred $120,000 expenses in the course of making a new waterproof and windproof material with the idea that it may be used for ski-wear.

(3) Ayplus Ltd has found that a chemical compound, known as XYX, is not harmful to the human body.

(4) Braynee Ltd has incurred a further $450,000 using flubber in creating prototypes of a new heat-resistant suit for stuntmen.

A   All of them

B   1 and 3

C   2 and 4

D   2 only

Test your understanding 3

This year, Deep Blue Sea Ltd has developed a new material from which the next generation of wetsuits will be made. This special material will ensure that swimmers are kept warmer than ever. The costs incurred meet the capitalisation criteria and by the 31 December 20X5 year end $250,000 has been capitalised.

The wetsuits are expected to generate revenue for five years from the date that commercial production commences on 1 January 20X6.

What amount is charged to the statement of profit or loss in the year ended 31 December 20X6?

A   nil

B $250,000

C $100,000

D $50,000

4 Measurement of intangible assets

Initial recognition and measurement

Initial recognition of an intangible asset is always at cost.

Subsequent measurement

IAS 38 does permit the valuation model to be applied for subsequent measurement of intangible assets. However, for this to apply, the intangible assets must be traded on an active market which effectively requires the intangible assets to be homogeneous (i.e. identical) in nature. This is very rarely the case and therefore, to all intents and purposes, intangible assets are accounted for using the cost model. In practical terms, capitalised development costs would not meet the criteria for the valuation model to apply and the cost model should always be applied.

In rare situations where the valuation model can be applied, in a similar way to IAS 16 dealing with revaluation of property, plant and equipment, any upward revaluation is recorded as an item of other comprehensive income for the year and taken to a separate revaluation surplus for intangible assets within equity on the statement of financial position.

5 IAS 38 disclosure requirements

The financial statements should disclose the following for capitalised development costs:

- the amortisation method used and the expected period of amortisation

- a reconciliation of the carrying amounts at the beginning and end of the period, showing new expenditure incurred, amortisation and amounts written off because a project no longer qualifies for capitalisation

- amortisation during the period.

In addition, the financial statements should also disclose the total amount of research and development expenditure recognised as an expense during the period.

The reconciliation of the carrying amount for intangible assets from the start of the year to the end of the year required by IAS 38 is similar to that required for property, plant and equipment in accordance with IAS 16 as follows:

	Development costs	Licences	Total
Cost or valuation:	$000	$000	$000
Balance b/fwd	X	X	X
Additions	X	X	X
Disposals	(X)	(X)	(X)
Balance c/fwd	X	X	X
Accumulated depreciation:			
Balance b/fwd	X	X	X
Charge for the year	X	X	X
Disposals	(X)	(X)	(X)
Balance c/fwd	X	X	X
Carrying amount 31 Dec 20X4	**X**	**X**	**X**
Carrying amount 31 Dec 20X3	**X**	**X**	**X**

Chapter summary

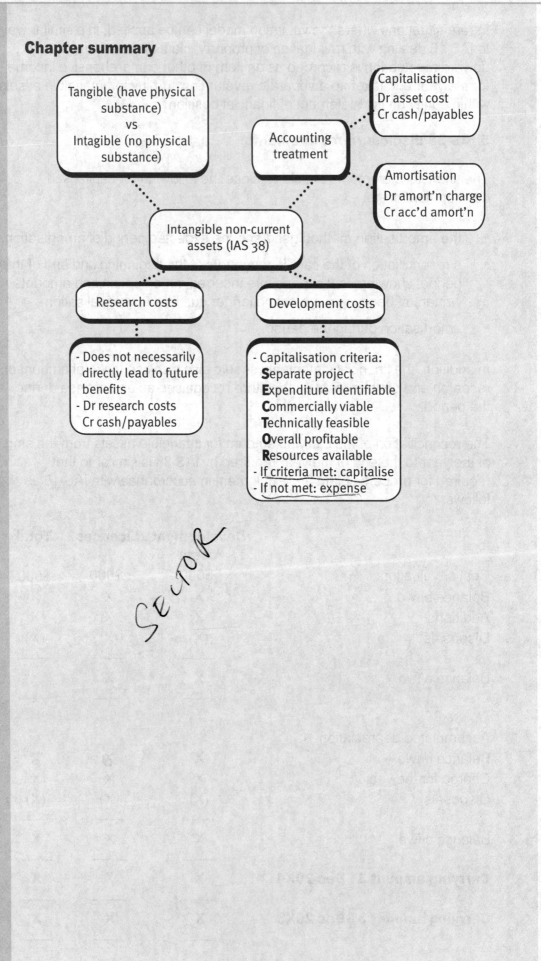

- Tangible (have physical substance)
  vs
  Intagible (no physical substance)

- Accounting treatment

- Capitalisation
  Dr asset cost
  Cr cash/payables

- Amortisation
  Dr amort'n charge
  Cr acc'd amort'n

- Intangible non-current assets (IAS 38)

- Research costs

- Development costs

- Does not necessarily directly lead to future benefits
- Dr research costs
  Cr cash/payables

- Capitalisation criteria:
  Separate project
  Expenditure identifiable
  Commercially viable
  Technically feasible
  Overall profitable
  Resources available
- If criteria met: capitalise
- If not met: expense

Test your understanding answers

Test your understanding 1

Statement of profit or loss

Amortisation	$2,000
($20,0000 / 10 years)	

Statement of financial position extract

Intangible assets	$18,000
($20,000 – $2,000)	

Test your understanding 2

The correct answer is C.

Both 1 and 3 involve researching materials, without any form of commercial production in mind.

Test your understanding 3

The correct answer is D.

Amortisation will be charged on a straight-line basis for each of the five years that revenue is generated.

Therefore the amortisation charge for each of the years ended 31 December 20X6 – 20Y0 will be:

$250,000/5 years = $50,000

10

Accruals and prepayments

Chapter learning objectives

Upon completion of this chapter you will be able to:

- understand how the matching concept applies to accruals and prepayments

- identify and calculate adjustments relating to accruals and prepayments

- record the appropriate adjustments for accruals and prepayments in the ledger accounts

- understand the impact of accruals and prepayments on profit and net assets.

1 Overview

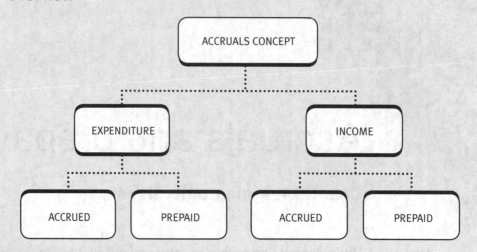

2 Accruals basis of accounting

The accruals basis of accounting means that to calculate the profit for the period, we must include all the income and expenditure relating to the period, whether or not the cash has been received or paid or an invoice received.

Profit is therefore:

Income earned	X
Expenditure incurred	(X)
	———
Profit	X

Accruals concept

The accruals concept is identified as an important accounting concept by IAS 1 Presentation of Financial Statements. The concept is that income and expenses should be matched together and dealt with in the statement of profit or loss for the period to which they relate, regardless of the period in which the cash was actually received or paid. Therefore all of the expenses involved in making the sales for a period should be matched with the sales income and dealt with in the period in which the sales themselves are accounted for.

Sales revenue

The sales revenue for an accounting period is included in the statement of profit or loss when the sales are made. This means that, when a sale is made on credit, it is recognised when the agreement is made and the invoice is sent to the customer rather than waiting until the cash for the sale is received. This is done by setting up a receivable in the statement of financial position for the amount of cash that is due from the sale (debit receivables and credit sales revenue).

Purchases

Similarly purchases are matched to the period in which they were made by accounting for all credit purchases when they took place and setting up a payable in the statement of financial position for the amount due (debit purchases and credit payables).

Cost of sales

The major cost involved in making sales in a period is the actual cost of the goods that are being sold. As we saw in a previous chapter, we need to adjust for opening and closing inventory to ensure that the sales made in the period are matched with the actual costs of those goods. Any goods unsold are carried forward to the next period so that they are accounted for when they are actually sold.

Expenses

The expenses of the period that the business has incurred in making its sales, such as rent, electricity and telephone, must also be matched with the sales for the period. This means that the actual expense incurred in the period should be included in the statement of profit or loss rather than simply the amount of the expense that has been paid in cash.

3 Accrued expenditure

An accrual arises where expenses of the business, relating to the year, have not been paid by the year end.

In this case, it is necessary to record the extra expense relevant to the year and create a corresponding statement of financial position liability (called an accrual):

Dr Expense account   X

Cr Accrual   X

An accrual will therefore reduce profit in the statement of profit or loss.

Illustration 1 – Accrued expenditure

A business' electricity charges amount to $12,000 pa. In the year to 31 December 20X5, $9,000 has been paid. The electricity for the final quarter is paid in January 20X6.

What year-end accrual is required and what is the electricity expense for the year?

Show the relevant entries in the ledger accounts.

Solution to Illustration 1

- The total expense charged to the statement of profit or loss in respect of electricity should be $12,000.

- The year-end accrual is the $3,000 expense that has not been paid in cash.

- The double entry required is:
- Dr Electricity expense $3,000
- Cr Accruals $3,000

Ledger accounts and accrued expenses

Method 1: know the accrual

Electricity expense

	$		$
Cash	9,000	Profit or loss (ß)	12,000
Accrual c/f	3,000		
	_____		_____
	12,000		12,000
	_____		_____
		Accrual b/f	3,000

Method 2: know the statement of profit or loss charge

Electricity expense

	$		$
Cash	9,000	Profit or loss	12,000
Accrual c/f (ß)	3,000		
	———		———
	12,000		12,000
	———		———
		Accrual b/f	3,000

Test your understanding 1

John Simnel's business has an accounting year end of 31 December 20X1. He rents factory space at a rental cost of $5,000 per quarter, payable in arrears.

During the year to 31 December 20X1 his cash payments of rent have been as follows:

- 31 March (for the quarter to 31 March 20X1) $5,000

- 29 June (for the quarter to 30 June 20X1) $5,000

- 2 October (for the quarter to 30 September 20X1) $5,000

The final payment due on 31 December 20X1 for the quarter to that date was not paid until 4 January 20X2.

Show the ledger accounts required to record the above transactions.

Accrued expenditure will reduce profit in the statement of profit or loss and will also create a current liability on the Statement of financial position.

For example, if we were to put through an accrual of $500 for telephone expenses. The double entry would be:

Dr Telephone expenses $500

Cr Accruals $500

The additional telephone expense would reduce profits by $500. The additional accrual would increase current liabilities by $500.

[handwritten margin notes:] Accrued ↑ AER → reduce profit / Expenditure

4 Prepaid expenditure

A prepayment arises where some of the following year's expenses have been paid in the current year.

In this case, it is necessary to remove that part of the expense which is not relevant to this year and create a corresponding statement of financial position asset (called a prepayment):

Dr Prepayment   X

Cr Expense account   X

A prepayment will therefore increase profit in the statement of profit or loss.

Illustration 2 – Prepaid expenditure

The annual insurance charge for a business is $24,000 pa. $30,000 was paid on 1 January 20X5 in respect of future insurance charges.

For the year-ended 31 December 20X5 what is the closing prepayment and the insurance expense for the year?

Show the relevant entries in the ledger accounts.

Solution to Illustration 2

- The total expense charged to the statement of profit or loss in respect of insurance should be $24,000.

- The year-end prepayment is the $6,000 that has been paid in respect of 20X6.

The double entry required is:

Dr Prepayment $6,000

Cr Insurance expense $6,000

Insurance – expense

	$		$
Cash	30,000	Profit or loss	24,000
		Prepayments c/f	6,000
	30,000		30,000

Test your understanding 2

Tubby Wadlow pays the rental expense on his market stall in advance. He starts business on 1 January 20X5 and on that date pays $1,200 in respect of the first quarter's rent. During his first year of trade he also pays the following amounts:

- 3 March (in respect of the quarter ended 30 June) $1,200

- 14 June (in respect of the quarter ended 30 September) $1,200

- 25 September (in respect of the quarter $1,400 ended 31 December)

- 13 December (in respect of the first quarter of 20X6) $1,400

Show these transactions in the rental expense account.

Prepaid expenditure increases profit on the Statement of profit or loss and also creates a current asset to be included on the Statement of financial position.

For example, if we were to put a prepayment of $1,000 in our financial statements for insurance, the double entry would be:

Dr Prepayments $1,000

Cr Insurance expense $1,000

The prepayments side would increase our current assets by the $1,000. The insurance expense would decrease by the $1,000, and hence increase our overall profits.

Proforma expense T-account

Expense

	$		$
Balance b/f (opening prepaid expense)	X	Balance b/f (opening accrued expense)	X
Bank (total paid during the year)	X	Profit or loss (total expense for the year)	X
Balance c/f (closing accrued expense)	X	Balance c/f (closing prepaid expense)	X
	X		X
Balance b/f (opening prepaid expense)	X	Balance b/f (opening accrued expense)	X

Notes to support the proforma

- There may be a debit balance brought forward (opening prepayment) or a credit balance brought forward (an accrual).

- Payments made during the year are debited to the expense account.

- If there is an accrual required at the end of the year, this is debited to the expense account (to increase the charge to profit or loss) and which is also carried forward at the end of the year as a credit balance.

- If there is a prepayment required at the end of the year, this is credited to the expense account (to reduce the charge to profit or loss) and which is also carried forward at the end of the year as a debit balance.

- In an expense account, there will be more debits than credits; when the account is balanced off, the net debit balance is taken to profit or loss for the year.

Test your understanding 3

On 1 January 20X5, Willy Mossop owed $2,000 in respect of the previous year's electricity. Willy made the following payments during the year ended 31 December 20X5:

- 6 February $2,800
- 8 May $3,000
- 5 August $2,750
- 10 November $3,100

At 31 December 20X5, Willy calculated that he owed $1,800 in respect of electricity for the last part of the year.

What is the electricity charge to the statement of profit or loss?

A $1,800

B $11,450

C $11,650

D $13,450

5 Accrued income

AIA

Accrued income arises where income has been earned in the accounting period but has not yet been received.

In this case, it is necessary to record the extra income in the statement of profit or loss and create a corresponding asset in the statement of financial position (called accrued income):

Dr Accrued income (SFP) X

Cr Income (P/L) X

Accrued income creates an additional current asset on our Statement of financial position. It also creates additional income on our Statement of profit or loss, and hence this will increase overall profits.

Illustration 3 – Accrued income

A business earns bank interest income of $300 per month. $3,000 bank interest income has been received in the year to 31 December 20X5.

What is the year-end asset and what is the bank interest income for the year?

Show the relevant entries in the ledger accounts.

Solution to Illustration 3

- The total amount credited to the statement of profit or loss in respect of interest should be $3,600 (12 × $300).
- The year-end accrued income asset is the $600 that has not yet been received.

The double entry required is:

Dr Accrued income (SFP) $600

Cr Bank interest income (P/L) $600

Bank interest income

	$		$
Profit or loss	3,600	Bank	3,000
		Accrued income c/f	600
	3,600		3,600
Accrued income b/f	600		

6 Prepaid income

Prepaid income arises where income has been received in the accounting period but which relates to the next accounting period.

KAPLAN PUBLISHING

In this case, it is necessary to remove the income not relating to the year from the statement of profit or loss and create a corresponding liability in the statement of financial position (called prepaid income):

Dr Income (P/L)   X

Cr Prepaid Income (SFP)   X

Illustration 4 – Prepaid income

A business rents out a property at an income of $4,000 per month. $64,000 has been received in the year ended 31 December 20X5.

What is the year-end liability and what is the rental income for the year?

Show the relevant entries in the ledger accounts.

Solution to Illustration 4

- The total amount credited to the statement of profit or loss in respect of rent should be $48,000 (12 × $4,000).

- The year-end prepaid income liability is the $16,000 ($64,000 – $48,000) that has been received in respect of next year.

The double entry required is:

Dr Rental income $16,000

Cr Prepaid income (SFP) $16,000

Rental income

	$		$
Profit or loss	48,000	Cash	64,000
Prepaid income c/f	16,000		
	———		———
	64,000		64,000
	———		———
		Prepaid income b/f	16,000

Prepaid income reduces income on the Statement of profit or loss and hence reduces overall profits too. It also creates a current liability on our Statement of financial position.

Proforma income T-account				

			Income	
	$			$
Balance b/f (opening accrued income)	X	Balance b/f (opening prepaid income)		X
Profit or loss (total revenue for the year)	X	Cash (total received during the year)		X
Balance c/f (closing prepaid income)	X	Balance c/f (closing accrued income)		X
	X			X
Balance b/f (opening accrued income)	X	Balance b/f (opening prepaid income)		X

Notes to support the proforma

- There may be a debit balance brought forward (opening accrued income) or a credit balance brought forward (opening prepaid income).

- Receipts received during the year are credited to the income account.

- If there is closing accrued income at the end of the year, this is credited to the income account (to increase income in profit or loss for the year) and which is also carried forward at the end of the year as a debit balance.

- If there is closing prepaid income at the end of the year, this is debited to the income account (to reduce income in profit or loss for the year) and which is also carried forward at the end of the year as a credit balance.

- In an income account, there will be more credits than debits; when the account is balanced off, the net credit balance is taken to profit or loss for the year.

Test your understanding 4

Accrued and prepaid income

10800·

Libby Farquar receives income from two rental units as follows:

Period	Unit 1 $	Received	Unit 2 $	Received
1.10.X4 – 31.12.X4	2,100	30.9.X4	1,300	2.1.X5
1.1.X5 – 31.3.X5	2,150	27.12.X4	1,300	4.4.X5
1.4.X5 – 30.6.X5	2,150	25.3.X5	1,300	1.7.X5
1.7.X5 – 30.9.X5	2,200	21.6.X5	1,400	6.10.X5
1.10.X5 – 31.12.X5	2,200	21.9.X5	1,400	2.1.X6
1.1.X6 – 31.3.X6	2,200	29.12.X5	1,400	4.4.X6

What is Libby's rental income in the statement of profit or loss for the year ended 31 December 20X5?

A $5,400

B $8,700

C $14,000

D $14,100

Chapter summary

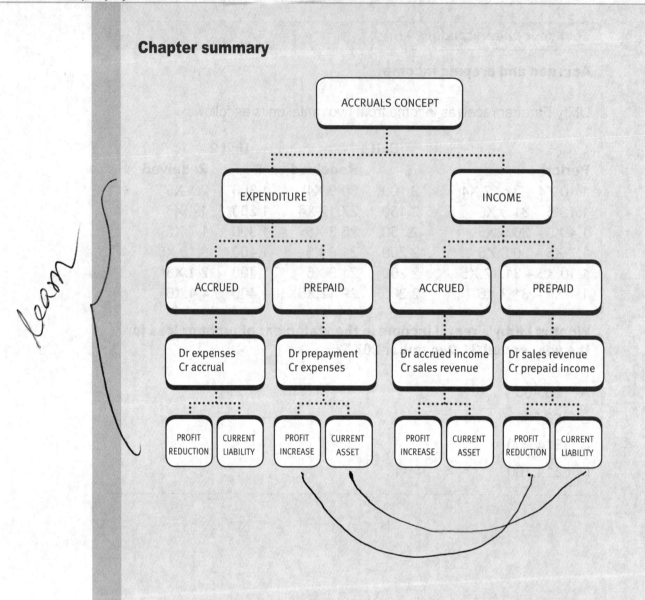

Test your understanding answers

Test your understanding 1

Rental expense

	$		$
31 March cash	5,000		
29 June cash	5,000		
2 October cash	5,000		
Accrual c/f	5,000	Profit or loss	20,000
	–––––		–––––
	20,000		20,000
	–––––		–––––
		Accrual b/f	5,000

Test your understanding 2

Rental expense

	$		$
1 January cash	1,200		
3 March cash	1,200		
14 June cash	1,200		
25 September cash	1,400	Profit or loss	5,000
13 December cash	1,400	Prepayment c/f	1,400
	–––––		–––––
	6,400		6,400
	–––––		–––––
Prepayment b/f	1,400		

Test your understanding 3

The correct answer is B.

Electricity expense

	$		$
6 February cash	2,800	Accrual b/f	2,000
8 May cash	3,000		
5 August cash	2,750		
10 November cash	3,100	Profit or loss	11,450
Accrual c/f	1,800		
	13,450		13,450
		Accrual b/f	1,800

Test your understanding 4

The correct answer is D.

Rental income (Unit 1)

	$		$
		Prepaid income b/f	2,150
		25.3.X5 cash	2,150
		21.6.X5 cash	2,200
Profit or loss	8,700	21.9.X5 cash	2,200
Prepaid income c/f	2,200	29.12.X5 cash	2,200
	10,900		10,900
		Prepaid income b/f	2,200

Rental income (Unit 2)			
	$		$
Accrued income b/f	1,300	2.1.X5 cash	1,300
		4.4.X5 cash	1,300
		1.7.X5 cash	1,300
Profit or loss	5,400	6.10.X5 cash	1,400
		Accrued income c/f	1,400
	———		———
	6,700		6,700
	———		———
Accrued income b/f	1,400		

Total income: $8,700 + $5,400 = $14,100

Receivables

Chapter learning objectives

Upon completion of this chapter you will be able to:

- explain and identify examples of receivables

- understand the purpose of aged receivables analysis

- record the adjustments in the ledger accounts to write of an irrecoverable debt and one that is consequently recovered

- record the adjustments in the ledger accounts to adjust the allowance for receivables

- identify the impact of the above adjustments on profits and net assets.

1 Overview

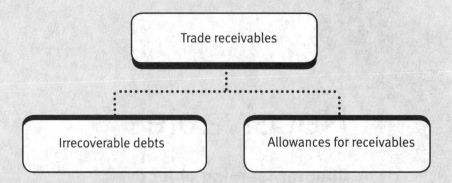

2 Cash and credit sales

If a sale is for cash, the customer pays for the goods/services at the point of sale. The double entry for a cash sales is:

Dr Cash

Cr Sales revenue

If the sale is on credit terms the customer will pay for the goods/services after receiving them. Typically trading terms allow customers 30 - 60 days when purchasing goods and services on credit.

Under the accruals concept, the sale is recorded in the ledger accounts when the right to the income is earned. That is usually the point at which the goods/services are delivered. Therefore when sales are made on credit the revenue is recorded with a corresponding asset that represents the customer's commitment to pay. The asset is referred to as a 'receivable.'

The double entry is recorded as follows:

Dr Receivables

Cr Sales revenue

When the customer eventually settles the debt the double entry will be:

Dr Cash account

Cr Receivables

This then clears out the balance on the customer's account.

The provision of credit facilities

The majority of businesses will sell to their customers on credit and state a defined time within which they must pay (a credit period). The main benefits and costs of doing so are as follows:

Benefits

- The business may be able to enter new markets.
- There is a possibility of increased sales.
- Customer loyalty may be encouraged.

Costs

- Can be costly in terms of lost interest since the business is accepting payment later.
- Cash flow of the business may deteriorate.
- There is a potential risk of irrecoverable debts.

Aged receivables analysis

Where credit facilities are offered, it is normal for a business to maintain an aged receivables analysis.

- Analysis is usually a list, ordered by name, showing how much each customer owes and how old their debts are.
- The credit control function of a business uses the analysis to keep track of outstanding debts and follow up any that are overdue.
- Timely collection of debts improves cash flow and reduces the risk of them becoming irrecoverable.

Credit limits

It is also normal for a business to set a credit limit for each customer. This is the maximum amount of credit that the business is willing to provide.

The use of credit limits may:

- reduce risk to business of irrecoverable debts by limiting the amount sold on credit
- help build up the trust of a new customer
- be part of the credit control strategy of a business.

3 Irrecoverable debts and allowances

The accruals concept dictates that when a sale is made, it is recognised in the accounts, regardless of whether or not the cash has been received. Occasionally customers either refuse to or cannot settle their outstanding debts. Not only does this lead to a loss of cash income for a business it also means that they have an asset on their statement of financial position that they are unlikely to be able to collect.

If it is highly unlikely that the amount owed by a customer will be received, then this debt is known as an irrecoverable debt. These are 'written' off by removing them from the ledger accounts completely. This course of action would be necessary if a customer was in formal liquidation proceedings and it was known that the outstanding debt will not be recovered.

If there is concern over whether a customer will pay but there is still hope that the amount (or at least some of it) can be recovered an 'allowance' is created. Unlike an irrecoverable debt, these items are left in the receivables ledger but a separate and opposite account (receivables are debits, the allowance is a credit) is set up that temporarily offsets the asset. If the balance is eventually paid the allowance can be easily removed. This course of action would be necessary if a customer was having cash flow difficulties but still felt they would be able to pay if given a little time.

4 Accounting for irrecoverable debts

An **irrecoverable debt** is a debt which is, or is considered to be, uncollectable.

With such debts it is prudent to remove them from the accounts and to charge the amount as an expense for irrecoverable debts to the statement of profit or loss. The original sale remains in the accounts as this did actually take place.

The double entry required to achieve this is:

    Dr Irrecoverable debts expense

    Cr Receivables

Test your understanding 1

Araf & Co have total accounts receivable at the end of their accounting period of $45,000. Of these it is discovered that one, Mr Xiun who owes $790, has been declared bankrupt, and another who gave his name as Mr Jones has totally disappeared owing Araf & Co $1,240.

Calculate the effect in the financial statements of writing off these debts as irrecoverable.

5 Accounting for irrecoverable debts recovered

There is a possible situation where a debt is written off as irrecoverable in one accounting period, perhaps because the customer has been declared bankrupt, and the money, or part of the money, due is then unexpectedly received in a subsequent accounting period.

When a debt is written off the double entry is:

Dr Irrecoverable debts expense

Cr Receivables (removing the debt from the accounts)

When cash is received from a customer the normal double entry is:

Dr Cash

Cr Receivables

When an irrecoverable debt is recovered, the credit entry (above) cannot be taken to receivables as the debt has already been taken out of the receivables balance.

Instead the accounting entry is:

Dr Cash

Cr Irrecoverable debts expense

Some businesses may wish to keep a separate 'irrecoverable debts recovered' account to separate the actual cost of irrecoverable debts in the period.

Test your understanding 2

4.

Celia Jones had receivables of $3,655 at 31 December 20X7. At that date she wrote off a debt from Lenny Smith of $699. During the year to 31 December 20X8 Celia made credit sales of $17,832 and received cash from her customers totalling $16,936. She also received the $699 from Lenny Smith that had already been written off in 20X7.

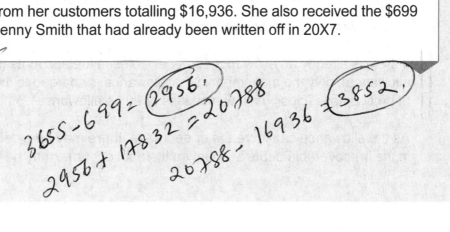

What is the final balance on the receivables account at 31 December 20X7 and 20X8?

	20X7	20X8
	$	$
A	2,956	3,852
B	2,956	3,153
C	3,655	4,551
D	3,655	3,852

6 Allowance for receivables

There may be some debts in the accounts where there is some cause for concern but they are not yet definitely irrecoverable.

It is prudent to recognise the possible expense of not collecting the debt in the statement of profit or loss, but the receivable must remain in the accounts in case the customer does, in fact, settle the amount outstanding.

An allowance is set up which is a credit balance. This is netted off against trade receivables in the statement of financial position to give a net figure for receivables that are probably recoverable.

The allowance should consist only of specific amounts where, for example, the customer is known to be in financial difficulty, or is disputing the invoice, or payment is already overdue, or is refusing to pay for some other reason (e.g. a faulty product), and therefore the amount owing may not be recovered. Therefore, an allowance can only be established where there is some objective evidence that a particular receivable may not be recovered in part or in full.

7 Accounting for the allowance for receivables

An allowance for receivables is set up with the following journal:

Dr Irrecoverable debts expense

Cr Allowance for receivables

If there is already an allowance for receivables in the accounts (opening allowance), only the movement in the allowance is charged to the statement of profit or loss (closing allowance less opening allowance).

As the allowance can increase or decrease, there may be a debit or a credit in the irrecoverable debts account so the above journal may be reversed.

When calculating and accounting for a movement in the allowance for receivables, the following steps should be taken:

(1) Write off irrecoverable debts.

(2) Calculate the receivables balance as adjusted for the write-offs.

(3) Ascertain the allowance for receivables required.

(4) Compare to the brought forward allowance.

(5) Account for the change in allowance to determine the expense or credit to the statement of profit or loss

(6) In the financial statements, deduct the closing allowance for receivables from the receivables balance.

Illustration 1

On 31 December 20X1 Jake Williams had receivables of $10,000. At that date, Jake estimated that there was evidence that amounts totalling $300 may not be recovered as those receivables were already overdue and he therefore wanted to make a specific allowance for this amount.

During 20X2, Jake made sales on credit totalling $100,000 and received cash from his customers of $94,000. At 31 December 20X2, Jake now considered that there was doubt regarding the recoverability of amounts totalling $700 which were overdue and which may not be recovered. The allowance for receivables should therefore be increased from $300 to $700.

During 20X3 Jake made sales of $95,000 and collected $96,000 from his receivables. At 31 December 20X3 Jake now considered that amounts totalling only $600 required an allowance for being overdue at that date. The allowance for receivables should therefore be adjusted from $700 to $600.

Calculate the allowance for receivables and the irrecoverable debt expense as well as the closing balance of receivables for each of the years 20X1, 20X2, 20X3.

Solution

20X1 Receivables

	$		$
At 31 December	10,000	Balance c/f	10,000
	10,000		10,000
Balance b/f	10,000		

Allowance required = $300

Allowance for receivables

	$		$
Balance c/f	300	31 Dec	
		Irrecoverable debts	300
	300		300
		Balance b/f	300

Irrecoverable debts expense

	$		$
31 Dec		31 Dec	
Allowance for receivables	300	Profit or loss	300
	300		300

Statement of financial position presentation

	$	$
Current assets		
Receivables		10,000
Less: Allowance for receivables		(300)
		9,700

20X2 Receivables

	$		$
Balance b/f	10,000		
Sales	100,000	Cash	94,000
		Balance c/f	16,000
	110,000		110,000
Balance b/f	16,000		
Allowance required $700			

Allowance for receivables

	$		$
		Balance b/f	300
		31 Dec	
Balance b/f	700	increase in allowance	400
	700		700
		Balance b/f	700

Irrecoverable debts expense

	$		$
31 Dec		31 Dec	
Allowance for receivables	400	Profit or loss	400
	400		400

Statement of financial position presentation

	$	$
Current assets		
Receivables	16,000	
Less: Allowance for receivables	(700)	
		15,300

20X3 Receivables

	$		$
Balance b/f	16,000		
Sales	95,000	Cash	96,000
		Balance c/f	15,000
	111,000		111,000
Balance b/f	15,000		

Allowance required: $600

Allowance for receivables

	$		$
31 Dec		Balance b/f	700
Decrease in allowance	100		
Balance c/f	600		
	700		700
		Balance b/f	600

Irrecoverable debts expense

	$		$
31 Dec		31 Dec	
Profit or loss	100	Allowance for receivables	100
	100		100

Statement of financial position presentation

	$	$
Current assets		
Receivables	15,000	
Less: Allowance for receivables	(600)	
		14,400

Test your understanding 3

John Stamp has opening balances at 1 January 20X6 on his trade receivables account and allowance for receivables account of $68,000 and $3,400 respectively. During the year to 31 December 20X6 John Stamp made credit sales of $354,000 and collected cash from his receivables of $340,000.

At 31 December 20X6 John Stamp reviewed his receivables listing and acknowledged that he is unlikely ever to receive debts totalling $2,000. These are to be written off as irrecoverable. In addition, at that date he estimated that amounts totalling $4,000 were overdue and that an allowance for receivables was required to cover these amounts.

What is the amount charged to John's statement of profit or loss for irrecoverable debt expense in the year ended 31 December 20X6?

A $2,700

B $6,100

C $2,600

D $6,000

What will the effect be of Irrecoverable debts on both the statement of profit or loss and the statement of financial position?

Chapter summary

Trade receivables

IRRECOVERABLE DEBTS

- Amounts that the business will not receive from its customers

ACCOUNTING FOR IRRECOVERABLE DEBTS

To recognise the expense in the statement of profit or loss

Dr   Irrecoverable debts expense

Cr   Receivables

ACCOUNTING FOR IRRECOVERABLE DEBTS RECOVERED

The debt has been taken out of receivables, the journal is:

Dr cash
Cr irrecoverable debts expense

ALLOWANCE FOR RECEIVABLES

- There may be some doubt as to the collectability of some of the business' receivables balances
- An allowance is made to recognise the possible expense of not receiving the cash

ACCOUNTING FOR THE ALLOWANCE FOR RECEIVABLES

To record an increase or setting up the allowance:

Dr   Irrecoverable debts expense

Cr   Allowance for receivables

The journal entry is reversed if the allowance is reduced

Test your understanding answers

As the two debts are considered to be irrecoverable, they must be removed from receivables:

Receivables

	$		$
Balance at period end	45,000	Irrecoverable debts	
		– Mr Xiun	790
		Irrecoverable debts	
		– Mr Jones	1,240
		Balance c/f	42,970
	45,000		45,000
Balance b/f	42,970		

Irrecoverable debts expense

	$		$
Receivables			
– Mr Xiun	790		
Receivables			
– Mr Jones	1,240	Profit or loss	2,030
	2,030		2,030

Note that the sales revenue account has not been altered and the original sales to Mr Xiun and Mr Jones remain. This is because these sales actually took place and it is only after the sale that the expense of not being able to collect these debts has occurred.

The correct answer is A.

20X7 Receivables

	$		$
31 Dec	3,655	Irrecoverable debts	
		– Lenny Smith	699
		Balance c/f	2,956
	3,655		3,655
Balance b/f	2,956		

20X7 Irrecoverable debts expense

	$		$
Receivables			
– Lenny Smith	699	Profit or loss	699
	699		699

20X8 Receivables

	$		$
Balance b/f	2,956		
Sales	17,832	Cash received	16,936
		Balance c/f	3,852
	20,788		20,788
Balance b/f	3,852		

20X8 Irrecoverable debts expense

	$		$
Profit or loss	699	Cash	699
	699		699

Test your understanding 3

The correct answer is C.

Receivables

20X6	$	20X6	$
1 Jan Balance b/f	68,000	31 Dec Cash	340,000
31 Dec Sales revenue	354,000	31 Dec Irrecoverable debts w/off	2,000
		31 Dec Balance c/f	80,000
	422,000		422,000
20X7			
1 Jan Balance b/f	80,000		

Irrecoverable debts expense

20X6	$	20X6	$
31 Dec Receivables	2,000		
31 Dec Increase in allowance for receivables	600	31 Dec Profit or loss	2,600
	2,600		2,600

Allowance for receivables

20X6	$	20X6	$
		1 Jan Balance b/f	3,400
31 Dec Balance c/f	4,000	31 Dec Irrecoverable debts	600
	4,000		4,000
		20X7	
		1 Jan Balance b/f	4,000

Note that only the one irrecoverable debts expense account is used both to write off irrecoverable debts and to increase or decrease the allowance for receivables. There is no need to use separate accounts for each type of expense.

Working – Allowance for receivables

$4000 – b/f $3,400 = increase of $600 ✓

The **statement of financial position** will show a receivables balance of 80,000. Underneath this separately the allowance for receivables c/f balance of $4,000 will be deducted to give a net receivables total of $76,000.

The **statement of profit or loss** will show the $2,600 as an expense. This expense will cause a decrease in overall profits.

Payables, provisions and contingent liabilities

Chapter learning objectives

Upon completion of this chapter you will be able to:

- classify items as current or non-current liabilities
- identify and explain examples of payables
- define and illustrate the different accounting treatments of 'provisions,' 'contingent liabilities,' and 'contingent assets'
- calculate and record provisions and movements in provisions.

1 Overview

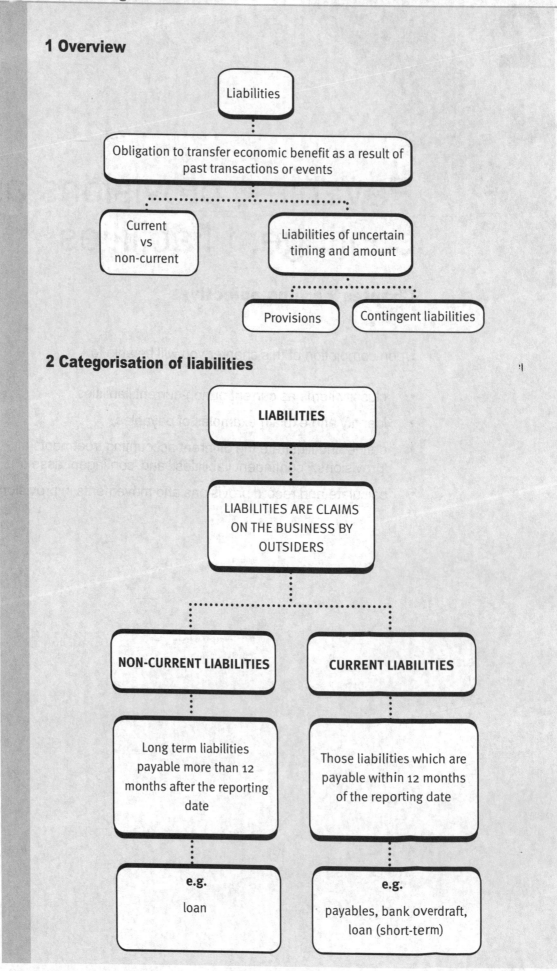

2 Categorisation of liabilities

It is important to consider the timing of settlement of a liability so that you can ensure you allocate it to the correct category of the statement of financial position. This can be significant to many multiple choice style questions, so take care when making adjustments for liabilities. Typically trade payables (liabilities for goods and services purchased), overdrafts and accruals are the main forms of current liability examined at F3 level. Loans are the main form of non-current liabilities.

Remember that a liability is defined as an obligation to transfer economic benefits as a result of a past transaction or event. The obligation must be capable of being reliably measured. The obligation may be a legal obligation or a constructive obligation. A constructive obligation may be established by a company having established or published policies and practices which creates a valid expectation on the part of others that the company will act in a certain way.

A good example of a constructive obligation is a retail store which allows customers to return unwanted goods, a policy which is in excess of the minimum legal obligations to only accept goods which are returned because they are faulty or defective in some way.

3 Cash and credit purchases

If a purchase is for cash, the business pays for the goods/services at the point of sale. The double entry for a cash purchase is:

Dr Purchases/expenses

Cr Cash

If the purchase is on credit terms the business will pay for the goods/services after receiving them. Typically trading terms allow 30 - 60 days to settle outstanding debts when purchasing goods and services on credit.

Under the accruals concept, the purchase is recorded in the ledger accounts when the expense has been incurred. That is usually the point at which the goods/services are received/rendered. Therefore when purchases are made on credit the cost is recorded with a corresponding liability that represents the obligation to pay the supplier of the goods/services. The liability is referred to as a 'payable.'

The double entry is recorded as follows:

Dr Purchases/expenses

Cr Payables

When the payable liability is actually paid the double entry to reflect this is:

Dr Payables

Cr Cash

 ## 4 Provisions

A **provision** can be defined as a liability of uncertain timing or amount.

For example, a company may face a legal action for a breach of health and safety law. The likely repercussion is that it may be fined if the court judgement is made against them. The timing and severity of the fine will be decided by a court at some future date. The key question is: should the company reflect this information in its financial statements?

If we assume that the potential fine could be significant (it could even lead to the closure of the business) should the potential consequences be disclosed to the shareholders in some way? As owners of the business, they are entitled to know about this potentially significant issue that could damage the profits and reputation of the business and, therefore, the financial value of their investment in the company.

Accounting for a provision

The first potential course of action management can take is to recognise a provision in the accounts. This is done by estimating the potential cost of the uncertain event and recognising it immediately. As the amount would be settled at a future date, a corresponding liability is recorded, as follows:

Dr Expenses

Cr Provision

The provision will need to be classified as either a current or non-current liability as befits the situation.

Criteria for recognising a provision

Given the uncertainty relating to provisions there is significant scope for accounting error, or even deliberate manipulation of provisions to alter profits.

To reduce this risk IAS 37 Provisions, Contingent Liabilities and Contingent Assets provides three criteria that must be met before a provision can be recognised in the financial statements:

- There must be a present obligation (legal or constructive) that exists as the result of a past event.

- There must be a probable transfer of economic benefits.
- There must be a reliable estimate of the potential cost.

Illustration 1

The criteria referred to above mean that a provision can only be recorded in an accounting period if recognition of a liability has been triggered at the year-end.

For example: Smith Ltd's year-end is 31 December 20X7. In November 20X7 they dismiss an employee. In February 20X8 a customer slips whilst on their premises and breaks her arm.

In March 20X8 both the employee and the injured customer sue Smith Ltd; the former for unfair dismissal and the latter for compensation for injuries suffered on Smith's premises.

Should an obligation be recognised at 31 December 20X7 for either of these lawsuits?

Solution to Illustration 1

There is a potential obligation at the year-end for the employee claiming unfair dismissal. This is because the triggering event happened in November 20X7, which is before the year-end.

There is no obligation to the injured customer at 31 December 20X7. The event happened after the year-end date of 31 December 20X7. Therefore, any financial consequences resulting from the claim made by the customer will be reflected in the financial statements for the year ended 31 December 20X8.

Obligations

Obligations can be triggered by either legally or constructively.

A legal obligation is an obligation that derives from:

- the terms of a contract
- legislation
- any other operation of law.

A constructive obligation is an obligation that derives from an entity's actions where:

- The entity has in some way indicated that it will accept certain responsibilities.

- The entity has created an expectation on the part of other parties that it will meet those responsibilities.

5 Contingent liabilities and contingent assets

A contingent liability is defined as:

(1) a **possible** obligation that arises from past events; or

(2) a probable obligation that arises from past events but the amount of the obligation **cannot be measured with sufficient reliability**.

When a provision is not recognised in the financial statements because it does not meet the criteria specified in IAS 37, it may still need to be disclosed as a contingent liability in the financial statements.

Examples of contingent liabilities include outstanding litigation where the potential costs cannot be estimated with any degree of reliability or when the likelihood of losing the litigation is only deemed possible (rather than probable).

A contingent asset is defined as a possible asset that arises from past events and whose existence will be confirmed only by the occurrence or non-occurrence of one or more uncertain future events not wholly within the control of the enterprise.

An example of a contingent asset is when a business claims compensation from another party and the outcome of the claim is uncertain at the reporting date.

Accounting for contingent liabilities and contingent assets

The requirements of IAS 37 regarding contingent liabilities and contingent assets are summarised in the following table:

Probability of occurrence	Contingent liabilities	Contingent assets
Virtually certain	Provide	Recognise
Probable	Provide	Disclosure note in financial statements
Possible	Disclosure note in financial statements	Ignore
Remote	Ignore	Ignore

- Note that the reporting standard gives no guidance regarding the meaning of the terms in the left-hand column. One possible interpretation is as follows:

    Virtually certain > 95%

    Probable 51% – 95%

    Possible 5% – 50%

    Remote < 5%

e.g

Illustration 2

A retail store has a policy of refunding purchases by dissatisfied customers, (e.g. when goods have been purchased and the customer decides that they are the wrong size, colour or style) even though it is under no legal obligation to do so. Its policy of making refunds is publicised in the store and in advertisements. The retail store has a year-end date of 31 December 20X6.

Should a provision be recognised in the financial statements for the year ended 31 December 20X6 for goods sold before the year-end which may be returned during 20X7?

Solution to Illustration 2

The policy is well known and creates a valid expectation that the store will give refunds to customers who return goods. At the year-end date, there is a constructive obligation. It is probable some refunds will be made.

The obligation can be reliably measured, perhaps by using expected values based upon past experience of what proportion or value of goods sold are actually returned by customers.

Conclusion: A provision is required and a reliable estimate of the amount should be made for inclusion in the financial statements.

Test your understanding 1

The draft financial statements of Madras, a limited liability company, for the year ended 31 December 20X6 are currently under review. The following points have been raised:

(i) An ex-employee has started an action against Madras for wrongful dismissal. The company's legal team have stated that the ex-employee is not likely to succeed. The following estimates have been given by the lawyers relating to the case:

    (a) Legal costs (to be incurred whether the claim is successful or not) $5,000

    (b) Settlement of claim if successful $15,000
        Currently no provision has been made by Madras in the financial statements.

(ii) Madras has a policy of refunding the cost of any goods returned by dissatisfied customers, even though it is under no legal obligation to do so. This policy of making refunds is generally known. At the year end, Madras reliably estimated that returns totalling $4,800 will be made after the year-end.

(iii) A customer has made a claim against Madras for injury suffered following the purchase and use of a defective product. Legal advisers have confirmed that Madras will probably have to pay financial compensation of $100,000 to the customer. In turn, Madras has made a counter-claim against the supplier of the defective product for $100,000 and believes it is probable that its claim against the supplier will be successful.

State with reasons what adjustments, if any, should be made by Madras in the financial statements.

Movement in provisions

Provisions should be reviewed at each statement of financial position date and adjusted to reflect the current best estimate.

Increase in provision:	Dr Relevant expense account
	Cr Provision
Decrease in provision:	Dr Provision
	Cr Relevant expense account

6 IAS 37 disclosure requirements

Reporting provisions in the final accounts

Provisions are reported as a liability in the statement of financial position.

They may be classed as either a current or non-current liability, depending upon the subject matter of the provision.

Disclosure

- Where the requirement is to provide for a contingent liability, the liability is reflected in the financial statements, but called a provision in order to highlight the uncertainty surrounding it

- The movement in this provision is recorded in the financial statements each year.

- When disclosure is made by note, the note should state:
    - the nature of the contingency
    - the uncertain factors that may affect the future outcome
    - an estimate of the financial effect, or a statement that such an estimate cannot be made.

Chapter summary

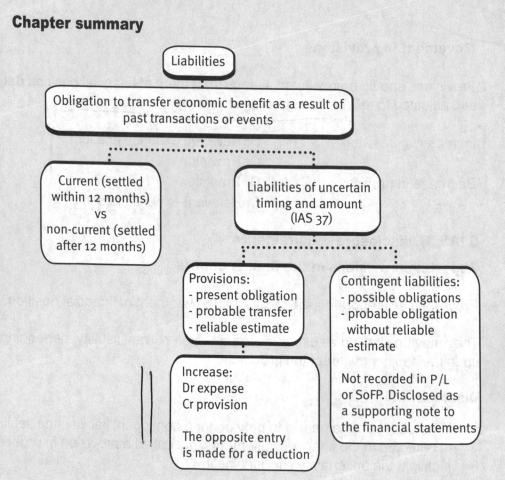

Test your understanding answers

Test your understanding 1

(i) IAS 37 defines a contingency as an obligation or an asset that arises from past events whose existence will be confirmed only by the occurrence or non-occurrence of one or more uncertain future events not wholly within the control of the enterprise. A provision should be made if:

    (a) There is an obligation.

    (b) A transfer is probable.

    (c) There is a reliable estimate.

The legal costs of $5,000 should therefore be provided for since they will have to be paid whatever the outcome of the legal case. However, the claim is not likely to succeed and so no provision should be made. A disclosure note should be made for the contingent liability (i.e. potential loss if Madras loses the court case) of $15,000.

(ii) IAS 37 states that an obligation can be legal or constructive. In this case the policy of refunds has created a constructive obligation and it has been reliably measured. A provision for $4,800 should therefore be made in the financial statements.

(iii) As it is regarded as probable that Madras will be required to pay compensation of $100,000 to the injured customer, it constitutes a present obligation as a result of a past obligating event, and should therefore be accounted for as a provision. The success of the counterclaim for $100,000 is also considered probable and would therefore need to be disclosed in the notes to the financial statements as a contingent asset (reimbursement). Only if it were considered virtually certain would the counterclaim be recognised as an asset in the statement of financial position. Note that, even if that was the case, the provision and contingent asset would be separately accounted for in the statement of financial position – they would not be netted off.

13

Capital structure and finance costs

Chapter learning objectives

Upon completion of this chapter you will be able to:

- understand the capital structure of a limited liability company
- record movements in share capital and share premium accounts
- define, discuss and record bonus issues and rights issues
- record dividends and finance costs in the ledger accounts
- identify and record other reserves
- record income tax in the accounting ledgers.

1 Overview

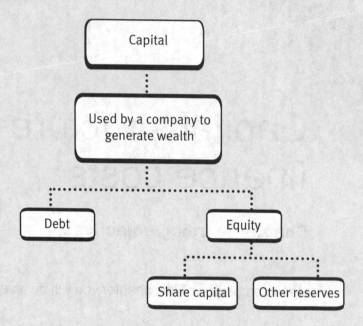

2 The capital structure of a limited liability company

All companies have to be financed, regardless of the type of company that they are. Without financing of any sort the business would not be able to begin trading; they would not be able to purchase raw materials, recruit staff, advertise products, or even put fuel in their vehicles.

Finance is provided by the capital invested in the business.

Capital is something that on its own has little or no use but can be employed in the generation of wealth.

Money is a form of financial capital; there is not an awful lot you can do with physical currency (except perhaps admire its shiny appearance or burn it if it is the paper sort) but it can be used in exchange for goods and services which can be put to good use. Most businesses will exchange money for raw materials, machinery, property, energy and labour, amongst other things. These can be used to create goods and services that can be sold to generate wealth for the business and its owners.

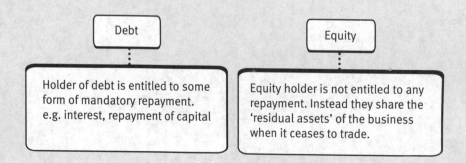

KAPLAN PUBLISHING

There are a number of ways that a business can attract financial capital but each has its own characteristics and consequences. In general all forms of finance can be loosely categorised into two distinct groups:

- Debt, which requires some form of mandatory transfer of economic benefit to the provider of the finance, or

- Equity, which gives the provider of the finance the rights to share in the residual assets of the business when it ceases to trade.

Most forms of finance are simple to categorise but some forms of finance have characteristics of both and it's not entirely clear whether they are debt, equity or both. For this syllabus you need to be aware of three forms of financial capital and how to record them in the financial statements:

(i) Ordinary ('equity') share capital: this is equity as the directors are under no obligation to repay the investors (shareholders) or to pay them a dividend. An ordinary shareholding is evidence of ownership of a company and the shareholders receive the residual interest in the business once it ceases to trade in proportion to the size of their shareholdings. Ordinary shares are shown under equity on the statement of financial position.

Directors may choose to pay the shareholders an annual dividend. These are recognised in the statement of changes in equity, not the statement of profit or loss. This is **not** a deduction from profit; it is a distribution of profit to the rightful owners of it.

(ii) Loan notes: under the terms of loan note agreements directors are usually required to pay the loan holder an annual interest amount and are obliged to repay the full debt at a fixed point in time. This is therefore a form of debt and appears as a liability on the statement of financial position.

The interest payment is treated as a finance charge, which is shown as an expense in the statement of profit or loss. This is a deduction from profit.

(iii) Preference shares: these can be either debt or equity, depending on their terms. If there is any obligation to repay the preference shareholder (redeemable) then this is evidence of a debt. These are shown as liabilities on the statement of financial position and any dividends paid to these shareholders would be treated as finance charges.

Irredeemable preference shares are shares that do not have to be repaid. They are therefore treated as equity in the statement of financial position. It must be made clear that they are not the same as ordinary shares as they do not entitle the owner to a residual interest in the business. The accompanying dividends are, however, treated the same as ordinary dividends in the financial statements.

3 Ordinary share capital

As stated above, ordinary share capital is treated as equity and the associated dividend payments are recorded in the statement of changes in equity.

Share capital terminology

Each share has a **nominal or par value**, often $1, 50c or 25c. This is an arbitrary value assigned to a share, which is often perceived as the share's minimum value. This value remains fixed, whereas the market value of the share (the value at which the share is actively traded) fluctuates over time. This value is often used as a means of calculating dividends to shareholders (paid as a percentage of the nominal value).

Shares are sold, in the first instance, by a company at an **issue price**. This is at least equal to the nominal value of the share, but often exceeds it. Once shares have been sold to the public the shareholders may then sell their shares privately. The value at which the shares are trading on the open market is referred to as the **market value**.

The market value of a share fluctuates according to the success and perceived expectations of a company. If a company is listed on the stock exchange, the value is determined by reference to recent transactions between buyers and sellers of shares. This value does not feature in the financial statements.

Other terminology to be aware of

- **Issued** share capital is the share capital that has actually been issued to shareholders. The number of issued shares is used in the calculation of dividends.

- **Called-up** share capital is the amount of the nominal value paid by the shareholder plus any further amounts that they have agreed to pay in the future.

- **Paid up** share capital is the amount of the nominal value which has been paid at the current date.

Accounting for the issue of shares

If a company were to issue shares at their nominal value the double entry to record this raising of finance would be:

Dr Cash   Issue price × no. of shares
Cr Share capital Nominal value × no. of shares

In reality companies generally issue shares at a price above their nominal value. This is referred to as issuing shares at a premium.

The double entry to record such an issue is:

Dr Cash   Issue price × no. of shares
Cr Share capital Nominal value × no. of shares
Cr Share   ß (i.e. the difference between the issue price and the
premium   nominal value × no. of shares sold).

Both the share capital and share premium accounts are shown on the statement of financial position within the 'Equity' section.

Test your understanding 1

Bourbon issued 200,000 25c shares at a price of $1.75 each.

Show this transaction using ledger accounts.

4 Rights issues

A **rights issue** is:

the offer of new shares to existing shareholders in proportion to their existing shareholding at a stated price (normally below market values).

The **advantages** are:

* A rights issue is the cheapest way for a company to raise finance through the issuing of further shares.

* A rights issue to existing shareholders has a greater chance of success compared with a share issue to the public.

The **disadvantages** are:

* A rights issue is more expensive than issuing debt.
* It may not be successful in raising the finance required.

A rights issue is accounted for in the same way as a normal share issue and therefore has exactly the same impact on the statement of financial position as an issue at full price.

Test your understanding 2

Upon incorporation in 20X4, The Jammy Dodger, a limited liability company, issues 1,000 50c shares at nominal value. Needing further funds, in 20X5 it makes a rights issue of 1 for 5 at $0.75. This offer is fully taken up.

What accounting entries are required in 20X4 and 20X5? Illustrate the relevant section of the statement of financial position at year end 20X5.

5 Bonus issues

A **bonus issue** is:

the issue of new shares to existing shareholders in proportion to their existing shareholding. No cash is received from a bonus issue.

The **advantages** are:

* Issued share capital is divided into a larger number of shares, thus making the market value of each one less, and so more marketable.

* Issued share capital is brought more into line with assets employed in the company by reducing stated reserves and increasing share capital.

The **disadvantages** are:

* the admin costs of making the bonus issue.

As no cash is received from a bonus issue, the issue must be funded from reserves. Any reserve can be used, though a non-distributable reserve such as the share premium account would be used in preference to reserves which can be distributed:

Dr Share premium   Nominal value

(or other reserve)

Cr Share capital   Nominal value

Test your understanding 3

Ginger Knut, a limited liability company, has 20,000 50c shares in issue (each issued for $1.25) and makes a 1 for 4 bonus issue, capitalising the share premium account.

What are the balances on the share capital and share premium accounts after this transaction?

	SC	SP
	$	$
A	15,000	10,000
B	12,500	12,500
C	25,000	Nil
D	22,500	2,500

Test your understanding 4

Rich T is a limited liability company with 200,000 25c shares in issue. At 1 January the balance on the share premium account is $75,000. The following transactions occur in the year ended 31 December 20X6:

31 January There is a fully taken-up 2 for 5 rights issue. The issue price is $1.80.

12 August There is a 1 for 10 bonus issue made using the share premium account.

What are the balances on the share capital and share premium accounts on 31 December 20X6?

	SC	SP
	$000	$000
A	308	111
B	77	84
C	154	93
D	77	192

6 Dividends

Dividends represent the distribution of profits to shareholders. They are usually expressed as an amount per share e.g. 10c per share or 10% of nominal value.

Dividends on preference shares are usually based on a pre-determined amount, such as 5% of the nominal value of the shareholding.

Ordinary dividends

A company may pay a mid-year or interim dividend. The double entry is:

Dr Retained earnings (and disclose in statement of changes in equity)   X
Cr Bank   X

At the end of the year companies may propose or declare a dividend to the ordinary shareholders (i.e. tell the shareholders the amount of a dividend to be paid after the year-end). This is a **final dividend**. These dividends have to be approved at the annual general meeting (AGM) and until this point the company have no obligation to pay them.

Therefore proposed dividends at the end of the year that have not been approved by shareholders **cannot be recorded as liabilities at the year-end.**

7 Loan notes (loan stock)

A limited company can raise funds by issuing loan notes. These are fixed term loans. The term 'loan note' simply refers to the document that is evidence of the debt, often a certificate that is issued to the lender.

Similar to shares, the loan note will have a set nominal value, e.g. $100. Individuals or organisations can buy the loan notes at an agreed price (this can be any value, it does not have to be the same as the nominal value). The life of the loan note will be fixed and the company issuing them will have to pay the loan note holder back at an agreed point in time.

The issuer will also have to pay interest to the loan note holder. The interest will be calculated based on the nominal value of the loan note (for example, 5% of the nominal value per annum). The interest incurred is included in 'finance costs' in the statement of profit or loss.

Accounting entries

When the finance is first received the company receiving the finance must recognise the obligation to repay the loan holder as follows:

Dr Cash

Cr Non-current liability

Every year the business should recognise a finance charge (i.e. interest) based upon the terms of the agreement as follows:

Dr Finance charges (P/L)

Cr Cash/current liabilities (depending on whether the interest has been paid or not).

Test your understanding 5

Custard Creameries is an incorporated business which needs to raise funds to purchase plant and machinery. On 1 March 20X5 it issues $150,000 10% loan notes, redeemable in 10 years' time. Interest is payable half yearly at the end of August and February.

What accounting entries are required in the year ended 31 December 20X5? Show relevant extracts from the statement of financial position.

8 Preference shares

If preference shares are redeemable they are treated the same as loan notes; i.e. they are recorded as a liability in the statement of financial position and dividend payments are treated the same as finance charges.

If the preference shares are irredeemable the shareholding and associated dividends are treated exactly the same as ordinary shareholdings, as explained above.

Test your understanding 6

Cracker, a company, has share capital as follows:

Ordinary share capital (50c shares) $200,000

8% Irredeemable preference share capital $50,000

The company pays an interim dividend (i.e. a dividend declared part way through the financial year) of 12.5c per share to its ordinary shareholders and pays the preference shareholders their dividend, although this is not mandatory. Before the year end the company proposes a final dividend of 36.5c per share to its ordinary shareholders.

Calculate the amounts shown in the statement of changes in equity (SOCIE) and statement of financial position (SFP) in relation to dividends for the year.

	SOCIE	SFP
	$000	$000
A	200	150
B	54	nil
C	200	146
D	101	72

9 Other reserves

In addition to using loan capital and share capital, companies can also use the capital created internally to generate wealth by reinvesting it back into the business. These capital sources represent the profits made by the business and the inflation in value of tangible non-current assets recognised in a revaluation. They are referred to as reserves or other components of equity.

They are included in the statement of financial position and movements in share capital and reserves for the accounting period are summarised and disclosed in the statement of changes in equity.

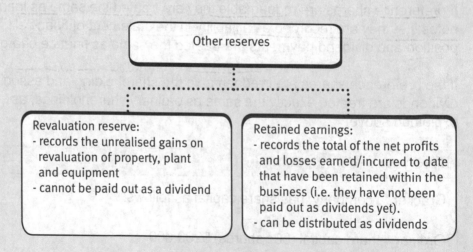

Other reserves

Revaluation reserve:
- records the unrealised gains on revaluation of property, plant and equipment
- cannot be paid out as a dividend

Retained earnings:
- records the total of the net profits and losses earned/incurred to date that have been retained within the business (i.e. they have not been paid out as dividends yet).
- can be distributed as dividends

Retained earnings

Retained profits are due (although generally not paid out) to the shareholders of the company. As they are the owners of the company the profits made by that company are their property. It therefore follows that they should be presented as part of the company's liability to the shareholders.

10 Income tax

In the same way that individuals are subject to tax on their income, the income generated by a business is also subject to tax.

Sole traders and partnerships

In the case of a sole trader or a partnership, the tax charge is imposed upon the individual, rather than the business. Consequently, if the business bank account is used to pay what is a personal tax liability, it will be accounted for as a form of drawings made from the business by the owner.

Limited liability companies

In the case of a limited liability company, as it is a separate legal entity, if it generates income, it will be subject to tax. Consequently, the tax charge tax must be reflected in the statement of profit or loss as an expense and any tax liabilities outstanding must be reflected in the statement of financial position.

This is normally referred to as **'income tax'** as it is a tax charge on the income of a company. In the UK, this was traditionally referred to as corporation tax, but is now more commonly referred to as income tax. It should not be confused with the income tax paid by individual employees on their salary and other earnings.

The charge for income tax is based upon the level of profits earned by the company and the tax rates in place at the time of calculation.

Company year-ends and tax year-ends rarely match. Therefore companies must estimate their income tax liability at the end of each accounting period and record an appropriate estimate of the liability likely to be paid.

These estimates are unlikely to be entirely accurate (they are usually a 'best estimate' when the accounts are being prepared) and, as such, companies tend to either over or under estimate the provision for income tax, which is adjusted for in the following year's accounts.

You will not be required to have any tax-related knowledge to calculate tax charges. For the purposes of Paper F3, you are required to understand how income tax charges and liabilities are accounted for in limited company financial statements. In many ways, it is similar to accounting for a provision – recognise a liability when required, with any movement in the liability accounted for in profit or loss.

Steps for recording income tax

Step 1

At the end of the year a company should make the following double entry for its estimate of the tax liability:

Dr Income tax charges (P&L)

Cr Income tax liability (SoFP – current liability)

Step 2

Following the year-end the actual tax liability will be calculated and paid. The associated double entry is:

Dr Income tax liability

Cr Cash

Step 3

It is unlikely the actual charge will match the estimated liability so the tax liability account will be left with a closing balance carried forward. This needs to be removed as the debt has been settled (i.e. there should not be any carried forward balances because the tax authorities have been paid the correct amount).

If there is an overprovision in the prior year (i.e. estimate was greater than the amount paid) there will be a closing credit balance carried forward. This is adjusted as follows:

Dr Income tax liability

Cr Income tax charge.

As the company overestimated, the charge for the following year is reduced by the appropriate amount so that, over the two-year period, the correct charge has been recorded.

If there is an underestimate in the prior year (i.e. estimate was less than the amount paid) there will be a closing debit balance carried forward. This is adjusted as follows:

Dr Income tax charge

Cr Income tax liability

As the company underestimated, the charge for the following year is increased by the appropriate amount, so that over the two-year period, the correct charge has been recorded.

Accounting entries – Further explanation

In simple terms, **the income tax liability on the statement of financial position should only ever be equal to the estimate of the tax liability at the end of the year**. (The under/over provision from the prior year should have been sorted out well before the year-end).

The charge to the statement of profit or loss can be calculated as follows:

	$000
Current tax estimate	X
Under/(over) provision in prior year	X/(X)
Total income tax charge for the year	X

Test your understanding 7

Garry Baldy commenced trade on 1 January 20X4 and estimates that the tax payable for the year ended 31 December 20X4 is $150,000.

In September 20X5, the accountant of Garry Baldy receives and pays a tax demand for $163,000 for the year ended 31 December 20X4. At 31 December 20X5 he estimates that the company owes $165,000 for corporation tax in relation to the year ended 31 December 20X5.

Draw up the tax charge and income tax payable accounts for the years ended 31 December 20X4 and 20X5 and detail the amounts shown in the statement of financial position and statement of profit or loss in both years.

Test your understanding 8

Choccychip estimated last year's tax charge to be $230,000. As it happened, their tax advisor settled with the tax authorities at $222,000. The difference arose because the financial statements were submitted sometime before the tax computation. Therefore the directors had to make a prudent estimate of the potential tax liability to put in the accounts.

This year, Choccychip estimate their tax bill to be $265,000, but they are a little confused as to how this should be reflected in the financial statements.

Which of the following is correct for the end of the current year?

	Statement of financial position liability ($)	Tax expenses ($)
A	257,000	265,000
B	273,000	265,000
C	265,000	257,000
D	265,000	273,000

Chapter summary

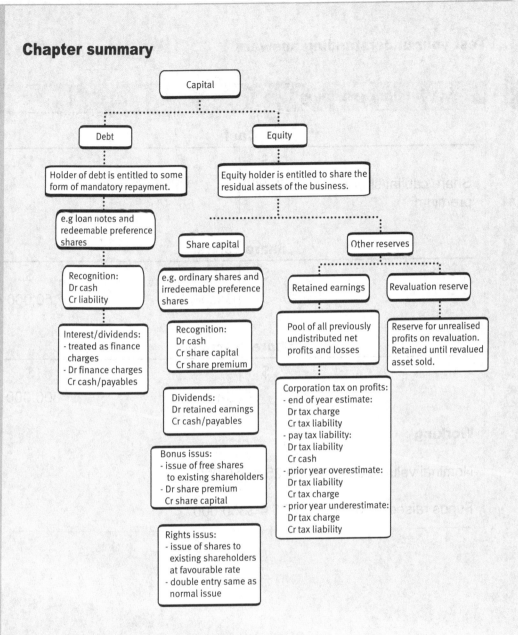

Test your understanding answers

Test your understanding 1

Cash

	$			$
Share capital/share premium	350,000			

Share capital

	$			$
		Cash		50,000

Share premium

	$			$
		Cash		300,000

Working

Nominal value: 200,000 × $0.25 = $50,000

Funds raised: 200,000 × $1.75 = $350,000

Test your understanding 2

20X4	Dr Cash	$500
	Cr Share capital	$500

20X5   For every five shares a shareholder owns, he or she is entitled to buy another one. The offer is fully taken up, meaning that 200 new shares are issued (1,000 shares/5 × 1).

Dr Cash (200 × $0.75)	$150
Cr Share capital (200 × $0.50)	$100
Cr Share premium	$50

(200×0.25) ↓ $(0.75 - 0.50)$

Statement of financial position

Capital and reserves:

	$
Share capital – 50c ordinary shares	600
Share premium	50
Accumulated profit	X

Test your understanding 3

The correct answer is B.

- For every four shares held, a new share is issued.
- Therefore 5,000 new shares are issued (20,000 shares/4 × 1)

Dr Share premium (5,000 × 50c)	$2,500
Cr Share capital	$2,500

Statement of financial position

Capital and reserves:

	$
Share capital – 50c ordinary shares (20,000 × $0.5) + $2,500	12,500
Share premium (20,000 × ($1.25 – $0.5)) – $2,500	12,500
Accumulated profit	X

Test your understanding 4

The correct answer is D.

Share capital

	$		$
		Balance b/f	50,000
		Rights issue (cash)	20,000
Balance c/f	77,000	Bonus issue	7,000
	———		———
	77,000		77,000
	———		———
		Balance b/f	77,000

Share premium

	$		$
		Balance b/f	75,000
Bonus issue (SC)	7,000	Rights issue (cash)	124,000
Balance c/f	192,000		
	———		———
	199,000		199,000
	———		———
		Balance b/f	192,000

Statement of financial position

Capital and reserves:	$
Share capital – 25c ordinary shares	77,000
Share premium	192,000
Retained earnings	X

Workings

Rights issue: (200,000/5) × 2 = 80,000 new shares

Proceeds: 80,000 × $1.80 = $144,000

Nominal value: 80,000 × 25c =$20,000

Bonus issue: (280,000/10) × 1 = 28,000 new shares

Nominal value: 28,000 × 25c = $7,000

Test your understanding 5

1 March 20X5 Dr Cash	$150,000
Cr 10% Loan notes	$150,000
31 August 20X5 Dr Finance cost	$7,500
Cr Cash	$7,500
$150,000 × 10% × 6/12 = $7,500	
31 December 20X5 Dr Finance cost	$5,000
Cr Interest accrual	$5,000
$150,000 × 10% × 4/12 = $5,000	

Statement of financial position

	$
Non-current liabilities	
10% Loan notes	150,000
Current liabilities	
Trade payables	X
Loan note interest payable	5,000

Test your understanding 6

The correct answer is B.

No. of ordinary shares = $200,000/50c = 400,000

Interim ordinary dividend;

400,000 × 12.5c = $50,000

Preference dividend:

50,000 × 8% = $4,000

Statement of changes in equity

	$
Retained earnings at start of year	X
dividends ($50,000 + $4,000)	(54,000)
At end of year	X

Note: The final dividend cannot be accounted for until approved at the AGM and therefore cannot be a liability at the year-end.

Test your understanding 7

Tax payable (statement of financial position)

	$		$
		20X4	
		Profit or loss	150,000
	150,000		150,000
Sept X5 Bank	163,000	20X5 Balance b/f	150,000
		Under-provision b/f	13,000
Balance c/f	165,000	20X5 Profit or loss	165,000
	328,000		328,000
		20X6 Balance b/f	165,000

Tax charge (statement of profit or loss)

	$		$
20X4 tax payable	150,000	Profit or loss	150,000
	150,000		150,000
20X5 Under-provision	13,000		
Tax payable	165,000	Profit or loss	178,000
	178,000		178,000

The tax charge in 20X5 is increased to reflect the under-provision made in 20X4.

Statement of financial position

	20X4	20X5
	$000	$000
Corporation tax liability	150	165

Statement of profit or loss

	20X4	20X5
Tax expense	150	178

Test your understanding 8

The correct answer is C.

- The liability in the statement of financial position= the estimated amount payable for the current year.

- The tax charge in the statement of profit or loss = the estimated amount payable for the current year – last year's overprovision.

Control account reconciliations

Chapter learning objectives

Upon completion of this chapter you will be able to:

- understand the purpose of, and prepare, control accounts for receivables and payables

- perform control account reconciliations and identify which errors would be highlighted by such a control

- identify and correct errors in control accounts.

1 Overview

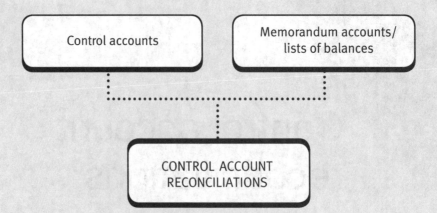

2 Control accounts

Control accounts are general ledger accounts that summarise a large number of transactions. As such they are part of the double entry system. They are used to prove the accuracy of the ledger accounting system. They are mainly used with regard to receivables and payables balances.

When a company transfers the daily total of the sales book into the general ledger the double entry is:

Dr Receivables ledger control account

Cr Sales revenue.

When they transfer the total of the purchase day book the double entry is:

Dr Purchases

Cr Payables ledger control account

At the same time most businesses will maintain what is referred to as a 'memorandum.' This is a separate list of individual receivable and payable amounts due from each customer and to each supplier, respectively. This simple 'list of balances' is used as a record so that companies know how much each customer is due to pay and how much they are due to pay each supplier. This assists with credit control and cash flow management.

A key control operated by a business is to compare the total balance on the control account at the end of the accounting period with the total of all the separate memorandum balances. In theory they should be identical. This is referred to as a **control account reconciliation**.

Note: The memorandum balances are often, confusingly, referred to as the 'receivables ledger' and the 'payables ledger.' Don't get these mixed up with the control accounts in the main/general ledger!

3 Illustrative control accounts

The receivables ledger control account may include any of the following entries:

Receivables ledger control account

Balance b/f	X	Balance b/f	X
Credit sales (SDB)	X	Sales returns (SRDB)	X
		Bank (CB)	X
Bank (CB) dishonoured cheques	X	Irrecoverable debts (journal)	X
Bank (CB) refunds of credit balances	X	Discounts allowed	X
Interest charged	X	Contra	X
Balance c/f	X	Balance c/f	X
	X		X
Balance b/f	X	Balance b/f	X

The payables ledger control account may include any of the following entries:

Payables ledger control account

Balance b/f	X	Balance b/f	X
Bank (CB)	X	Credit purchases (PDB)	X
Purchases returns (PRDB)	X	Bank (CB) refunds of debit balances	X
Discounts received	X		
Contra	X		
Balance c/f	X	Balance c/f	X
	X		X
Balance b/f	X	Balance b/f	X

Abbreviation key:

SDB Sales day book

PDB Purchases day book

SRDB Sales returns day book

PRDB Purchases returns day book

CB Cash book

Note that any entries to the control accounts must also be reflected in the individual accounts within the accounts receivable and payable ledgers.

Recording contra entries

Contra entries

The situation may arise where a customer is also a supplier. Instead of both owing each other money, it may be agreed that the balances are contra'd, i.e. cancelled.

The double entry for this type of contra is:

Dr Payables ledger control account

Cr Receivables ledger control account

The individual receivable and payable memorandum accounts must also be updated to reflect this.

Recording credit balances

Credit balances on the receivables ledger control account

Sometimes the receivables ledger control account may show a credit balance, i.e. we owe the customer money. These amounts are usually small and arise when:

- The customer has overpaid.
- Credit notes have been issued for fully-paid-for goods.
- Payment is received in advance of raising invoices.

The payables ledger control account may show a debit balance for similar reasons.

Technically such balances should not exist and should be transferred to the correct account. Thus a credit in a receivable account should be adjusted as follows:

Dr Receivables

Cr Payables

Debit balances in the payables ledger will be adjusted using exactly the same double entry.

Test your understanding 1

Jones prepares monthly Receivables and Payables ledger control accounts. At 1 November 2005 the following balances existed in the company's records.

	Dr $	Cr $
Receivables ledger control account	54,000	1,000
Payables ledger control account	200	43,000

The following information is extracted in November 2005 from the company's records:

	$
Credit sales	251,000
Cash sales	34,000
Credit purchases	77,000
Cash purchases	29,000
Credit sales returns	11,000
Credit purchases returns	3,000
Amounts received from credit customers	242,000
Dishonoured cheques	500
Amounts paid to credit suppliers	74,000
Cash discounts allowed	3,000
Cash discounts received	2,000
Irrecoverable debts written off	1,000
Increase in allowances for receivables	1,200
Interest charged to customers	1,400
Contra settlements	800

At 30 November 2005 the balances in the Receivables and Payables ledgers, as extracted, totalled:

	Dr	Cr
	$	$
Receivables ledger balances	To be calculated	2,000
Payables ledger balances	200	To be calculated

Prepare the receivables ledger control account and the payables ledger control account for the month of November 2005 to determine the closing debit and closing credit balances on the receivables ledger control account and payables ledger control account respectively.

4 Control account reconciliations

As stated above, the reconciliation is a working to ensure that the entries in the ledger accounts (memorandum) agree with the entries in the control account. The totals in each should be exactly the same. If not it indicates an error in either the memorandum account or the control account. All discrepancies should be investigated and corrected.

Test your understanding 2

Suggest reasons why there might be a difference between the balance on the receivables ledger control account and the total of the list of accounts receivable ledger balances.

5 Preparing a control account reconciliation

The format of a control account reconciliation, in this case for receivables, is as follows:

Receivables ledger control account

	$		$
Balance given by the examiner	X	Adjustments for errors	X
Adjustments for errors	X	Revised balance c/f	X
	—		—
	X		X

Reconciliation of individual receivables balances with control account balance

	$
Balance as extracted from list of receivables	X
Adjustments for errors	X/(X)
Revised total agreeing with balance c/f on control account	X

- The examiner will provide details of the error(s).

- You must decide for each whether correction is required in the control account, the list of individual balances or both.

- When all errors have been corrected, the revised balance on the control account should agree to the revised total of the list of individual balances.

- Due to the nature of the F3/FFA exam, you will not be asked to produce a full control account reconciliation, however you may be asked for the revised balance on the control account / list of individual balances after one or two errors have been corrected.

Illustration 1 – Preparing a control account reconciliation

Alston's payables ledger control account is an integral part of the double entry system. Individual ledger account balances are listed and totalled on a monthly basis, and reconciled to the control account balance. Information for the month of March is as follows:

(1) Individual ledger account balances at 31 March have been listed out and totalled $19,766.

(2) The payables ledger control account balance at 31 March is $21,832.

(3) On further examination the following errors are discovered:

- The total of discount received for the month, amounting to $1,715, has not been entered in the control account but has been entered in the individual ledger accounts.

- On listing-out, an individual credit balance of $205 has been incorrectly treated as a debit.

- A petty cash payment to a supplier amounting to $63 has been correctly treated in the control account, but no entry has been made in the supplier's individual ledger account.

- The purchases day book total for March has been undercast (understated) by $2,000.

- Contras (set-offs) with the receivables ledger, amounting in total to $2,004, have been correctly treated in the individual ledger accounts but no entry has been made in the control account.

(i) **Prepare the part of the payables ledger control account reflecting the above information.**

(ii) **Prepare a statement reconciling the original total of the individual balances with the corrected balance on the control account.**

Solution to Illustration 1

The best way to approach the question is to consider each of the points above in turn and ask to what extent they affect (i) the payables ledger control account and (ii) the listing of payables ledger balances.

Step 1

The total of discount received in the cash book should have been debited to the payables ledger control account and credited to discount received. Thus, if the posting has not been entered in either double entry account it clearly should be. As this has already been entered into the individual ledger accounts, no adjustment is required to the list of balances.

Step 2

Individual credit balances are extracted from the payables ledger. Here, this error affects the ledger accounts balance. No adjustment is required to the control account, only to the list of balances.

Step 3

The question clearly states that the error has been made in the individual ledger accounts. Amendments should be made to the list of balances. Again, no amendment is required to the control accounts.

Step 4

The total of the purchases day book is posted by debiting purchases and crediting payables ledger control account. If the total is understated, the following bookkeeping entry must be made, posting the $2,000 understatement:

Dr Purchases

   Cr Payables ledger control account

As the individual ledger accounts in the payables ledger are posted individually from the purchases day book, the total of the day book being understated will not affect the listing of the balances in the payables ledger.

Step 5

Here it is clear that the error affects the control account, not the payables ledger. Correction should be made by the bookkeeping entry:

Dr Payables ledger control account

Cr Receivables ledger control account

Payables ledger control account

20X9	$	20X9	$
Discount received	1,715	31 Mar	
Sales receivable ledger control	2,004	Balance	21,832
Balance c/f	20,113	Purchase	2,000
	23,832		23,832

Reconciliation of individual balances with control account balance

	Cr $
Balances as extracted	19,766
Credit balance incorrectly treated 2 × $205	410
Petty cash payment	(63)
Net total agreeing with control account	20,113

Test your understanding 3

Rayneydaze is a business selling umbrellas branded with corporate logos. The umbrellas are sold on credit, rather than for cash. The accountant is carrying out a reconciliation of the receivables ledger control account balance, which is $172,120 to the total of the balances on the individual accounts in the receivables ledger, which is $176,134.

The following has been found:

(1) A contra item of $1,500 has not been entered in the receivables ledger control account.

(2) A cheque for $555 from a customer has been dishonoured. The correct double entry has been posted but the individual accounts have not been updated.

(3) A payment of $322 from a customer has incorrectly been entered in the accounts receivable ledger as $233.

(4) Discounts allowed totalling $120 have not been entered in the control account.

(5) Cash received of $800 has been debited to the individual customer's account in the accounts receivable ledger.

(6) Total credit sales of $4,500 to a large accountancy firm, Close & Counter have been posted correctly to the ledger account but not recorded in the control account.

Correct the receivables ledger control account and reconcile this to the sum total of the individual accounts in the accounts receivable ledger.

Test your understanding 4

Tonga received a statement from a supplier, Cook, showing a balance of $14,810. Tonga's Payables ledger shows a balance due to Cook of $10,000. Investigation reveals the following:

(1) Cash paid to Cook of $4,080 has not been recorded by Cook.

(2) Tonga's recorded the fact that a $40 cash discount was not allowed by Cook, but forgot to record this in the payables ledger.

What discrepancy remains between Tonga and Cook's records after allowing for these items?

A $9,930

B $9,850

C $770

D $690

Supplier statements

These statements are issued to a business by suppliers to summarise the transactions that have taken place during a given period, and also to show the balance outstanding at the end of the period.

- Their purpose is to ensure that the amount outstanding is accurate and agrees with underlying documentation.

- The payables (individual) ledger account should agree with the total of the supplier statement.

- As such, these are a further way to prove the accuracy of accounting records.

Supplier statement reconciliations

It is also possible to reconcile a supplier statement to the control account.

The purpose for doing this is as follows:

- before any payments are made to suppliers it is important to ensure that the suppliers statement is correct – else we could make over or under payments.

- each invoice and credit note listed on the statement should be checked to the original documentation for accuracy.

- once accuracy has been established, it is then possible to decide which invoices need paying and when by.

Below is an example extract of a statement from a supplier:

STATEMENT					
Date	Transaction	Total $	Current $	30+ $	60+ $
10 May 20X9	Invoice 100	94.50			94.50
1 June 20X9	CN 2008	(24.56)			(24.56)
4 July 20X9	Invoice 110	101.99		101.99	
15 July 20X9	Invoice 156	106.72	106.72		
	TOTALS	278.65	106.72	101.99	69.94
May I remind you that our credit terms are 30 days.					

Here is the payables ledger which corresponds with this supplier:

Nino Ltd

		$				$
1 June 20X9 CN		24.56	10 May 20X9	Invoice 100		94.50
			4 July 20X9	Invoice 110		110.99
			15 July 20X9	Invoice 156		106.72

You can see that the invoice dated 4 July 20X9 in the ledger is of a total $110.99, however in the statement it appears as $101.99.

The purchase invoice itself should be reviewed to check which is the correct amount. If the suppliers statement is incorrect, then a polite telephone call to the supplier should be made or a letter sent explaining the problem.

If it is the ledger that is incorrect then it should be updated.

Chapter summary

CONTROL ACCOUNTS

- Control accounts include a summary of transactions that have occurred in the period.
- They are a means of checking that the information in the ledger accounts is correct.
- They are part of the double entry system.

MEMORANDUM ACCOUNTS

- Ledger accounts include a separate account for each credit customer/ credit supplier.
- They are memorandum accounts and not part of the double entry system.

CONTROL ACCOUNT RECONCILIATIONS

- These are a means of checking that the balance on the control account agrees with the balance on the ledger account.
- There may be errors in the ledger account, the control account or both.

PREPARING A CONTROL ACCOUNT RECONCILIATION

- Compare the balance on the ledger account with the control account.
- Review the list of errors to see which account needs amending.
- Set up a T account for the control accounts.
- Prepare a reconciliation for the ledger account.

Test your understanding answers

Test your understanding 1

Receivables ledger control account

	$		$
Balance b/f	54,000	Balance b/f	1,000
Credit sales	251,000	Sales returns	11,000
Dishonoured cheques	500	Cash received	242,000
Interest charged	1,400	Discounts allowed	3,000
		Irrecoverable debts	1,000
		Contra	800
Balance c/f	2,000	Balance c/f	50,100
	308,900		308,900
Balance b/f	50,100	Balance b/f	2,000

Payables ledger control account

	$		$
Balance b/f	200	Balance b/f	43,000
Purchases returns	3,000	Credit purchases	77,000
Cash paid	74,000		
Discounts received	2,000		
Contra	800		
Balance c/f	40,200	Balance c/f	200
	120,200		120,200
Balance b/f	200	Balance b/f	40,200

Test your understanding 2

The following are reasons why the accounts receivable control account may not agree with the ledger account:

- The sales day book, sales returns day book or cash receipts book have been incorrectly totalled.

- A total from a book of prime entry has been transferred to the control account as a different figure.

- An individual entry from a book of prime entry has been transferred to the individual customer's account as a different figure.

- An entry in the control account or the individual customer's account has been omitted or posted to the wrong side of the account.

- The double entry for a day book total has been incorrectly made.

- An individual customer's account has been incorrectly balanced.

- The list of accounts receivable ledger balances has been incorrectly totalled.

- An entry has been made in either the control account or the individual customer's account but not in both.

- An individual customer's balance has been omitted from the list of balances.

Test your understanding 3

Receivables ledger control account

	$		$
Balance b/f	172,120	Contra (1)	1,500
Credit sales (6)	4,500	Discounts (4)	120
		Balance c/f	175,000
	176,620		176,620
Balance b/f	175,000		

Receivables ledger reconciliation

Balance per accounts receivable ledger	176,134
Dishonoured cheque (2)	555
Misposting (3)	(89)
Cash received (5)	(1,600)
Revised balance	175,000

Test your understanding 4

The correct answer is D.

	Cook $	Tonga $	
Difference			
Balance per question	14,810	10,000	
Adjustment	(4,080)	40	
Revised balance	10,730	10,040	690

chapter

15

Bank reconciliations

Chapter learning objectives

Upon completion of this chapter you will be able to:

- understand the purpose of bank reconciliations
- identify the main reasons for differences between the cash book and the bank statement
- correct cash book errors and/or omissions
- prepare bank reconciliation statements
- derive bank statement and cash book balances from given information
- identify the bank balance to be reported in the final accounts.

1 Overview

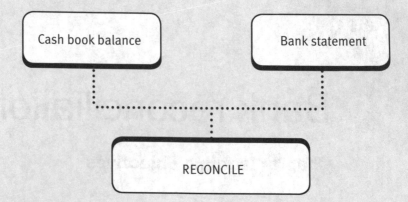

2 The bank reconciliation

The objective of a bank reconciliation is to reconcile the difference between:

- the cash book balance, i.e. the business' record of their bank account, and

- the bank statement balance, i.e. the bank's record of the bank account.

The cash book is the double entry record of cash and bank balances contained within the nominal ledger accounting system. It is, in effect, the cash control account.

 Note that debits and credits are reversed in bank statements because the bank will be recording the transaction from its point of view, in accordance with the business entity concept.

Reasons to prepare a bank reconciliation statement

Nature and purpose of a bank reconciliation statement

The cash book records all transactions with the bank. The bank statement records all the bank's transactions with the business.

The contents of the cash book should be exactly the same as the record provided by the bank in the form of a bank statement, and therefore the business' records should correspond with the bank statement.

This is in fact so, but with three important provisos:

(1) The ledger account maintained by the bank is the opposite way round to the cash book. This is because the bank records balances from their perspective. Therefore if a client has a positive bank balance the bank would display this as a credit balance because they have a liability to pay it back to the client. If the client is overdrawn this would be shown as a debit because the bank are owed a repayment from the client.

(2) Timing differences must inevitably occur. A cheque payment is recorded in the cash book when the cheque is despatched. The bank only records such a cheque when it is paid by the bank, which may be several days later.

(3) Items such as interest may appear on the bank statement but are not recorded in the cash book as the business is unaware that they have arisen.

The existence of the bank statement provides an important check on the most vulnerable of a company's assets – cash. However, the differences referred to above make it essential to reconcile the balance on the ledger account with that of the bank statement.

The reconciliation is carried out frequently, usually at monthly intervals.

3 Differences between the bank statement and the cash book

When attempting to reconcile the cash book with the bank statement, there are three differences between the cash book and bank statemont:

- unrecorded items
- timing differences
- errors

Cash book adjustments

Unrecorded items

These are items which arise in the bank statements before they are recorded in the cash book. Such 'unrecorded items' may include:

- interest
- bank charges
- dishonoured cheques.

They are not recorded in the cash book simply because the business does not know that these items have arisen until they see the bank statement.

The cash book must be adjusted to reflect these items.

Test your understanding 1

On which side of the cash book should the following unrecorded items be posted?

- bank charges
- direct debits/standing orders
- direct credits
- dishonoured cheques received from customers
- bank interest received.

Bank statement adjustments

Timing differences

These items have been recorded in the cash book, but due to the bank clearing process have not yet been recorded in the bank statement:

- Outstanding/unpresented cheques (cheques sent to suppliers but not yet cleared by the bank).
- Outstanding/uncleared lodgements (cheques received by the business but not yet cleared by the bank).

The bank statement balance needs to be adjusted for these items:

	$
Balance per bank statement	X
Less: Outstanding/unpresented cheques	(X)
Add: Outstanding/uncleared lodgements	X
	——
Balance per cash book (revised)	X

Errors in the cash book

The business may make a mistake in their cash book. The cash book balance will need to be adjusted for these items.

Errors in the bank statement

The bank may make a mistake, e.g. record a transaction relating to a different person within our business' bank statement. The bank statement balance will need to be adjusted for these items.

Outstanding payments and receipts

Outstanding or unpresented cheques

Suppose a cheque relating to a payment to a supplier of Poorboy is written, signed and posted on 29 March. It is also entered in the cash book on the same day. By the time the supplier has received the cheque and paid it into his bank account, and by the time his bank has gone through the clearing system, the cheque does not appear on Poorboy's statement until, say, 6 April. Poorboy would regard the payment as being made on 29 March and its cash book balance as reflecting the true position at that date.

Outstanding deposits/lodgements

In a similar way, a trader may receive cheques by post on 31 March, enter them in the cash book and pay them into the bank on the same day. Nevertheless, the cheques may not appear on the bank statement until 2 April. Again the cash book would be regarded as showing the true position. Outstanding deposits are also known as outstanding lodgements.

4 Proforma bank reconciliation

Cash book

Bal b/f	X	Bal b/f	X
Adjustments	X	Adjustments	X
Revised bal c/f	X	Revised bal c/f	X
	——		——
	X		X
	——		——
Revised bal b/f	X	Revised bal b/f	X

Bank reconciliation statement as at .....

	$
Balance per bank statement	X
Outstanding cheques	(X)
Outstanding lodgements	X
Other adjustments to the bank statement	X/(X)
	——
Balance per cash book (revised)	X

- Beware of overdrawn balances on the bank statement.

- Beware of debits/credits to bank statements.

- Beware of aggregation of deposits in a bank statement.

- **Note that the bank balance on the statement of financial position is always the balance per the revised cash book**.

Test your understanding 2

In preparing a company's bank reconciliation statement, the accountant finds that the following items are causing a difference between the cash book balance and bank statement balance:

(1) Direct debit $530.

(2) Lodgements not credited $1,200.

(3) Cheque paid in by the company and dishonoured $234.

(4) Outstanding cheques $677.

(5) Bank charges $100.

(6) Error by bank $2,399 (cheque incorrectly credited to the account).

KAPLAN PUBLISHING

Which of these items will require an entry in the cash book?

A   3, 4 and 6

B   1, 3 and 5

C   1, 2 and 4

D   2, 5 and 6

Test your understanding 3

The following information has been extracted from the records of N Patel:

Bank account

		$			Chq no	$
1 Dec	Balance b/f	16,491	1 Dec	Alexander	782	857
2 Dec	Able	962	6 Dec	Burgess	783	221
	Baker	1,103	14 Dec	Barry	784	511
10 Dec	Charlie	2,312	17 Dec	Cook	785	97
14 Dec	Delta	419	24 Dec	Hay	786	343
21 Dec	Echo	327	29 Dec	Rent	787	260
23 Dec	Cash sales	529				
30 Dec	Fred	119	31 Dec	Balance c/f		19,973
		22,262				22,262

High Street Bank

Bank Statement – N. Patel

Date	Details	With-drawals	Deposits	Balance
		$	$	$
1 December	Balance b/f			17,478
2 December	780	426		
2 December	781	737		16,315
2 December	Deposit		176	16,491
5 December	782	857		
5 December	Bank charges	47		15,587
6 December	Deposit		2,065	17,652
10 December	Standing order (rates)	137		17,515
11 December	783	212		17,303
13 December	Deposit		2,312	19,615
17 December	784	511		19,104
17 December	Deposit		419	19,523
23 December	Deposit		327	19,850
24 December	Deposit		528	20,378
28 December	786	343		20,035
30 December	310923	297		19,738
31 December	Balance c/f			19,738

(a) **Prepare a bank reconciliation statement at 1 December.**

(b) **Update the cash book for December.**

(c) **Prepare a bank reconciliation statement at 31 December.**

Test your understanding 4

The following is a summary of Ami's cash book as presented to you for the month of December 20X6:

Bank account

	$		$
Receipts	1,469	Balance b/f	761
Balance c/f	554	Payments	1,262
	2,023		2,023

All receipts are banked and payments made by cheque.

On investigation you discover:

(1) Bank charges of $136 entered on the bank statement had not been entered in the cash book.

(2) Cheques drawn amounting to $267 had not been presented to the bank for payment.

(3) A cheque for $22 had been entered as a receipt in the cash book instead of as a payment;

(4) A cheque drawn for $6 had been incorrectly entered in the cash book as $66.

What balance is shown on the bank statement at 31 December 20X6?

A $913

B $941 overdraft

C $941

D $407 overdraft

Chapter summary

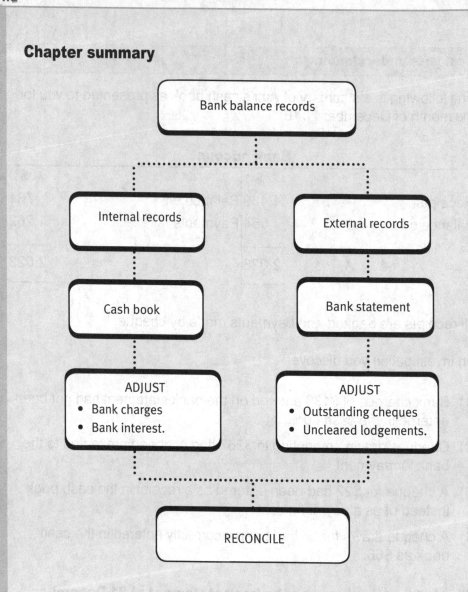

Test your understanding answers

Test your understanding 1

Cash book

	$		$
Bank interest	X	Bank charges	X
Direct credits	X	Direct debits/	X
		standing orders	
		Dishonoured cheques	X

Test your understanding 2

The correct answer is B.

Test your understanding 3

Bank reconciliation statement as at 1 December	$
Balance per bank statement	17,478
Less: Outstanding cheques ($426 + $737)	(1,163)
Add: Outstanding lodgements	176
Balance per cash book	
	16,491

Bank account

	$		$
Balance b/f	19,973	Deposit difference	
		($529 – 528)	1
Error – cheque 783		Bank charges	47
($221–212)	9		
		Rates – s/order	137
		Revised balance c/f	19,797
	19,982		19,982
Revised balance b/f	19,797		

Bank reconciliation statement as at 31 December	$
Balance per bank statement	19,738
Less: Outstanding cheques ($97 + 260)	(357)
Add: Outstanding lodgements (Fred)	119
Bank error (Cheque 310923)	297
Balance per cash book	
	19,797

Test your understanding 4

The correct answer is D.

Cash book

	$		$
Adjustment re cheque (4)	60	Balance b/f	554
Balance c/f	674	Bank charges (1)	136
		Adjustment re paid cheque entered as receipt (3)	44
	734		734
		Balance b/f	674

Bank reconciliation statement as at 31 December 20X6

	$
Balance per bank statement at 31 December 20X6 (derived)	(407)
Less: Cheques issued but not yet presented (2)	(267)
Balance per cash book at 31 Dec 20X6	
	(674)

The trial balance, errors and suspense accounts

Chapter learning objectives

Upon completion of this chapter you will be able to:

- identify the purpose of and prepare a trial balance
- identify the types of error which may occur in bookkeeping systems
- identify the types of error which would and would not be highlighted by a trial balance
- understand the purpose of a suspense account
- prepare journal entries to correct errors and clear out a suspense account
- understand and calculate the impact of errors on the financial statements.

1 Overview

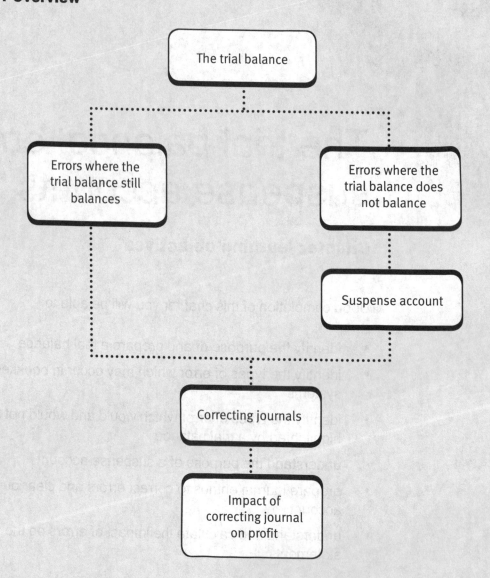

2 The trial balance

At the end of the year, once all ledger accounts have been balanced off, the closing balances are summarised on a long list of balances. This is referred to as a trial balance.

All the closing debit balances are summarised in one column and the closing credit balances in another. Given the nature of the double entry system described in this text the totals of both columns should agree. If not the discrepancy must be investigated and corrected.

This is another control in the accounting system to ensure that the balances reported in the financial statements are accurate. The layout of a trial balance is illustrated below:

Trial balance as at 31 December 20X5

	Dr	Cr
	$	$
Revenue		X
Purchases	X	
Administrative expenses	X	
Non-current assets	X	
Trade receivables	X	
Cash	X	
Share capital		X
Loans		X
Trade payables		X
	___	___
	X	X

3 The process of preparing financial statements

The process for preparing financial statements can be illustrated as follows:

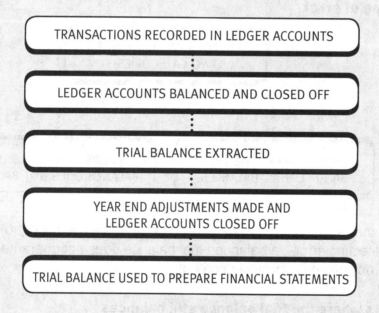

Examination questions may draw on any particular stage of this process.

Test your understanding 1

Gateway Ltd sets up as a company and in the first nine days of trading the following transactions occurred:

1 January	They issue $10,000 share capital for cash.
2 January	They purchase goods for $4,000 and pay by cheque.
3 January	They buy a delivery van for $2,000 and pay by cheque.
4 January	They purchase $1,000 of goods on credit.
5 January	They sell goods for $1,500 cash.
6 January	They sell all remaining goods for $5,000 on credit.
7 January	They pay $800 to suppliers by cheque.
8 January	They pay rent of $200 by cheque.

(a) **Complete the relevant ledger accounts.**

(b) **Extract a trial balance.**

4 Type of error

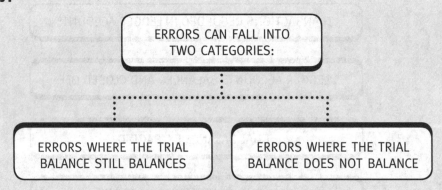

This shows that whilst the trial balance provides a useful control mechanism for detecting errors, a balanced trial balance does not guarantee the accuracy of the financial statements.

Errors where the trial balance still balances

- **Error of omission:** A transaction has been completely omitted from the accounting records, e.g. a cash sale of $100 was not recorded.

- **Error of commission**: A transaction has been recorded in the wrong account, e.g. rates expense of $500 has been debited to the rent account in error.

- **Error of principle:** A transaction has conceptually been recorded incorrectly, e.g. a non-current asset purchase of $1,000 has been debited to the repair expense account rather than an asset account.

- **Compensating error:** Two different errors have been made which cancel each other out, e.g. a rent bill of $1,200 has been debited to the rent account as $1,400 and a casting error on the sales account has resulted in sales being overstated by $200.

- **Error of original entry:** The correct double entry has been made but with the wrong amount, e.g. a cash sale of $76 has been recorded as $67.

- **Reversal of entries:** The correct amount has been posted to the correct accounts but on the wrong side, e.g. a cash sale of $200 has been debited to sales and credited to bank.

When correcting these errors, a good approach is to consider:

(1) What should the double entry have been? ('should do').

(2) What was the double entry? ('did do').

(3) Therefore what correction is required? ('to correct').

Always assume that if one side of the double entry is not mentioned, it has been recorded correctly.

Test your understanding 2

Provide the journal to correct each of the following errors:

(1) A cash sale of $100 was not recorded.

(2) Rates expense of $500, paid in cash has been debited to the rent account in error.

(3) a non-current asset purchase of $1,000 on credit has been debited to the repairs expense account rather than an asset account.

(4) A rent bill of $1,200 paid in cash has been debited to the rent account as $1,400 and a casting error on the sales account has resulted in sales being overstated by $200.

(5) A cash sale of $76 has been recorded as $67.

(6) A cash sale of $200 has been debited to sales and credited to cash.

Errors where the trial balance does not balance

- Single sided entry – a debit entry has been made but no corresponding credit entry or vice versa.

- Debit and credit entries have been made but at different values.

- Two debit or two credit entries have been posted.

- An incorrect addition in any individual account, i.e. miscasting.

- Opening balance has not been brought down.

- Extraction error – the balance in the trial balance is different from the balance in the relevant account or the balance from the ledger account has been placed in the wrong column of the TB.

If there is a difference on the trial balance, then a suspense account is used to make the total debits equal the total credits:

	$	$
Non-current assets	5,000	
Receivables	550	
Inventory	1,000	
Cash	200	
Payables		600
Loan		2,000
Share capital		4,000
Suspense account		150
	6,750	6,750

The balance on the suspense account must be cleared before final accounts can be prepared.

Corrections to any of the six errors mentioned above will affect the suspense account.

5 Suspense accounts

A suspense account is an account in which debits or credits are held temporarily until sufficient information is available for them to be posted to the correct accounts.

There are two main reasons why suspense accounts may be created:

- On the extraction of a trial balance the debits are not equal to the credits and the difference is put to a suspense account.

- When a bookkeeper performing double entry is not sure where to post one side of an entry they may debit or credit a suspense account and leave the entry there until its ultimate destination is clarified.

Approach to questions:

- Take the same approach as before.

- In the 'did do' section use the suspense account to balance off the entry that was made (remember: the double entry must have been unbalanced for the TB not to balance)

- In the correcting journal reverse this suspense account entry.

E.g. The purchase of a non-current asset costing $100 has been recorded by debiting $10 to the non-current assets account and crediting $100 to cash.

What should the double entry have been? ('Should do')		What was the double entry? ('Did do')		Correcting journal	
Dr NCA	$100	Dr NCA	$10	Dr NCA	$90
Cr Cash	$100	Dr Suspense (bal. fig)	$90	Cr Suspense	$90
		Cr Cash	$100		

- Where an opening balance has not been brought down, journal it in and send the opposite entry to suspense.

- The correction journal must always include an equal debit and credit.

Illustration 1 – Suspense accounts

On extracting a trial balance, the accountant of ETT discovered a suspense account with a debit balance of $1,075 included therein; she also found that the debits exceeded the credits by $957. She posted this difference to the suspense account and then investigated the situation. She discovered:

(1) A debit balance of $75 on the postage account had been incorrectly extracted on the list of balances as $750 debit.

(2) A payment of $500 to a credit supplier, X, had been correctly entered in the cash book, but no entry had been made in the payables control account.

(3) When a motor vehicle had been purchased during the year the bookkeeper did not know what to do with the debit entry so he made the entry Dr Suspense, Cr Bank $1,575.

(4) A credit balance of $81 in the sundry income account had been incorrectly extracted on the list of balances as a debit balance.

(5) A receipt of $5 from a credit customer, Y, had been correctly posted to his account but had been entered in the cash book as $625.

(6) The bookkeeper was not able to deal with the receipt of $500 from the owner's own bank account, and he made the entry Dr Bank and Cr Suspense.

(7) No entry has been made for a cheque of $120 received from a credit customer M.

(8) A receipt of $50 from a credit customer, N, had been entered into the receivables control account as $5 and into the cash book as $5.

What journals are required to correct the errors and eliminate the suspense account?

Solution to Illustration 1

Process of clearing a suspense account

The starting position we have is as follows (once we have posted our $957):

Suspense account

	$		$
Balance b/f	1,075	Trial balance difference	957

We now need to work our way through the information given in numbered points 1 to 8 to try and clear this suspense account.

You need to ask yourself the following questions for each point:

(a) what should the double entry have been?

(b) what was the double entry that has been made?

(c) what is the journal we need to correct this?

(1) (a) It should have been: Dr postage 75, Cr bank 75

(b) They have posted Dr postage 750, Cr bank 75, so the other Dr of 675 will automatically go to the suspense a/c

(c) correction = Dr suspense a/c 675, Cr postage 675

(2) (a) It should have been: Dr payables 500, Cr cash 500

  (b) They have posted Dr suspense a/c 500, Cr cash 500

  (c) correction = Dr payables 500, Cr suspense a/c 500

(3) (a) It should have been Dr Motor vehicles cost 1575, Cr bank 1575

  (b) They have posted: Dr suspense a/c 1575, Cr cash 1575

  (c) correction = Dr motor vehicles 1575, Cr suspense a/c 1575

(4) (a) should have been: Dr bank/cash 81. Cr sundry income 81

  (b) They have posted Dr sundry income 81, Dr bank 81 Cr suspense a/c 162

  (c) Correction = Dr suspense a/c 162, Cr sundry income 162

(5) (a) Should have been Dr cash 5, Cr receivables 5

  (b) They have posted Dr cash 625, Cr receivables 5, so Cr suspense a/c 620

  (c) Correction = Dr suspense a/c 620, Cr cash 620

(6) (a) Should have been: Dr bank 500, Cr capital 500

  (b) They have posted Dr bank 500, Cr suspense a/c 500

  (c) correction = Dr suspense a/c 500, Cr capital 500

(7) (a) They should have posted Dr bank 120, Cr receivables 120

  (b) They have posted nothing

  (c) Correction = Dr bank 120, Cr receivables 120

(8) (a) Should have been Dr cash 50, Cr receivables 50

  (b) They have posted Dr cash 5, Cr receivables 5

  (c) Correction = Dr cash 45, Cr receivables 45

Now you can post all of the journals that you have listed under the (c) corrections which affect the suspense a/c.

Then you can balance off your suspense a/c and it should balance on both the debit and credit sides. Hence, this will clear your suspense a/c and leave it with a nil balance.

Once you have done so, you should get the following result:

Suspense account

	$		$
Balance b/f	1,075	Trial balance difference	957
Postage (1)	675	Payable (2)	500
Sundry income (4)	162	Motor vehicle cost (3)	1,575
Cash (5)	620		
Capital (6)	500		
	_____		_____
	3,032		3,032

Test your understanding 3

The debit side of a company's TB totals $1,200 more than the credit side.

Which of the following errors would fully account for the difference?

A   The petty cash balance of $1,200 has been omitted from the TB

B   A receipt of $1,200 for commission receivable has been omitted from the records

C $600 paid for plant maintenance has been correctly entered into the cash book and credited to the plant cost account

D   Discount received of $600 has been debited to the discount allowed account

Test your understanding 4

Bond's TB failed to agree and a suspense account was opened for the difference. Bond does not maintain control accounts for sales and purchases. The following errors were found in Bond's accounting records:

(1) In recording the sale of a non-current asset, cash received of $33,000 was credited to the disposals account as $30,000.

(2) An opening accrual of $340 had been omitted.

(3) Cash of $8,900 paid for plant repairs was correctly accounted for in the cash book but was credited to the plant cost account.

(4) A cheque for $12,000 paid for the purchase of a machine was debited to the machinery account as $21,000.

Which of the errors will require an entry to the suspense account to correct them?

A   1, 3 and 4 only

B   All

C   1 and 4 only

D   2 and 3 only

6 Adjustments to profit

The correction journal may result in a change in profit, depending on whether the journal debits or credits the statement of profit or loss:

Dr Statement of financial position account Cr Statement of financial position account	No impact on profit
Dr Profit or loss account Cr Profit or loss account	No impact on profit
Dr Profit or loss account Cr Statement of financial position account	Profit decreases
Dr Statement of financial position account Cr Profit or loss account	Profit increases

For this purpose the suspense account is defined as a statement of financial position account.

Errors where the trial balance still balances

Even if the trial balance still balances, there may be errors of posting into the ledger accounts. This may distort the information presented in the statement of financial position and statement of profit or loss.

Consider the example of accounting for a cash sale of $1,000 with the following accounting entries made in the ledgers:

Debit   Non-current assets $1,000   Credit Trade payables $1,000

An equal value of debits and credits have been posted into the ledgers, and the trial balance will agree, but the accounting entries are wrong. Consequently, the balances for non-current assets and trade payables will be overstated by $1,000. In addition, the balances for the bank balance and sales revenue will be understated by $1,000. This will be corrected by a journal adjustment.

In this example, the net effect is that sales revenue and profit for the year in the statement of profit or loss has been understated by $1,000. In the statement of financial position, non-current assets and trade payables have been overstated, and the bank balance has been understated, each by $1,000.

The correcting entries required are as follows:

Debit   Cash account $1,000   Credit Non-current assets $1,000
Debit   Trade payables $1,000   Credit Sales revenue $1,000

Errors where the trial balance does not balance

If the trial balance does not balance, there will be one or more errors posting into the ledger accounts. This will distort the information presented in the statement of financial position and statement of profit or loss.

Consider the example of accounting for a cash sale of $1,000 with the following accounting entry made in the ledgers:

Debit Cash account $1,000 with no credit entry made.

An unequal value of debits and credits have been posted into the ledgers, and the trial balance will not agree, which will require creation and clearance of a suspense account in due course.

Initially, sales revenue and therefore profit for the year has been understated. A suspense account will be created with a credit balance of $1,000.

In this example, the net effect is that sales revenue and profit for the year in the statement of profit or loss has been understated by $1,000. In the statement of financial position, the suspense account with a credit balance has been created and will be cleared by a journal adjustment as follows:

Debit Suspense account $1,000 Credit Sales revenue $1,000

Test your understanding 5

The following correction journals have been posted by Boris Brokovitch, a self-employed plumber:

(1) Dr Suspense $4,000
    Cr Rent $4,000

(2) Dr Payables $2,500
    Cr Suspense $2,500

(3) Dr Loan interest $1,000
    Cr Loan $1,000

(4) Dr Suspense $650
    Cr Sundry income $650

(5) Dr Suspense $6,000
    Cr Cash $6,000

Boris' draft profit figure prior to the posting of these journals is $355,000.

What is the revised profit figure?

A $354,000

B $358,650

C $356,150

D $358,000

What affect will these correction journals have on the Statement of financial position?

7 Statement of comprehensive income

Your correction journals may also affect other comprehensive income. In F3/FFA only journals involving revaluation adjustments would affect this.

Chapter summary

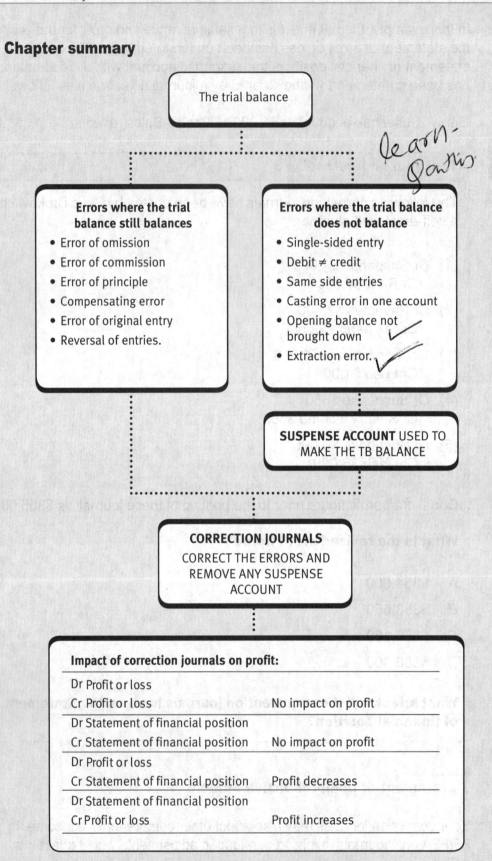

The trial balance

learn-parties

Errors where the trial balance still balances
- Error of omission
- Error of commission
- Error of principle
- Compensating error
- Error of original entry
- Reversal of entries.

Errors where the trial balance does not balance
- Single-sided entry
- Debit ≠ credit
- Same side entries
- Casting error in one account
- Opening balance not brought down ✓
- Extraction error. ✓

SUSPENSE ACCOUNT USED TO MAKE THE TB BALANCE

CORRECTION JOURNALS
CORRECT THE ERRORS AND REMOVE ANY SUSPENSE ACCOUNT

Impact of correction journals on profit:

Dr Profit or loss	
Cr Profit or loss	No impact on profit
Dr Statement of financial position	
Cr Statement of financial position	No impact on profit
Dr Profit or loss	
Cr Statement of financial position	Profit decreases
Dr Statement of financial position	
Cr Profit or loss	Profit increases

Test your understanding answers

Test your understanding 1

Cash

		$			$
1 Jan	Share capital	10,000	2 Jan	Purchases	4,000
5 Jan	Revenue	1,500	3 Jan	Delivery van	2,000
			7 Jan	Payables	800
			8 Jan	Rent	200
				Balance c/f	4,500
		11,500			11,500
	Balance b/f	4,500			

Ordinary share capital

	$			$
Balance c/f	10,000	1 Jan	Cash	10,000
	10,000			10,000
			Bal b/f	10,000

Purchases

		$		$
2 Jan	Cash	4,000	To P/L	5,000
4 Jan	Payables	1,000		
		5,000		5,000

Delivery van

		$			$
3 Jan	Cash	2,000		Balance c/f	2,000
		2,000			2,000
	Balance b/f	2,000			

Payables

		$			$
7 Jan	Cash	800	4 Jan	Purchases	1,000
	Balance c/f	200			
		1,000			1,000
				Balance b/f	200

Revenue

		$			$
	To P/L	6,500	5 Jan	Cash	1,500
			6 Jan	Receivables	5,000
		6,500			6,500

Receivables

		$			$
7 Jan	Revenue	5,000		Balance c/f	5,000
		5,000			5,000
	Balance b/f	5,000			

Rent

	$		$
8 Jan Cash	200	To P/L	200
	200		200

Trial balance as at 9 January

	Dr	Cr
	$	$
Cash	4,500	
Ordinary share capital		10,000
Purchases	5,000	
Delivery van	2,000	
Payables		200
Revenue		6,500
Receivables	5,000	
Rent	200	
	16,700	16,700

Test your understanding 2

	What should the double entry have been?	What was the double entry?	Correcting journal
(1)	Dr cash $100 Cr sales $100		Dr cash $100 Cr sales $100 to record both sides of the sale correctly
(2)	Dr rates $500 Cr cash $500	Dr rent $500 Cr cash $500	Dr rates $500 to record the rates expense correctly Cr rent $500 to reverse the incorrect debit to the rent account

(3)	Dr NC asset $1,000 Cr payables $1,000	Dr repairs $1,000 Cr payables $1,000	DR NC asset $1,000 to record the asset correctly Cr repairs $1,000 to reverse the incorrect debit to the repairs account
(4)	Dr rent $1,200 Cr cash $1,200	Dr rent $1,400 Cr cash $1,200	Cr rent $200 to reverse the extra £200 debited to the rent account Dr sales $200 to correct the casting error
(5)	Dr cash $76 Cr sales $76	Dr cash $67 Cr sales $67	Dr cash $9 Cr sales $9 to record the extra $9 sales not previously recorded
(6)	Dr cash $200 Cr sales $200	Dr sales $200 Cr cash $200	Dr cash $400 Cr sales $400 to firstly reverse the error of $200 and then record the sale of $200 correctly in both accounts

Test your understanding 3

The correct answer is D.

A and C would result in the credit side of the TB being $1,200 higher than the debit side.

B would have no effect on the TB since neither the debit nor the credit side of the transaction has been accounted for.

Test your understanding 4

The correct answer is B.

An entry to the suspense account is required wherever an account is missing from the trial balance or the initial incorrect entry did not include an equal debit and credit.

Test your understanding 5

The correct answer is B.

	Increase $	Decrease $	$
Draft profit			355,000
1 Rent	4,000		
2 No impact			
3 Loan interest		1,000	
4 Sundry income	650	———	
	———		
5 No impact			
			3,650
			———
Revised profit			358,650

Statement of financial position

Journal 1
The Dr entry would go towards clearing any suspense a/c balance.

Journal 2
The Dr payables would decrease the current liabilities. The Cr suspense a/c would go towards clearing the account balance.

Journal 3
The Cr loan would increase the loan liability balance. It does not state whether it is current or non-current.

Journal 4
The Dr suspense a/c would work towards clearing any balance left.

Journal 5
Dr suspense a/c would completely clear the balance in this account. The Cr cash would decrease the cash balance held, which is a current asset.

Preparing basic financial statements

Chapter learning objectives

Upon completion of this chapter you will be able to:

- prepare a statement of financial position and statement of profit or loss and other comprehensive income (or extracts) from given information

- understand, identify and report reserves in a company statement of financial position

- understand the interrelationship between the main financial statements

- identify items requiring separate disclosure on the face of the statement of profit or loss

- explain the purpose of disclosure notes

- define and classify events after the reporting period as adjusting or non-adjusting.

1 Overview

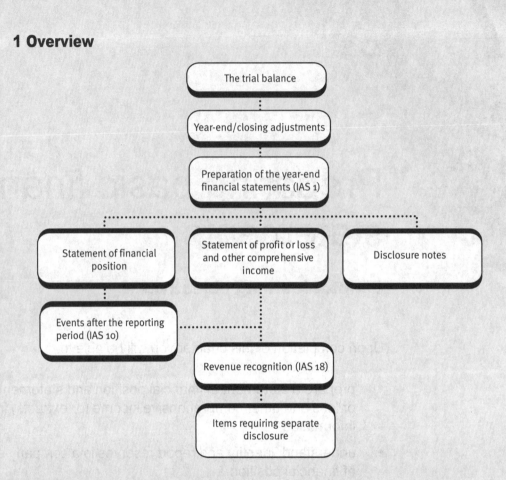

The trial balance

Year-end/closing adjustments

Preparation of the year-end financial statements (IAS 1)

Statement of financial position

Statement of profit or loss and other comprehensive income

Disclosure notes

Events after the reporting period (IAS 10)

Revenue recognition (IAS 18)

Items requiring separate disclosure

2 The process of preparing financial statements

In the previous chapter we introduced the process for preparing financial statements:

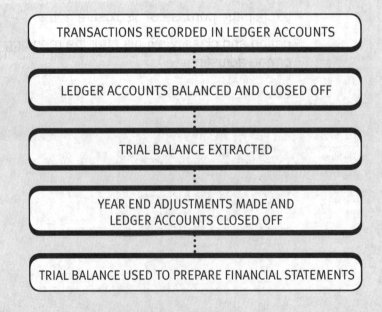

TRANSACTIONS RECORDED IN LEDGER ACCOUNTS

LEDGER ACCOUNTS BALANCED AND CLOSED OFF

TRIAL BALANCE EXTRACTED

YEAR END ADJUSTMENTS MADE AND LEDGER ACCOUNTS CLOSED OFF

TRIAL BALANCE USED TO PREPARE FINANCIAL STATEMENTS

By this stage you should be familiar with the double entry bookkeeping process, closing off the ledger accounts and extracting a trial balance. In this chapter we will explore the adjustments commonly made at the end of the accounting period after the initial trial balance has been drafted and then look at how the financial statements are prepared from this information.

3 Adjustments to the initial trial balance

As well as adjusting the trial balance figures for any errors identified there are also a number of common adjustments made at the end of the accounting period. These include:

- closing inventory
- depreciation for the year
- accruals and prepayments
- irrecoverable debts and allowances for doubtful debts
- income tax
- provisions and contingent liabilities, and
- events after the reporting period.

These adjustments need to be processed before the financial statements can be created.

Common accounting adjustments (recap)

Here is a reminder of the accounting entries for the more common adjustments required when preparing the financial statements:

(i) Closing inventory (Chapter 6)

Dr Inventory (SFP)

Cr Cost of sales (P/L)

(ii) Depreciation charge for the year (Chapter 7)

Dr Depreciation expense (P/L)

Cr Accumulated depreciation (SFP)

(iii) Accruals (Chapter 10)

Dr Expenses (P/L)

Cr Accrual (Liability) (SFP)

(iv) Prepayments (Chapter 10)

Dr Prepayment (Current Asset) (SFP)

Cr Expenses (P/L)

(v) Irrecoverable debts (Chapter 11)

Dr Irrecoverable debt expense (P/L)

Cr Receivables (SFP)

(vi) Allowance for receivables (Chapter 11)

Increase in allowance

Dr Irrecoverable debt expense (P/L)

Cr Allowance for receivables (SFP)

Decrease in allowance

Dr Allowance for receivables (SFP)

Cr Irrecoverable debt expense (P/L)

(vii) Tax estimate for the year (Chapter 13)

Dr Tax charge (P/L)

Cr Current tax liabilities (SFP)

(viii) Adjustments for prior year tax estimates (Chapter 13)

Overprovision in prior year

Dr Current tax provision (SFP)

Cr Tax charge for the year (P/L)

Underprovision in prior year

Dr Tax charge for the year (P/L)

Cr Current tax provision (SFP)

4 IAS 1 Presentation of Financial Statements

The required formats for published company financial statements are provided by IAS 1. This requires the following components to be presented:

- a statement of financial position
- a statement of profit or loss
- a statement of profit or loss and other comprehensive income
- a statement of changes in equity
- notes to the accounts, and
- a statement of cash flows.

5 The statement of financial position (SFP)

This summarises the asset, liability and equity balances (i.e. the financial position of the company) at the end of the accounting period.

Note that IAS 1 requires assets and liabilities to be classified as either current or non-current.

Statement of financial position for XYZ at 31 December XXXX

	$m	$m
Non-current assets		
Property, plant and equipment	X	
Investments	X	
Intangibles	X	
	–––	
		X
Current assets		
Inventories	X	
Trade and other receivables	X	
Prepayments	X	
Cash	X	
	–––	
		X
		–––
Total assets		**X**
		–––

Equity

Ordinary share capital	X
Irredeemable preference share capital	X
Share premium	X
Reserves:	
Retained earnings	X

    X

Non-current liabilities

Loan notes	X

Current liabilities

Trade and other payables	X
Overdrafts	X
Tax payable	X

    X

Total equity and liabilities	**X**

Current assets and current liabilities

The suggested statement of financial position format makes a distinction between current and non-current assets and liabilities. IAS 1 sets down the rules to be applied in making this distinction.

Current assets

An asset should be classified as a current asset if it is:

- held primarily for trading purposes

- expected to be realised within 12 months of the statement of financial position date; or

- cash or a cash equivalent (i.e. a short term investment, such as a 30 day bond).

All other assets should be classified as non-current assets.

Note that this definition allows inventory or receivables to qualify as current assets under (a) above, even if they may not be realised into cash within twelve months.

Current liabilities

The rules for current liabilities are similar to those for current assets.

A liability should be classified as a current liability if:

- it is expected to be settled in the normal course of the enterprise's operating cycle
- it is held primarily for the purpose of being traded
- it is due to be settled within 12 months of the statement of financial position date or
- the company does not have an unconditional right to defer settlement for at least 12 months after the statement of financial position date.

All other liabilities should be classified as non-current liabilities.

6 The statement of profit or loss

This summarises the incomes earned and expenses incurred during the financial period.

XYZ Group

Statement of profit or loss for the year ended 31 December XXXX

	$
Revenue	X
Cost of sales	(X)
	—
Gross profit	X
Distribution costs	(X)
Administrative expenses	(X)
	—
Profit from operations	X
Investment income	X
Finance costs	(X)
	—
Profit before tax	X
Tax expense	(X)
	—
Net profit for the period	X
	—

7 The statement of profit or loss and other comprehensive income

This is simply an extension of the statement of profit or loss. The reason for this is that some gains the business makes during the year are not realised gains. The main example is the revaluation of tangible assets. The gain is not realised until the asset is sold and converted into cash. The revaluation represents a hypothetical gain (i.e. what gain would a company make if the asset was sold).

For this reason it should not be included in net profit for the period, which represents the profit earned from realised sales. Instead the unrealised gains are added onto the end of the statement of profit or loss, as follows:

Statement of profit or loss and other comprehensive income for XYZ for the year ended 31 December XXXX

	$m
Revenue	X
Cost of sales	(X)
Gross profit	X
Distribution costs	(X)
Administrative expenses	(X)
Profit from operations	X
Investment income	X
Finance costs	(X)
Profit before tax	X
Tax expense	(X)
Net profit for the period	X

Other comprehensive income

Items that will not be reclassified to profit or loss in future periods:

Gain/loss on property revaluation	X/(X)
Total comprehensive income for the year	**X**

Items requiring separate disclosure

Certain items need to be separately disclosed on the face of the statement of profit or loss so that they are clearly visible to the users of the financial statements. The main items requiring such treatment are significant, one-off transactions or events. They need to be disclosed because they are not part of the normal trading activity of the business and could significantly distort the reported profits or losses for the year. They include:

- restructuring or reorganisation of the company

- profits or losses on disposal of property, plant and equipment (or investments), and

- impairments of inventory, property, plant and equipment.

All such items should be included on their own, separate line in the statement of profit or loss.

Relationship between the statement of profit or loss and statement of financial position

The link between the statement of financial position and the statement of profit or loss is shown below:

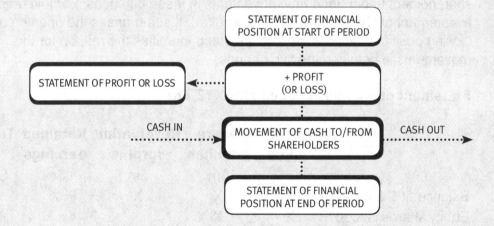

8 The statement of changes in equity

Equity represents the owners' interests in the company. An alternative way of defining it is that it represents what is left in the business when it ceases to trade, all the assets are sold off and all the liabilities are paid. This can then be distributed to the equity holders (ordinary shareholders).

It is made up primarily of share capital (including share premium) and reserves. The main reserves are the revaluation surplus and retained earnings.

Revaluation surplus

This is created to recognise the surplus arising when tangible non-current assets (normally land and buildings) are revalued (for more detail see Chapter 8). The gain is not real so cannot be included in the profit reserves of the business. However, the gain would still form part of the value repaid to the equity holders if the business were sold off at that point in time.

Retained earnings

This represents the sum total of all the profits and losses made by the business since its incorporation and that have not yet been paid to shareholders as a dividend.

As these elements are particularly relevant to shareholders (it helps them value their wealth or 'share of the pie') it is important to ensure the shareholders understand any movements in these balances. For this reason a statement of changes in equity is required. It summarises the opening and closing positions on all these accounts and identifies the reason for the movements in between the two periods.

Statement of changes in equity for XYZ Ltd

	Share capital $m	Share premium $m	Revaluation surplus $m	Retained earnings $m	Total $m
Balance at 1 January	X	X	X	X	X
Equity shares issued	X	X			X
Revaluation surplus in year			X		X
Net profit				X	X
Dividends				(X)	(X)
Bal at 31 Dec	X	X	X	X	X

9 Disclosure notes

Disclosure notes are required for a variety of reasons, including:

- to explain the accounting policies used in preparing the accounts
- to explain the movement between the opening and closing balances of major statement of financial position items
- to show how certain balances are calculated, and
- to provide further detail/explanation to users of the financial statements, as necessary for the accounts to be understandable to the users.

For this exam you do not need to know the presentation of all the relevant disclosure notes that support the financial statements. The notes you do need to know and the chapters they are described in are:

- Non-current tangible and intangible assets (Chapters 7 & 8).
- Provisions (Chapter 12).
- Events after the reporting period (this chapter), and
- Inventory (Chapter 6).

10 Preparation of financial statements and the exam

The following example requires the preparation of a statement of profit or loss and a statement of financial position from a trial balance and adjustments.

Illustration 1 – Preparation of financial statements

The trial balance of Crown as at 31 December 20X5 was as follows:

	Dr	Cr
	$	$
Ordinary share capital		100,000
Sales and purchases	266,800	365,200
Inventory at 1 January 20X5	23,340	
Returns	1,200	1,600
Wages	46,160	
Rent	13,000	
Motor expenses	3,720	
Insurance	760	
Irrecoverable debts	120	
Allowance for receivables		
1 January 20X5		588
Discounts	864	1,622
Light and heat	3,074	
Bank overdraft interest	74	
Motor vehicles at cost	24,000	
– accumulated depreciation		
1 Jan 20X5		12,240
Fixtures and fittings at cost	28,000	
– accumulated depreciation		
1 Jan 20X5		16,800
Land	100,000	
Receivables and payables	17,330	23,004
Bank	3,312	
Income tax underprovision	100	
Buildings at cost	100,000	
– aggregate depreciation:		
1 Jan 20X5		6,000
Retained earnings at 1 Jan 20X5		104,800
	———	———
	631,854	631,854
	———	———

You are given the following additional information:

(1) Inventory at 31 December 20X5 was $25,680.

(2) Rent was prepaid by $1,000 and light and heat owed was $460 at 31 December 20X5.

(3) Land is to be revalued to $250,000 at 31 December 20X5.

(4) Following a final review of the receivables at 31 December 20X5, Crown decides to write off another debt of $130. The company also wants to maintain the allowance for receivables at 3% of the year end balance.

(5) Crown estimated that the income tax charge on profit for the year was $7,300.

(6) Depreciation is to be provided as follows:

(a) building – 2% annually, straight-line

(b) fixtures & fittings – straight line method, assuming a useful economic life of five years with no residual value

(c) motor vehicles – 30% annually on a reducing balance basis.

A full year's depreciation is charged in the year of acquisition and none in the year of disposal.

Prepare a statement of profit or loss and other comprehensive income for the year ended 31 December 20X5 and a statement of financial position as at that date for Crown.

Statement of profit or loss and other comprehensive income for the year ended 31 December 20X5

	$
Revenue (365,200 – 1,200)	364,000
Cost of sales (W1)	(262,860)
Gross profit	101,140
Administrative expenses (W2)	(76,796)
Profit before tax	24,344
Income tax charge (W3)	(7,400)
Profit for the year	16,944
Other comprehensive income	
Revaluation surplus in year	150,000
Total comprehensive income	166,944

Statement of financial position as at 31 December 20X5

	$	$
Non-current assets		
Property, plant and equipment (W5)		355,832
		355,832
Current assets		
Inventory	25,680	
Trade receivables (W6)	16,684	
Prepayments	1,000	
Cash at bank	3,312	
		46,676
		402,508

Equity

Ordinary share capital	100,000	
Revaluation surplus (250,000 – 100,000)	150,000	
Retained earnings (104,800 + 16,944)	121,744	
	———	
		371,744

Current liabilities

Income tax liability (W3)	7,300	
Trade payables	23,004	
Accrued expenses	460	
	———	
		30,764
		———
		402,508
		———

Workings:

(W1) Cost of sales

	$
Opening Inventory	23,340
Purchases	266,800
Returns out	(1,600)
	———
	288,540
Closing inventory	(25,680)
	———
	262,860
	———

(W2) Administrative expenses

	$
Wages	46,160
Rent ($13,000 – 1,000)	12,000
Motor expenses	3,720
Insurance	760
Irrecoverable debts ($120 + 130)	250
Decrease in allowance for receivables (W6)	(72)
Discounts allowed	864
Light and heat ($3,074 + 460)	3,534
Bank interest	74
Sundry income	(1,622)
Depreciation (W4)	11,128
	———
	76,796
	———

(W3) Income tax

	$
Overprovision re previous year per trial balance	100
Income tax on profit for year (and year-end liability)	7,300
	7,400

(W4) Depreciation charge for year

	P&L charge	Prov'n b/fwd	Prov'n c/fwd
	$	$	$
Buildings ($100,000 × 2%)	2,000	6,000	8,000
Fixtures and fittings ($28,000 × 20%)	5,600	16,800	22,400
Motor vehicles (($24,000 – $12,240) × 30%)	3,528	12,240	15,768
	11,128		

(W5) Non-current assets

	Cost or val'n	Acc dep'n	CV
	$	$	$
Land (valuation in year)	250,000	–	250,000
Buildings	100,000	8,000 (W4)	92,000
Fixtures and fittings	28,000	22,400 (W4)	5,600
Motor vehicles	24,000	15,768 (W4)	8,232
	402,000	46,168	355,832

(W6) Trade receivables

	$
Receivables ($17,330 – 130 w/off)	17,200
Allowance for receivables c/fwd (17,200 × 3%)	(516)
	16,684

Movement in allowance for receivables:	
Balance b/fwd	588
Balance c/fwd (as per above)	516
Decrease in allowance to P&L	(72)

KAPLAN PUBLISHING

Test your understanding 1

The trial balance of Penguin, a limited liability company, as at 31 December 20X5 was as follows:

	Dr $	Cr $
Sales and purchases	20,000	50,000
Inventory	8,000	
Distribution costs	8,000	
Administration expenses	15,550	
Receivables and payables	10,000	20,000
Fundamental reorganisation costs	2,400	
Cash at bank	7,250	
Ordinary shares 50c		8,000
10% irredeemable preference shares $1		9,000
10% loan notes		8,000
Non-current assets at net book value	35,000	
Share premium		3,000
Accumulated profits at 1 January 20X5		3,000
Loan note Interest paid	800	
Preference dividend paid	900	
Interim ordinary dividend paid	1,600	
Tax		500
Suspense		8,000
	———	———
	109,500	109,500

The following is to be taken into account.

(1) A building whose net book value is currently $5,000 is to be revalued to $11,000.

(2) A final ordinary dividend of 10c per share is to be proposed.

(3) The balance on the income tax account represents an overprovision of tax for the previous year. Tax for the current year is estimated at $3,000.

(4) Closing inventory is $12,000.

(5) The balance on the suspense account represents the proceeds from the issue of 4,000 ordinary shares.

Prepare the following financial statements for the year ended 31 December 20X5:

(1) **statement of profit or loss and other comprehensive income**

(2) **statement of financial position**

(3) **statement of changes in equity**

Test your understanding 2

Phillipa Page prints and publishes study materials. She has prepared the following trial balance as at 30 June 20X7:

	Dr $	Cr $
Purchases	60,000	
Inventory at 1 July 20X6	10,000	
Sales		120,000
Distribution costs	13,200	
Administrative and selling expenses	5,600	
Trade receivables	12,200	
Discount allowed	1,550	
Bank balance		4,150
Capital account at 1 July 20X6		73,100
Discount received		2,500
6% Bank loan		10,000
Non-current assets at carrying amount	102,500	
Capital introduced in the year		5,000
Loan interest paid	300	
Drawings	8,000	
Trade payables		5,600
Wages	15,000	
Suspense		8,000
	─────	─────
	228,350	228,350
	─────	─────

The following is to be taken into account.

(1) Inventory valuation at 30 June 20X7 was $12,000.

(2) Phillipa decided to write off an irrecoverable receivable of $1,000. This should be accounted for as an administrative and selling expense.

(3) The wages cost should be split equally between cost of sales and administrative and selling expenses.

(4) Discounts allowed should be accounted for as an administrative and selling expense.

(5) The bank loan was taken out on 1 July 20X6.

(6) The depreciation charge for the year of $5,000 on property, plant and equipment has not yet been accounted for. It should be classified as a cost of sale.

(7) The balance on the suspense account represents the proceeds from the disposal of an item of property, plant and equipment. At the date of disposal, that item had a net carrying amount of $10,000. The gain or loss on disposal should be accounted for as a cost of sale.

Prepare the statement of profit or loss for the year ended 30 June 20X7, together with the statement of financial position as at 30 June 20X7 on behalf of Phillipa Page.

11 Events after the reporting period (IAS 10)

Events after the reporting period can be defined as those material events which occur between the statement of financial position date and the date on which the financial statements are published.

Adjusting and non-adjusting events

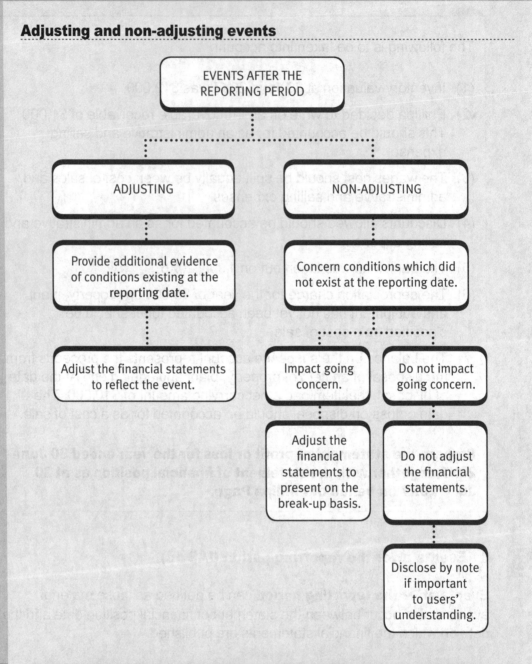

EVENTS AFTER THE REPORTING PERIOD

ADJUSTING

Provide additional evidence of conditions existing at the reporting date.

Adjust the financial statements to reflect the event.

NON-ADJUSTING

Concern conditions which did not exist at the reporting date.

Impact going concern.

Adjust the financial statements to present on the break-up basis.

Do not impact going concern.

Do not adjust the financial statements.

Disclose by note if important to users' understanding.

Adjusting and non-adjusting events

Adjusting events

These events provide additional evidence of conditions existing at the reporting date. For example, irrecoverable debts arising one or two months after the reporting date may help to quantify the allowance for receivables as at the reporting date. If an adjusting event is identified the financial statements must be amended to reflect the relevant condition.

Examples of adjusting events

- The settlement after the reporting date of a court case which confirms a year end obligation.

- The receipt of information after the reporting date that indicates that an asset was impaired at the reporting date.

- The bankruptcy of a customer after the reporting date that confirms that a year-end debt is irrecoverable.

- The sale of inventories after the reporting period at a price lower than cost.

- The determination after the reporting date of the cost of assets purchased or proceeds from assets sold before the reporting date.

- The discovery of fraud or errors showing that the financial statements are incorrect.

Non-adjusting events

These are events arising after the reporting date but which do not concern conditions existing at the reporting date. Such events will not, therefore, have any effect on items in the statement of profit or loss or statement of financial position. However, in order to prevent the financial statements from presenting a misleading position, some form of additional disclosure is required if the events are material, by way of a note to the financial statements giving details of the event.

Examples of non-adjusting events

- Announcing a plan to discontinue an operation.

- Major purchases of assets.

- The destruction of assets after the reporting date by fire or flood.

- Entering into significant commitments or contingent liabilities.

- Commencing a court case arising out of events after the reporting date.

Test your understanding 3

Which of the following are adjusting events for BigCo Ltd? The year end is 30 June 20X6 and the accounts are approved on 18 August 20X6.

(1) Sales of year-end inventory on 2 July 20X6 at less than cost.

(2) The issue of new ordinary shares on 4 July 20X6.

(3) A fire in the main warehouse occurred on 8 July 20X6. All inventory was destroyed.

(4) A major credit customer was declared bankrupt on 10 July 20X6

(5) All of the share capital of a competitor, TeenyCo Ltd was acquired on 21 July 20X6.

(6) On 1 August 20X6, $500,000 was received in respect of an insurance claim dated 13 February 20X6.

A   1, 4 and 6

B   1, 2, 4 and 6

C   1, 2, 5 and 6

D   1, 4, 5 and 6

Disclosure of material, non-adjusting events

If a non-adjusting event is identified and it is material (i.e. significant to the decision making of users) it should be disclosed by way of a note to the financial statements. The note should describe:

(i) the nature of the event

(ii) an estimate of the financial effect, or a statement that such an estimate cannot be made.

12 Revenue (IAS 18)

Recognition of revenue is vital to the fair presentation of the financial statements. With most transactions it is easy to identify when revenue is earned but for some, for example where a company agrees to provide cleaning services for a period of three years, it can be more difficult identifying when the revenue has been earned and, therefore, when it can be recognised in the financial statements.

IAS 18 Revenue defines when revenue from various sources may be recognised. It deals with revenue arising from three types of transaction or event:

- sale of goods

- rendering of services

- interest, royalties and dividends from the assets of the enterprise.

Sale of goods

Revenue from the sale of goods should be recognised when all the following conditions have been satisfied:

(a) All the significant risks and rewards of ownership have been transferred to the buyer.

(b) The seller retains no effective control over the goods sold.

(c) The amount of revenue can be reliably measured.

(d) The benefits to be derived from the transaction are likely to flow to the enterprise.

(e) The costs incurred or to be incurred for the transaction can be reliably measured.

Revenue recognition

Conditions (a) and (b) are usually met at the time when legal ownership passes to the buyer, but there are four examples in IAS 18 where the seller retains significant risks:

- when the seller has an obligation for unsatisfactory performance beyond normal warranty provisions

- when the receipt of the cash for the sale is contingent upon the buyer selling the goods on and receiving cash

- when the goods are to be installed at the buyer's site and this has not yet been completed

- when the buyer has the right to cancel the contract.

Revenue and associated costs are recognised simultaneously in accordance with the matching concept.

Rendering of services

The provision of a service is likely to be spread over a period of time.

IAS 18 states that revenue from services may be recognised according to the stage of completion of the transaction at the statement of financial position date.

As with the sale of goods, conditions must be satisfied:

(a) The amount of the revenue can be measured reliably.

(b) The benefits from the transaction are likely to flow to the enterprise.

(c) The stage of completion of the work can be measured reliably.

(d) The costs incurred or to be incurred for the transaction can be reliably measured.

When a partly completed service is in its early stages, or the outcome of the transaction cannot be reliably estimated, revenue should be recognised only up to the amount of the costs incurred to date, and then only if it is probable that the enterprise will recover in revenue at least as much as the costs.

If it is probable that the costs of the transaction will not be recovered, no revenue is to be recognised.

Other revenues

Interest, royalties and dividends

Provided the amount of revenue can be reliably measured and the receipt of the income is reasonably assured, these items should be recognised as follows:

- Interest should be recognised on a time-proportion basis taking account of the yield on the asset.

- Royalties should be recognised on an accruals basis in accordance with the relevant agreement.

- Dividends should be recognised when the shareholder's right to receive payment has been established.

Disclosure

- The accounting policy for revenue recognition, including the methods used to determine the stage of completion of service transactions.

- The amount of revenue recognised for each of the five categories above.

- The amount, if material, in each category arising from exchanges of goods or services.

Chapter summary

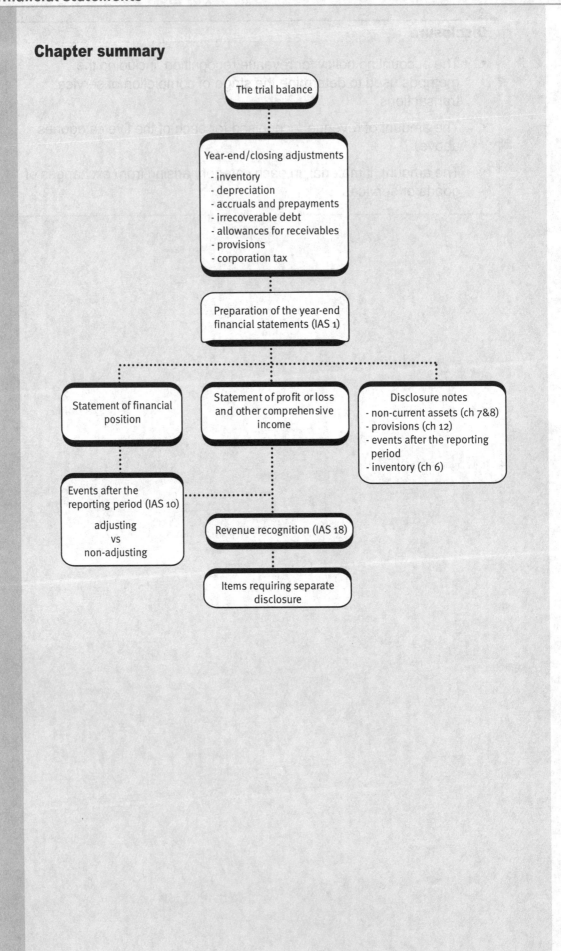

Test your understanding answers

Test your understanding 1

Penguin

Statement of profit or loss and other comprehensive income for the year ended 31 December 20X5

	$
Sales revenue	50,000
Cost of sales (8,000 + 20,000 – 12,000)	(16,000)
Gross profit	34,000
Distribution costs	(8,000)
Administrative expenses	(15,550)
Operating profit	10,450
Fundamental reorganisation costs	(2,400)
	8,050
Finance charges	(800)
Profit before taxation	7,250
Taxation (3,000 – 500)	(2,500)
Profit for the year	4,750

Other Comprehensive Income

Items that will not be reclassified to profit or loss in future periods:

Revaluation surplus in the year	6,000
Total Comprehensive Income	10,750

Statement of financial position at 31 December 20X5

	$	$
Non-current assets		
Tangible assets (35,000 + 6,000)		41,000
Current assets		
Inventory	12,000	
Trade receivables	10,000	
Cash at bank and in hand	7,250	
		29,250
Total assets		70,250
Equity		
Ordinary share capital (8,000 + 2,000)		10,000
10% irredeemable preference share capital		9,000
Share premium account (3,000 + 6,000)		9,000
Revaluation surplus		6,000
Retained earnings		5,250
		39,250
Non-current liabilities		
10% loan notes		8,000
Current liabilities		
Trade payables	20,000	
Taxation	3,000	
		23,000
		70,250

KAPLAN PUBLISHING

Statement of changes in equity
for the year ended 31 December 20X5

	Ordinary share capital	Irredeemable pref capital	Share premium	Revaluation surplus	Retained earnings	Total
	$	$	$	$	$	$
Balance at 1 Jan 20X5	8,000	9,000	3,000	–	3,000	23,000
Revaluation of building				6,000		6,000
Profit for the year					4,750	4,750
Dividends (900 + 1,600)					(2,500)	(2,500)
Issue of share capital *	2,000		6,000			8,000
Balance at 31 Dec 20X5	10,000	9,000	9,000	6,000	5,250	39,250

* The issue of 4,000 shares for $8,000 means they were issued at $2 each. If the nominal value is $0.50 then the premium per share was $1.50. Therefore the increase in share capital was 4,000 shares × $0.50 = $2,000 and the increase in share premium was 4,000 shares × $1.50 = $6,000.

Note that the irredeemable preference share capital has been accounted for as equity in both the SOFP and SOCIE. There is no obligation to redeem or repay this share capital – therefore, it is classified as equity.

Test your understanding 2

Phillipa Page

Statement of profit or loss for the year ended 30 June 20X7

	$
Sales revenue	120,000
Cost of sales (W1)	(72,500)
Gross profit	47,500
Discount received	2,500
Distribution costs	(13,200)
Administrative and selling expenses (W2)	(15,650)
Operating profit	21,150
Finance costs (W3)	(600)
Profit for the year	20,550

Statement of financial position at 30 June 20X7

	$	$
Non-current assets		
Tangible assets (102,500 – 10,000 – 5,000)		87,500
Current assets		
Inventory	12,000	
Trade receivables (12,200 – 1,000)	11,200	
		23,200
Total assets		110,700
Capital account		
Balance brought forward at 1 July 20X6		73,100
Capital introduced in the year		5,000
Profit for the year		20,550
Drawings		(8,000)
		90.650

Non-current liabilities

6% bank loan		10,000
Current liabilities		
Trade payables	5,600	
Bank overdraft	4,150	
Interest accrual	300	
	———	10,050
		———
		110,700
		———

Workings

(W1) Cost of sales	$
Opening inventory	10,000
Purchases	60,000
Closing inventory	(12,000)
Wages (50% × 15,000)	7,500
Loss on disposal of non-current asset (10,000 – 8,000 proceeds)	2,000
Depreciation charge	5,000
	———
	72,500
	———

(W2) Administrative and selling expenses	$
Per trial balance	5,600
Wages (50% × 15,000)	7,500
Irrecoverable receivable written off	1,000
Discount allowed	1,550
	———
	15,650
	———

(W3) Loan interest	$
Charge for the year: 10,000 × 6%	600
Amount paid per trial balance	(300)
	———
Accrual required	300
	———

Test your understanding 3

The correct answer is A.

(1)	Sales of year end inventory at less than cost	Adjusting	Closing inventory must be valued at the lower of cost and net realisable value. The post-year-end sale provides evidence of the net realisable value. Therefore closing inventory must be adjusted to reflect the reduction in value.
(2)	Share issue	Non-adjusting	
(3)	Fire in warehouse	Non-adjusting	If this is BigCo's only or main warehouse and the fire affects going concern, the event will be reclassified as adjusting.
(4)	Bankruptcy of major customer	Adjusting	The bankruptcy of the customer provides evidence of their inability to pay their debt at the year-end. The amount outstanding from the customer at 30 June 20X6 should therefore be written off in the year-end accounts.
(5)	Acquisition of TeenyCo Ltd	Non-adjusting	
(6)	Receipt of insurance monies	Adjusting	The receipt of insurance monies provides evidence of a year-end asset. The amount subsequently received should be reflected as such in the year-end accounts.

Incomplete records

Chapter learning objectives

Upon completion of this chapter you will be able to:

- understand and apply techniques used in incomplete record situations:
    - (i)   use of accounting equation
    - (ii) use of ledger accounts to calculate missing figures
    - (iii) use of cash and/or bank summaries
    - (iv) use of given gross profit percentage to calculate missing figures.

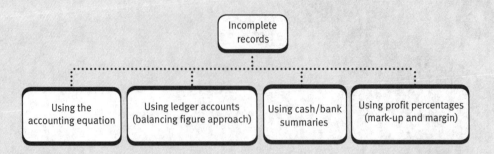

1 Incomplete records

When you are preparing a set of accounts, it is likely that you may not have all of the information available to you to complete a set of financial statements.

It is likely that you may have an incomplete ledger or control accounts system.

If this is the case, you will have to use the best information that is available to you and 'guestimate' any missing figures.

There are a number of different ways which we can use to calculate missing figures and balances, such as:

- Accounting equation method
- Balancing figure approach
- Using cash/banking data, and
- Profit ratios – mark-up and margin.

2 Using the accounting equation

If a business has recorded very little information of its transactions it may only be possible to calculate net profit for the year. This can be done using the accounting equation as follows:

Assets = equity + liabilities

This can be expanded as follows:

Total assets = share capital + retained earnings + other reserves + total liabilities

We could expand this further to disclose each non-current/current asset and liability. However, that is not necessary as all this represents is the captions on the statement of financial position. The only figure worth expanding is retained earnings (RE):

Closing RE = the prior year's RE figure +/– this year's profit/loss – dividends

By working out the value of closing assets, liabilities and share capital (using a valuation exercise) we should be able to work out the retained earnings figure. If we know the previous year's retained earnings (from last year's statement of financial position) we should be left with the profit/loss for the year as the missing figure.

Test your understanding 1

The statement of Andy Carp Ltd at 31 December 20X8 shows the following balances:

- Non-current assets – $10,000
- Current assets – $3,400
- Share capital – $200
- Non-current liabilities – $2,100
- Current liabilities – $1,700

The sales, purchases and expense records of Andy Carp have unfortunately been destroyed and the directors need help estimating the net profit for the year so that they can estimate their tax liability. They have informed you that the retained earnings at 31 December 20X7 were $7,350.

What was the profit/loss (before tax) made by Andy Carp Ltd during the year ended 31 December 20X8?

A $2,250

B $2,450

C $2,050

D $9,400

3 The ledger account (balancing figure) approach

The balancing figure approach, using ledger accounts, is commonly used in the following way:

Ledger account	Missing figure
Receivables	Credit sales, Money received from receivables
Payables	Credit purchases, Money paid to payables
Cash at bank	Drawings, Money stolen
Cash in hand	Cash sales, Cash stolen

Cash at bank

	$		$
Cash received from customers	X	Cash paid to suppliers	X
Bankings from cash in hand	X	Expenses	X
Sundry income	X	Drawings	X
		Money stolen	X
		Balance c/f	X
	—		—
Balance b/f	X		X
	—		—

Cash in hand

	$		$
Cash sales	X	Cash purchases	X
Sundry income	X	Sundry Expenses	X
		Bankings	X
		Money stolen	X
		Balance c/f	X
	—		—
Balance b/f	X		X
	—		—

In the case of receivables and payables, you may need to use total receivables and total payables accounts where information given cannot be split between cash and credit sales and purchases:

Total receivables

	$		$
Balance b/f	X	Total cash received in respect of sales (from cash and credit customers)	X
Total sales (cash and credit)	X		
	X	Balance c/f	X
Balance b/f	X		X

Total payables

	$		$
		Balance b/f	
Total cash paid in respect of purchases (cash purchases and payments to credit suppliers)	X	Total purchases (cash and credit)	X
Balance c/f	X	Balance b/f	X

Test your understanding 2

Suppose that opening receivables for B Rubble's business are $30,000. There have been total receipts from customers of $55,000 of which $15,000 relates to cash sales and $40,000 relates to receipts from receivables. Discounts allowed in the year totalled $3,000 and closing receivables were $37,000.

What are total sales for the year?

A $65,000

B $50,000

C $47,000

D $62,000

Test your understanding 3

The opening payables of Dick Dastard-Lee's business are $15,000. Total payments made to suppliers during the year were $14,000. Discounts received were $500 and closing payables were $13,000.

What are total purchases for the year?

A $16,500

B $16,000

C $12,000

D $12,500

Questions may require you to calculate 'missing' figures from the statement of profit or loss, for example rent and rates values, from a list of information including payments and opening/closing accruals and prepayments.

To calculate the missing value for each expense use either:

*   T-accounts, or

*   Equations

Test your understanding 4

The following information relates to Ivor Big-Head's business:

On 1 January	Electricity accrued	$250
	Rent prepaid	$300
Cash paid in the year	Electricity	$1,000
	Rent	$2,000
On 31 December	Electricity accrued	$300
	Rent prepaid	$400

What are the charges for electricity and rent in the statement of profit or loss for the year?

	Electricity $	Rent $
A	1,050	2,100
B	1,050	1,900
C	950	1,900
D	950	2,100

Test your understanding 5

On 1 January Elma Fudd's bank account is overdrawn by $1,367. Payments in the year totalled $8,536 and on 31 December the closing balance is $2,227 (positive).

What are total receipts for the year?

A $4,942

B $7,676

C $9,396

D $12,130

Test your understanding 6

On 1 January, Daisee Chain's business had a cash float of $900. During the year cash of $10,000 was banked, $1,000 was paid out as drawings and wages of $2,000 were paid. On 31 December the float was $1,000.

How much cash was received from customers for the year?

A $12,900

B $14,900

C $13,100

D $6,900

4 Using cash/bank summaries

The use of bank summaries is similar to the ledger account approach. This method assumes that, whilst data may be missing from the ledger accounts, a company can always reconstruct their cash inflows and outflows using either the cash book or bank statements, or both.

Illustration 1

During the year ended 31 July 20X9 Collins Ltd lost some of their accounting data due to a computer virus. Whilst they have managed to reconstruct elements of their financial statements they need some help determining their sales revenue for the year.

Their closing trade receivables figure at 31 July 20X8, taken from the prior year's statement of financial position, was $98,425. You have reviewed the list of receivables (the memorandum) and calculated that the receivables outstanding at 31 July 20X9 total $107,550. After discussions with management you also determine that shortly prior to the year-end $1,500 of trade receivables were written off as irrecoverable. This has not been reflected in the list of balances/memorandum.

To assist you one of your bookkeepers has reconciled the cash books with the bank statements for the year and has calculated that $245,675 has been received from customers during the year. Cash till receipts confirm that $53,435 was received during the year from cash sales. The remainder constitutes receipts from credit customers.

What was the total sales revenue of Collins Ltd for the year ended 31 July 20X9?

$...............................

Solution to Illustration 1

This, at first, may seem like a daunting question. It is no more difficult than any other question about ledger accounts but it does involve a number of calculations that must be performed to obtain the correct answer. It is therefore important to identify which figures you need to calculate to be able to arrive at the answer.

In this case we need to determine the total sales of Collins Ltd for the year. This includes both cash and credit sales. We already know the total cash sales – they are $53,435. We therefore need to determine credit sales.

To do this we can use a receivables ledger control account:

RLCA

	$		$
B/f at 1 Aug 20X8			
Credit sales for year		Cash received from credit customers	
		Bal c/f at 31 July 20X9	

To be able to complete the RLCA account we need four figures:

(1) Receivables at 1 August 20X8.

(2) Cash received from credit customers.

(3) Receivables at 31 July 20X9, and

(4) Credit sales for the year.

Let's now work through each of these figures in turn:

(1) Receivables at 1 August 20X8 (opening receivables) will be the same as last year's closing figure of $98,425.

(2) If total cash received during the year was $245,675 and $53,435 relates to cash sales then the remaining $192,240 ($245,675 – $53,435) of the receipts relate to payments from credit customers.

(3) Closing receivables per the list/memorandum were $107,550. However, $1,500 needs to be deducted from this for irrecoverable debts. Therefore the closing receivables figure is $106,550.

(4) Credit sales can now be worked out by filling in the T-account, as follows:

RLCA

	$		$
B/f at 1 Aug 20X8	98,425		
Credit sales for year (bal. fig)	199,865	Cash received from credit customers	192,240
		Bal c/f at 31 July 20X9	106,050
	———		———
	298,290		298,290
	———		———

Therefore the correct answer for **total sales** is as follows:

	$
Cash sales	53,435
Credit sales	199,865
	———
Total sales	**253,300**
	———

5 Ratios – Mark-up and margin

Gross profit can be expressed as a percentage of either sales or cost of sales:

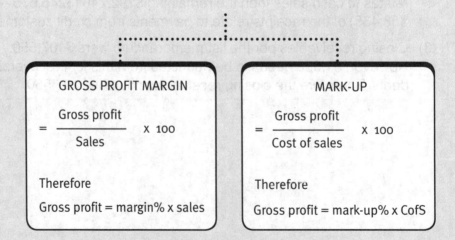

GROSS PROFIT MARGIN

$$= \frac{\text{Gross profit}}{\text{Sales}} \times 100$$

Therefore

Gross profit = margin% x sales

MARK-UP

$$= \frac{\text{Gross profit}}{\text{Cost of sales}} \times 100$$

Therefore

Gross profit = mark-up% x CofS

E.g.

Sales $5,000
Cost of sales   ($4,000)
Gross profit $1,000

- Gross profit margin = (1,000/5,000) × 100 = 20%
- Mark-up = (1,000/4,000) × 100 = 25%

Test your understanding 7

Padraig O'Flaherty has sales of $1,000. He makes a margin of 25%.

What is the cost of sales figure?

A $200

B $800

C $750

D $250

Test your understanding 8

Ratios

Lorna McDuff has cost of sales of $600 and a 25% mark up.

What is her sales figure?

A $750

B $800

C $250

D $200

Using margin and mark up

Exam questions will often provide you with information about gross profit figures and ratios. You will then be required to calculate a missing figure. This can be done using the following 'relationship' columns:

(**Note:** Sales of $5,000 have been used in both examples to illustrate the difference between the mark-up and margin.)

Margin	$	Ratio	Mark up	$	Ratio
Sales	5,000	100%	Sales	5,000	125%
Cost of sales	4,000	80%	Cost of sales	(4,000)	100%
Gross profit	1,000	20%	Gross profit	1,000	25%

If we know either the mark-up or margin percentage and one of either sales, cost of sales and gross profit we should be able to calculate the remaining figures.

Test your understanding 9

Jethro Longhorn can tell you the following with regard to his business:

Margin 5%

Opening inventory $800

Closing inventory $600

Purchases $2,840

Complete Jethro's statement of profit or loss with the above figures.

Missing inventory figures

Traditionally (before the adoption of powerful computerised accounting systems) many businesses did not keep an accounting record of inventories. They would keep records of quantities but, given the proliferation of raw materials, would not complicate matters by keeping accounting records of costs and valuations. Instead they would perform a year-end reconciliation of valuations using the principles discussed earlier in this book.

It is also possible to use the methods described in this chapter to calculate the value of inventory. Remember that cost of sales is equal (in simple terms) to opening inventory + purchases – closing inventory. We have just illustrated how to work out cost of sales using margins and mark ups. We can also use ledger accounts and cash records to reconstruct total purchases for the year. In combination we can use these methods to identify the value of either opening or closing inventory.

Test your understanding 10

Jack Spratt provides the following information about his business:

Margin	20%
Sales	$100,000
Opening inventory	$10,000
Purchases	$82,000
Closing inventory after fire	$3,000

What is the cost of inventory lost in the fire?

A $12,000

B $9,000

C $69,000

D $5,667

Double entries for inventory and lost inventory

Actual closing inventory is posted by:

Dr Inventory (SFP)   X
Cr Profit or loss   X

Lost inventory will still be credited to the statement of profit or loss so that it is removed from cost of sales. However, the debit side of the entry will depend on whether or not the lost inventory has been insured:

If insured: Dr Insurance company   (Other receivables/current asset)
                  Cr Profit or loss   (Cost of sales)

If not insured: Dr Profit or loss   (Expense)
                  Cr Profit or loss   (Cost of sales)

Test your understanding 11

Fred lost his entire inventory in a fire. His unsigned insurance policy is still in the pocket of his good suit. Fred has supplied you with the following information:

Mark up 25%

Sales $10,000

Opening inventory $2,000

Purchases $7,500

Prepare Fred's statement profit or loss and show the journal to record closing inventory.

KAPLAN PUBLISHING

Chapter summary

Incomplete records

Using ledger accounts
(balancing figure approach)

Using cash/bank summaries

Reconstruct the relevant
ledger account as far as
possible using the
information given to reveal
one missing figure.

Use cash inflows and
outflows to help determine
sales and purchases figures.
Used in conjunction with
ledger account reconciliation.

Using the accounting
equation

Using profit percentages
(mark-up and margin)

Assets = equity + liabilities

Gross profit = margin% x sales

Gross profit = mark-up% x CofS

Test your understanding answers

Test your understanding 1

The correct answer is C.

Total assets = share capital + retained earnings + other reserves + total liabilities

$13,400 = $200 + retained earnings + $3,800

If we re-arrange this formula we end up with:

$13,400 – $200 – $3,800 = retained earnings

Retained earnings = $9,400

Closing retained earnings = prior year retained earnings + current year profits:

$9,400 = $7,350 + current year profits

$9,400 – $7,350 = current year profits

= **$2,050**

Test your understanding 2

The correct answer is A.

	Receivables		
	$		$
Balance b/f	30,000	Bank	40,000
Credit sales (ß)	50,000	Discount allowed	3,000
		Balance c/f	37,000
	80,000		80,000
Balance b/f	37,000		

Receivables

Total sales = credit sales + cash sales = $50,000 + $15,000 = **$65,000**

OR

Total receivables

	$		$
Balance b/f	30,000	Bank (total cash rec'd)	55,000
Total sales (ß)	65,000	Discount allowed	3,000
		Balance c/f	37,000
	95,000		95,000

Test your understanding 3

The correct answer is D.

Total payables

	$		$
Bank	14,000	Balance b/f	15,000
Discount received	500	Purchases (ß)	12,500
Balance c/f	13,000		
	27,500		27,500
		Balance b/f	13,000

Test your understanding 4

The correct answer is B.

Statement of profit or loss (extracts):

Expenses

Electricity (−250 + 1,000 + 300) = $1,050

Rent (300 + 2,000 − 400) = $1,900

Test your understanding 5

The correct answer is D.

Bank

	$		$
Receipts (ß)	12,130	Balance b/f	1,367
		Payments	8,536
		Balance c/f	2,227
	―――		―――
	12,130		12,130
	―――		―――
Balance b/f	2,227		

Test your understanding 6

The correct answer is C.

Cash in till

	$		$
Balance b/f	900	Bank	10,000
Receipts	13,100	Drawings	1,000
		Wages	2,000
		Balance c/f	1,000
	―――		―――
	14,000		14,000
	―――		―――
Balance c/f	1,000		

Test your understanding 7

The correct answer is C.

Gross profit: $1,000 × 25% = $250
Cost of sales:

	$
Sales	1,000
Cost of sales (ß)	(750)
Gross profit	
	250

Test your understanding 8

The correct answer is A.

Gross profit: $600 × 25% = $150

Sales	
	$
Sales (ß)	750
Cost of sales	(600)
Gross profit	
	150

Test your understanding 9

	$	$	%
Sales:		3,200	100
Cost of sales:	800		
Opening inventory	2,840		
Purchases	(600)		
		(3,040)	(95)
Gross profit:		160	5

Test your understanding 10

The correct answer is B.

	$	$	%
Sales:		100,000	100
Cost of sales:			
Opening inventory	10,000		
Purchases	82,000		
Closing inventory	(3,000)		
Inventory lost (ß)	(9,000)		
		(80,000)	(80)
Gross profit:		20,000	20

Test your understanding 11

	$	$	%
Sales:		10,000	125
Cost of sales:			
Opening inventory	2,000		
Purchases	7,500		
Inventory lost (ß)	(1,500)		
		(8,000)	(100)
Gross profit:		2,000	25
Dr Profit or loss (expense):		1,500	
Cr Profit or loss (cost of sales):		1,500	

Being the recording of uninsured inventory destroyed by the fire.

Statement of cash flows

Chapter learning objectives

Upon completion of this chapter you will be able to:

- differentiate between profit and cash flows
- recognise the benefits and drawbacks to users of financial statements of a statement of cash flows
- calculate the figures needed for the statement of cash flows
- calculate cash flows from operating activities using the indirect and direct method
- prepare statements of cash flows and/or extracts from given information.

1 Overview

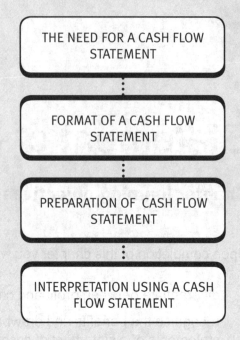

THE NEED FOR A CASH FLOW STATEMENT

FORMAT OF A CASH FLOW STATEMENT

PREPARATION OF CASH FLOW STATEMENT

INTERPRETATION USING A CASH FLOW STATEMENT

2 The need for a statement of cash flows

Profit and cash

Whilst a business might be profitable this does not mean it will be able to survive. To achieve this a business needs cash to be able to pay its debts. If a business could not pay its debts it would become insolvent and could not continue to operate.

The main reason for this problem is that profit is not the same as cash flow. Profits (from the statement of profit or loss) are calculated on the accruals basis. Most goods and services are sold on credit so at the point of sale revenue is recognised but no cash is received. The same can be said of credit purchases. There are also a number of expenses that are recognised that have no cash impact - depreciation is a good example of this. Therefore, it is possible for a business to be profitable but have insufficient cash available to pay its suppliers.

For this reason it is important that users of the financial statements can assess the cash position of a business at the end of the year but also how cash has been used and generated by the business during the accounting period. In the case of limited liability companies, IAS 7 requires that (with very few exceptions) a statement of cash flows is included as part of the annual financial statements made available to shareholders and other users of that information.

Cash flow management

As mentioned above, cash flow is vital to the survival of a company both in the long and the short term. To reflect this, one of the key measures of the health of a business is solvency or liquidity. These concepts will be discussed at greater length in the interpretations chapter.

In summary management have various liquid assets at their disposal that they can use to settle their debts in the short term. These include inventory, receivables and cash (i.e. current assets). They are used to pay off overdrafts, trade payables, loan interest and tax balances (i.e. current liabilities).

Management should maintain sufficient current assets to be able to pay their current liabilities as they fall due. If they do not, they will default their payments, lose supplier goodwill or suffer fines and sanctions. In the worst case scenario a supplier, lender or tax authority may even have a company put into administration or liquidation in an attempt to recover amounts due to them.

To ensure an effective balance, management must consider inventory production and storage cycles and have an effective system of credit control to ensure cash is received into the business as soon as possible. On the flip side they must also manage the level of debt they expose the business to.

IAS 7 Statement of Cash Flows

The objectives of IAS 7 are to ensure that companies:

- report their cash generation and cash absorption for a period by highlighting the significant components of cash flow in a way that facilitates comparison of the cash flow performance of different businesses.

- provide information that assists in the assessment of their liquidity, solvency and financial adaptability.

The benefits of a statement of cash flows

A statement of cash flows is needed as a consequence of the differences between profits and cash, as explained earlier. It helps to assess:

- liquidity and solvency – an adequate cash position is essential in the short term both to ensure the survival of the business and to enable debts and dividends to be paid.

- financial adaptability – will the company be able to take effective action to alter its cash flows in response to any unexpected events?

- future cash flows – an adequate cash position in the longer term is essential to enable asset replacement, repayment of debt and fund further expansion.

The bottom line is: cash flow means survival. A company may be profitable but, if it does not have an adequate cash position, it may not be able to pay its debts, purchase goods for resale, pay its staff etc.

The cash flow statement also highlights where cash is being generated, i.e. either from operating, financing or investing activities. A business must be self-sufficient in the long term; in other words it must generate operating cash inflows or it will be reliant on the sale of assets or further finance to keep it afloat.

Cash flows are also objective; they are matters of fact, whereas the calculation of profit is subjective and easy to manipulate.

The drawbacks of a statement of cash flow

- The statement of cash flows uses historic cash flows (a limitation that can be levied at all components of the financial statements). Users of the accounts are particularly interested in the future.

- No interpretation of the statement of cash flows is provided within the accounts. Users are required to draw their own conclusions as to the relevance of the figures contained within it.

- Non-cash transactions, e.g. bonus issues of shares and revaluations of assets are not highlighted in the statement of cash flows (although they are disclosed elsewhere within the accounts). These are of interest to users as they may impact future cash flows.

3 Format of a statement of cash flows

IAS 7 Statement of Cash Flows requires companies to prepare a statement of cash flows as part of their annual financial statements. The cash flow must be presented using standard headings. **Note:** There are two methods of reconciling cash from operating activities, which will be discussed later in this chapter.

You should ensure that you understand the items that are included within each of the three sections of the statement of cash flows, together with the reconciliation of the net increase or decrease in cash and equivalents for the year.

Statement of cash flows for the period ended 31 December XXX

	$000	$000
Cash flows from operating activities		
Cash generated from operations (see note below)	X	
Interest paid	(X)	
Income taxes paid	(X)	
	———	
Net cash flow from operating activities		X or (X)
Cash flows from investing activities		
Purchase of property, plant and equipment	(X)	
Proceeds of sale of equipment	X	
Interest received	X	
Dividends received	X	
	———	
Net cash flow from investing activities		X or (X)
Cash flows from financing activities		
Proceeds of issue of shares	X	
Receipt of new loans	X	
Repayment of loans	(X)	
Dividends paid	(X)	
	———	
Net cash flow from financing activities		X or (X)
		———
Net increase (decrease) in cash and cash equivalents		X or (X)
Cash and cash equivalents at the beginning of the period		X or (X)
		———
Cash and cash equivalents at the end of the period		X or (X)
		———

Note re 'Cash generated from operations': This is based upon a reconciliation beginning with profit before tax from the statement of profit or loss which is adjusted for items included in arriving at profit before tax, but which are not reflected by an inflow or outflow of cash. The reconciliation of items from 'Profit before tax' to 'Cash inflow from operating activities' can be shown either on the face of the statement of cash flows itself or as a separate working. This will be explained and illustrated within the chapter.

Key points

- Operating activities are the principal revenue-producing activities of the business. This section of the statement begins with profit before tax and is adjusted for various items which have been taken into account in arriving at profit before tax but which do not involve the movement of cash to arrive at 'Cash generated from operations'. This, in turn, is further adjusted to deduct interest paid and tax paid in the year to arrive at 'Net cash flow from operations'. Note that 'Net cash flow from operating activities can be calculated using either the direct or indirect method, and both will be explained and illustrated as the chapter progresses.

- Investing activities are cash spent on non-current assets, proceeds of sale of non-current assets and income from investments.

- Financing activities include the proceeds of issue of shares and long-term borrowings made or repaid.

- Net increase or decrease in cash and cash equivalents is the overall increase (or decrease) in cash and cash equivalents during the year. This can be calculated by comparing the level of cash and cash equivalents included in the statement of financial position at the start and at the end of the accounting period.

- Cash is defined as cash in hand and bank current account balances, including overdrafts.

- Cash equivalents are defined as current asset investments (short-term, highly liquid investments, e.g. a 30 day bond).

4 Cash generated from operations

There are two methods of presenting cash flows from operations. You need understand both methods of presentation and be able to apply either method in the examination if required.

The direct method provides more detailed information and is based upon cash flow information extracted directly from the accounting records. As this method discloses information that would otherwise remain confidential, most companies do not use the direct method.

Example using the direct method

Example of calculations using direct method

The gross cash flows necessary for the direct method can be derived:

(1) from the accounting records of the entity by totalling the cash receipts and payments directly, or

(2) from the opening and closing statements of financial position and statement of profit or loss for the year by constructing summary control accounts for:

- sales (to derive cash received from customers)

- purchases (to derive cash payments to suppliers)

- wages (to derive cash paid to and on behalf of employees).

Example using control accounts

The statements of financial position of a business were as follows:

	This year $	Last year $
Non-current assets	149,364	153,364
Inventories		
Receivables	346,000	265,840
Cash	165,166	
	660,530	419,204

	This year $	Last year $
Share capital	200,000	200,000
Reserves	141,640	
	341,640	200,000
Current liabilities	318,890	219,204
	660,530	4,19,204

Extracts from the statement of profit or loss for the year are:

	$	$
Sales revenue		1,589,447
Cost of sales:		
Purchases (no inventory)	1,105,830	
Wages and salaries	145,900	
		(1,251,730)
Administration:		
Purchases	96,077	
Salaries	100,000	
		(196,077)
Operating profit and retained profit for the year		141,640

Additional information

(1) Payables consist of

	This year $	Last year $
Payables ledger		
Re non-current assets	46,000	
Other	258,240	210,564
Wages accrued	14,650	8,640

(2) Purchase invoices relating to the acquisition of non-current assets totalling $80,000 have been posted to the payables ledger during the year.

Calculate the net cash flow from operating activities using the direct method.

Solution

	$
Operating activities	
Cash received from customers (W1)	1,509,287
Cash payments to suppliers (W2)	(1,154,231)
Cash paid to and on behalf of employees (W3)	(239,890)
	———
Net cash inflow from operating activities	115,166

Workings

(W1)

Receivables ledger control account

	$		$
Balance b/f	265,840	Cash receipts (ß)	1,509,287
Sales revenue	1,589,447	Balance c/f	346,000
	———		———
	1,855,287		1,855,287
	———		———

(W2)

Payables ledger control account
(excluding non-current asset purchases)

	$		$
Cash paid (ß)	1,154,231	Balance b/f	210,564
Balance c/f	258,240	Purchases	
		– Cost of sales	1,105,830
		– Administration	96,077
	———		———
	1,412,471		1,412,471
	———		———

Tutorial note: Information relating to non-current assets is not included in the payables ledger control account above in order to compute cash paid to suppliers of operating costs.

(W3)

Wages control

	$		$
Net wages paid (ß)	239,890	Balance b/f	8,640
Balance c/f	14,650	Cost of sales	145,900
		Administration	100,000
	254,540		254,540

Test your understanding 1

The following information relates to Flute, an entity.

Statement of financial position for the year ended 30 September – extracts

	20X8	20X7
	$	$
Trade receivables	31,250	35,633
Trade payables	14,195	13,750
Accrued wages expense	1,015	835
Interest payable	350	300
Income tax payable	1,250	1,075

Statement of profit or loss for the year ended 30 September 20X8 – extracts

	20X8
	$
Sales	427,915
Purchases	165,000
Wages	52,750
Interest expense	325
Income tax charge	1,515

Note: At 30 September 20X8, Flute had agreed to, but not yet accounted for, a contra between trade receivables and trade payables amounting to $230.

Using the direct method of presentation, prepare the net cash flow from operating activities extract of the statement of cash flows of Flute for the year ended 30 September 20X8.

Indirect method

The indirect method of presenting cash flows from operating activities relies upon information that is disclosed in the financial statements, or can be calculated from information disclosed in the financial statements. The starting point is normally profit before tax, which is then adjusted to remove any non-cash items or accruals-based figures included in the statement of profit or loss. The following are examples of adjustments which are normally required when preparing cash flows from operating activities using the indirect method:

- Depreciation – added back to profit before tax because it is a non-cash expense

- Loss on disposal of non-current assets - the loss a non-cash expense and is added back to profit before tax: the cash proceeds on disposal will be classified as an investing activity cash inflow. Note that a gain on disposal is deducted from profit before tax

- Interest payable expense – added back to profit before tax because it is not part of cash generated from operations (the cash payment is deducted elsewhere in the statement of cash flows - refer to the proforma statement)

- Increase / decrease in inventory – inventory represents purchases made in one accounting period, but which will be charged against profit in another accounting period. An increase in inventory is deducted from profit before tax as it represents a cash outflow to pay for the additional inventory. A decrease in inventory is added to profit before tax as it represents a cash inflow from disposing of inventory

- Increase / decrease in trade receivables – trade receivables represent revenue recognised in profit or loss in one accounting period, whilst the cash will be received in the following accounting period. An decrease in receivables is added to profit before tax as it represents a cash inflow as more cash has been collected from receivables. An increase in trade receivables is therefore deducted from profit before tax

- Increase / decrease in trade payables – trade payables represent purchases made in one accounting period which will be paid for in the following accounting period. An increase in trade payables means that the company has had the use or benefit of goods and services provided, but not yet paid for them. As such, it preserves cash resources within the business and is added back to profit before tax. A decrease in trade payables indicates that more payables have been paid off, and will therefore be deducted from profit before tax as a cash outflow.

In order to prepare a statement of cash flows, information from the current and prior year statement of financial position together with the current year statement of profit or loss is used.

The following financial statements provide the source data for the requirements of Test your understanding questions 2–7 inclusive within this chapter.

Test your understanding 2

Statement of financial position of Geronimo at 31 December

	20X6	20X5
	$000	$000
Non-current assets	1,048	750
Accumulated depreciation	(190)	(120)
	858	630
Current assets		
Inventory	98	105
Trade receivables	102	86
Dividend receivable	57	50
Cash	42	18
	299	259
Total assets	1,157	889
Equity and liabilities:		
Share capital	200	120
Share premium	106	80
Revaluation surplus	212	12
Retained earnings	283	226
	801	438
Non-current liabilities:		
Loan	200	300
Current liabilities:		
Trade payables	77	79
Interest accrual	3	5
Tax payable	76	67
	156	151
Total equity and liabilities	1,157	889

Statement of profit or loss for of Geronimo for the year ended 31 December 20X6

	$000
Sales revenue	1,100
Cost of sales	(678)
Gross profit	422
Operating expenses	(309)
Operating profit	113
Investment income	
– interest	15
– dividends	57
Finance charge	(22)
Income tax	(71)
Net profit for year	92

- Operating expenses include a loss on disposal of non-current assets of $5,000.

- During the year and item of plant was disposed of. The plant originally cost $80,000 and had accumulated depreciation to the date of disposal of $15,000.

Calculate the cash flow generated from operations using the indirect method.

5 Cash from operating activities

Cash flows may include:

- interest paid
- income taxes paid.

Calculation of interest / income taxes paid

The cash flow should be calculated by reference to:

- the charge to profits for the item (shown in the statement of profit or loss); and

- any opening or closing payable balance shown on the statement of financial position.

A T-account working may be useful:

e.g. Interest/tax payable account

	$		$
		Interest accrual b/f	X
Cash paid (ß)	X	P/L	
		Interest charge	X
Interest accrual c/f	X		
	⎯⎯		⎯⎯
	X		X
	⎯⎯		⎯⎯

If there is no change to the opening or closing then it should be the statement of financial position payable amount.

Test your understanding 3

Identify and calculate the cash flows relating to interest paid an income tax paid for inclusion under the heading 'Cash flows from operating activities' within Geronimo's statement of cash flows.

6 Investing activities cash flows

Investing activities cash inflows may include:

- interest received
- dividends received
- proceeds of sale of non-current assets.

Cash outflows may include:

- purchase of property, plant and equipment.

Calculation of interest and dividends received

Again, the calculation should take account of both the income shown in the statement of profit or loss and any relevant receivables balance from the opening and closing statements of financial position.

A T-account working may be useful:

Remember & learn

e.g. Interest receivable

	$		$
Interest receivable b/f	X		
P/L interest receivable	X	Cash received (ß)	X
		Interest receivable c/f	X
	X		X

Test your understanding 4

Identify and calculate the dividends and interest received to be shown under the heading 'Cash flows from investing activities' within Geronimo's statement of cash flows.

✓

Calculation of purchase of property, plant and equipment and proceeds of sale of equipment

ask Tutor

These amounts are often the trickiest to calculate within a statement of cash flows. It is therefore recommended that T-account workings are used.

The following T-accounts will be required for each class of assets:

- cost account
- accumulated depreciation account
- disposals account (where relevant).

Data provided in the source financial statements should then be entered into these T-accounts and the required cash flows found – often as balancing figures.

NB: If there is evidence of a revaluation, remember to include the uplift in value on the debit side of the asset T-account.

In some cases, insufficient detail is provided to produce separate asset and accumulated depreciation accounts. Instead, a carrying amount account should be used:

NCA – Carrying amount

	$		$
Carrying amount b/f	X		
Additions at carrying amount (= cash to purchase PPE)	X	Disposals at carrying amount	X
Revaluation	X	Depreciation charge for year	X
		Carrying amount c/f	X
	——		——
	X		X
	——		——

Test your understanding 5

Identify and calculate the cash outflow to purchase property, plant and equipment and the proceeds from the sale of equipment to be shown under the heading 'Cash flows from investing activities' within Geronimo's statement of cash flows.

7 Cash from financing activities

Cash inflows from financing activities may include:

- proceeds of the issue of shares
- proceeds of receipt of loans/debentures.

Cash outflows may include:

- repayment of loans/debentures
- dividends paid
- interest paid.

Note that IAS 7 permits interest paid to be classified as a cash outflow within either operating activities or as a financing activity. The important point is to ensure that the cash outflow for interest paid in the year is classified either within operating activities or within financing activities and not included twice within the statement of cash flows.

Calculation of the proceeds from the issue of shares is derived by comparison of the amounts included in the statement of financial position brought forward and carried forward on two accounts:

- share capital
- share premium.

Note that, if there is a bonus issue made in the year, this will not result in a cash inflow.

Calculation of proceeds or repayment of a loan

This cash flow is derived by comparing the brought forward balance with the balance carried forward. A fall in the amount outstanding indicates that all or part of the loan has been repaid in the year (a cash outflow). An increase indicates that there has been a further loan received in the year (a cash inflow). Note that this is one of the few cash flows that could be either a cash inflow or a cash outflow.

Dividends paid

A company can only account for dividends paid to its own shareholders on a cash basis in the financial statements. As dividends paid are effectively paid out of retained earnings, it is usually necessary to reconcile the opening and closing balances on retained earnings to identify any dividend paid in the year as a balancing figure.

Test your understanding 6

Identify and calculate each of the amounts to be shown under the heading 'Cash flows from financing activities' within Geronimo's statement of cash flows.

Test your understanding 7

Complete the following proforma statement of cash flows for Geronimo using your answers to Test your understanding questions 2–6.

Statement of cash flows for Geronimo for year ended 31 December 20X6

	$000	$000
Cash flows from operating activities		
Cash generated from operations		
Interest paid		
Tax paid		
		———
Net cash from operating activities		
Cash flows from investing activities		
Proceeds of sale of equipment		
Purchase of property, plant and equipment		
Interest received		
Dividends received		
		———
Net cash used in investing activities		
Cash flows from financing activities		
Proceeds of issue of shares		
Repayment of loans		
Dividends paid		
		———
Net cash used in financing activities		
Net increase in cash and cash equivalents		
		———
Cash and cash equivalents at beginning of period		
		———
Cash and cash equivalents at end period		

Test your understanding 8

You are given below, in summarised form, the accounts of Algernon, an entity, for 20X6 and 20X7.

	20X6			20X7		
	Cost	Dep'n	CV	Cost	Dep'n	CV
	$	$	$	$	$	$
Plant	10,000	4,000	6,000	11,000	5,000	6,000
Buildings	50,000	10,000	40,000	90,000	11,000	79,000
			46,000			85,000
Investments at cost			50,000			80,000
Land			43,000			63,000
Inventory			55,000			65,000
Receivables			40,000			50,000
Bank			3,000			
			237,000			343,000
Ordinary shares of $1 each			40,000			50,000
Share premium			12,000			14,000
Revaluation surplus (land)			–			20,000
Retained earnings			45,000			45,000
10% Loan notes			100,000			150,000
Payables			40,000			60,000
Bank			–			4,000
			237,000			343,000

Statement of profit or loss

	20X6	20X7
	$	$
Sales	200,000	200,000
Cost of sales	(100,000)	(120,000)
	100,000	80,000
Expenses	(50,000)	(47,000)
	50,000	33,000
Interest	(10,000)	(13,000)
Net profit for year	40,000	20,000

Notes:

A $20,000 dividend has been paid in the year.

Required:

(a) **Prepare a statement of cash flows for Algernon for 20X7, to explain as far as possible the movement in the bank balance. The statement of cash flows should be prepared using the direct method.**

(b) **Using the summarised accounts given, and the statement you have just prepared, comment on the position, progress and direction of Algernon.**

Test your understanding 9

Part of an entity's statement of cash flows is shown below:

	$000
Profit before tax	1,255
Loss on disposal	(455)
Increase in receivables	(198)
Increase in payables	340

The following criticisms of the extract have been made:

(1) The loss on disposal should have been added, not deducted.

(2) Increase in receivables should have been added, not deducted.

(3) Increase in payables should have been deducted, not added.

Which of the criticisms is valid?

A   1, 2 and 3

B   1 only

C   2 and 3 only

D   none of them

Test your understanding 10

Which of the following could appear in an entity's statement of cash flows?

(1) Proposed dividend

(2) Dividends received

(3) Bonus issue of shares

(4) Surplus on revaluation of non-current assets

A   1 and 2

B   1,2 and 3

C   2 only

D   2 and 3

Test your understanding 11

The following details were provided by Caddyshack, an entity, which had a profit before tax of $434,850 for the year ended 31 December 20X6.

(1) Depreciation of $37,400 was charged to the statement of profit or loss; this included an amount of $7,600 which was the loss on disposal of a non-current asset.

(2) Finance costs of $35,000 were charged to the statement of profit or loss.

(3) The following extract of the statement of financial position at 31 December 20X5 and 20X6 was provided:

	31 Dec 20X6	31 Dec 20X5
	$000	$000
Inventory	145	167
Trade receivables	202	203
Prepayments	27	16
Trade payables	196	212
Interest payable	6	28

What was the cash generated from operations?

A $468,250

B $511,250

C $476,250

D $503,250

Chapter summary

The need for a statement of cash flows
- Helps to assess liquidity of a company.
- Helps to assess future cash flows.
- User can see cash flows in and out of the business.

Format of a statement of cash flows
IAS 7 requires the cash flow statement to have three headings:
- Operating activities
- Investing activities
- Financing activities.

Preparation of a statement of cash flows
The cash movement is simply the movement between the current and previous year's balance in the statement of financial position. Watch out for trickier areas such as taxation, and non-current assets where a working will need to be done.

Interpretation using a statement of cash flows
The cash flow provides useful information including:
- how a business spends and receives cash
- whether operating activities yield a positive cash flow
- whether the business has the ability to generate cash in the future.

Test your understanding answers

Test your understanding 1

Operating activities	$
Cash received from customers (W1)	432,298
Cash payments to suppliers (W2)	(164,555)
Cash paid to and on behalf of employees (W3)	(52,570)
	————
Cash inflow from operations	215,173
Interest paid (W4)	(275)
Income tax paid (W5)	(1,340)
	————
Net cash inflow from operating activities	213,558
	————

Workings

(W1)

Receivables ledger control account

	$		$
Balance b/f	35,633	Cash receipts (ß)	432,298
		Contra with payables	230
Sales revenue	427,915	Balance c/f (31,250 – 230)	31,020
	————		————
	463,548		463,548
	————		————

(W2)

Payables ledger control account

	$		$
Cash paid (ß)	164,555	Balance b/f	13,750
Contra with receivables	230	Purchases	165,000
Balance c/f (14,195 – 230)	13,965		
	————		————
	178,750		178,750
	————		————

(W3)

Wages control

	$		$
Net wages paid (ß)	52,570	Balance b/f	835
Balance c/f	1,015	Profit or loss	52,750
	53,585		53,585

(W4)

Interest payable

	$		$
Interest paid (ß)	275	Balance b/f	300
Balance c/f	350	Profit or loss	325
	625		625

(W5)

Income tax

	$		$
Net wages paid (ß)	1,340	Balance b/f	1,075
Balance c/f	1,250	Profit or loss	1,515
	2,590		2,590

Note: When the contra is accounted for, it will reduce the balance outstanding at the year-end of both trade receivables and trade payables.

Test your understanding 2

	$000
Profit before tax (92 + 71) i.e. as per properly formatted P&L)	163
Add: Finance charge per P&L	22
Less: Investment income per P&L	(72)
Add: Depreciation (W1)	85
Add: Loss on disposal of plant	5
Add: Decrease in inventory (105 – 98)	7
Less: Increase in trade receivables (86 – 102)	(16)
Less: Decrease in trade payables (79 – 77)	(2)
Cash flow generated from operations	192

Note that interest paid and income tax paid would need to be deducted to arrive at 'Net cash flow from operations'.

(W1)

Accumulated depreciation

	$000		$000
Disposals	15	Balance b/f	120
Balance c/f	190	Depreciation charge (ß)	85
	205		205

Test your understanding 3

Interest paid

Interest payable

	$000		$000
		Interest accrual b/f	5
Cash paid (ß)	24		
Interest accrual c/f	3	P/L finance charge	22
	27		27

Income tax payable

	$		$
		Tax payable b/f	67
Cash paid (ß)	62	P/L tax charge	71
Tax payable c/f	76		
	138		138

Test your understanding 4

There is no balance for interest receivable at the start or end of the year; therefore interest received must equal interest receivable in the statement of profit or loss.

Interest received $15,000

Dividends received

Dividends receivable

	$		$
Dividends receivable b/f	50	Cash received (ß)	50
P/L dividends receivable	57	Dividends receivable c/f	57
	X		X

Test your understanding 5

PPE cost

	$000		$000
Balance b/f	750		
Additions (= Cash to purchase PPE)	178	Disposals	80
Revaluation (212 – 12)	200	Balance c/f	1,048
	1,128		1,128

Disposals

	$000		$000
Cost	80	Accumulated depreciation	15
		Loss on disposal	5
		Proceeds (ß)	60
	80		80

Test your understanding 6

	20X6	**20X5**	
	$000	$000	$000
Share capital	200	120	
Share premium	106	80	
	306	200	
Proceeds of share issue			106

306 – 200 = 106

Repayment of loan

- Balance on loan account was $300,000 in 20X5; in 20X6 it is ✓ $200,000.
- Therefore $100,000 has been repaid. ✓

Dividends paid

Retained earnings

	$000		$000
		Balance b/f	226
Dividends paid (bal. fig)	35	Profit for the year (P/L)	92
Balance c/f	283		
	318		318

Test your understanding 7

Statement of cash flows for Geronimo for year ended 31 December 20X6

	$000	$000
Cash flows from operating activities		
Cash generated from operations (TYU 1)	192	
Interest paid (TYU 2)	(24)	
Tax paid (TYU 2)	(62)	
	―――	
		106
Net cash generated from operating activities		
Cash flows from investing activities		
Proceeds of sale of equipment (TYU 4)	60	
Purchase of property, plant and equipment (TYU 4)	(178)	
Interest received (TYU 3)	15	
Dividends received (TYU 3)	50	
	―――	
Net cash used in investing activities		(53)
Cash flows from financing activities		
Proceeds of issue of shares (TYU 5)	106	
Repayment of loans (TYU 5)	(100)	
Dividends paid (TYU 5)	(35)	
	―――	
Net cash generated from financing activities		(29)
		―――
Net increase in cash and cash equivalents		24
Cash and cash equivalents at beginning of period		18
		―――
Cash and cash equivalents at end of period		42
		―――

Test your understanding 8

(a)

Statement of cash flows for Algernon for year ended 31 December 2007

	$	$
Cash flows from operating activities		
Cash receipts from customers (W1)	190,000	
Cash paid to suppliers and employees (W2)	(155,000)	
	———	
Cash generated from operations	35,000	
Interest paid	(13,000)	
Dividends paid	(20,000)	–
Net cash from operating activities	———	2,000
Cash flows from investing activities		
Purchase of tangible non-current assets (1,000 + 40,000)	(41,000)	
Purchase of investments	(30,000)	
Net cash used for investing activities	———	(71,000)
Cash flows from financing activities		
Issue of shares (10,000 + 2,000)	12,000	
Loan notes	50,000	
Net cash from financing activities	———	62,000
		———
Net decrease in cash and cash equivalents		(7,000)
Cash and cash equivalents at 1 January 20X7		3,000
		———
Cash and cash equivalents at 31 December 20X7		(4,000)
		———

	31 December	
	20X6	**20X7**
	$	$
Balance at bank	3,000	(4,000)
	———	———

Workings

(W1) Receipts from sales

Receivables control

	$		$
Balance b/f	40,000	Cash receipts (ß)	190,000
Sales revenue	200,000	Balance c/f	50,000
	240,000		240,000

(W2) Payables and wages control

Payable and wages control

	$		$
Cash paid (ß)	155,000	Balance b/f	40,000
Depreciation	2,000	Purchases re cost of sales (W3)	130,000
Balance c/f	60,000		
		Expenses	47,000
	217,000		217,000

(W3) Cost of sales

Cost of sales

	$		$
Opening inventory	55,000	Cost of sales	120,000
Purchases and wages (ß)	130,000	Closing inventory	65,000
	185,000		185,000

KAPLAN PUBLISHING

(b) Algernon has invested substantially in buildings, investments, inventory and receivables in the year. The finance has come from new share capital in part but mainly from loans. The equity to assets ratio of the company has thus decreased. The working capital has been financed by an equal increase in trade payables.

The profits have been fully distributed as dividends despite the halving of profits from last year. It might have been wiser to cut back on dividends in the period of expansion until the benefits of the expansion are seen in the form of higher profits.

Test your understanding 9

The correct answer is B.

A loss on disposal should be added back to profit as it is a non-cash expense.

Test your understanding 10

The correct answer is C.

Dividends received involve a cash receipt. The other transactions do not involve a movement of cash.

Test your understanding 11

The correct answer is D.

	$
Profit before tax	434,850
Depreciation and loss on disposal charged in P&L	37,400
Decrease in inventory	22,000
Decrease in trade receivables	1,000
Increase in prepayments	(11,000)
Decrease in trade payables	(16,000)
Finance costs charged in P&L	35,000
	———
Cash generated from operations	503,250

Note that the finance costs charged in the statement of profit or loss are included in the reconciliation to identify cash generated from operations. However, the cash paid in the year relating to finance costs is only relevant when calculating the net cash flow from operations.

Interpretation of financial statements

Chapter learning objectives

Upon completion of this chapter you will be able to:

- describe how the interpretation and analysis of financial statements is used in a business environment

- explain the purpose of the interpretation of ratios

- calculate and interpret the relationship between the following key accounting ratios
    - profitability
    - liquidity
    - efficiency
    - position

- explain the interrelationships between ratios

- draw valid conclusions from the information contained within the financial statements.

1 Overview

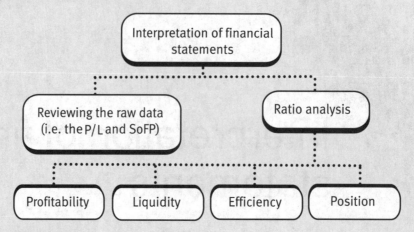

2 Interpreting financial information

Introduction

Financial statements on their own are of limited use. If you were to identify that a business has made profits of $1 million what does that tell you about the business? Does it suggest the business is a success? It might, but not if in the previous year they made profits of $50 million and their closest rival earned profits of $60 million.

It is important that users of financial statements can interpret the financial statements to be able to draw out valid conclusions. Typically this involves the use of comparisons to prior years, forecasts and competitors. Users can compare sales and expense figures, asset and liability balances and cash flows to perform this analysis.

Ratio analysis is widely used to support this process of comparison. Don't forget though that ratios are calculated using the figures already present in the financial statements. The raw data is equally useful when performing analysis. Ratios are simply a tool to try and assist understanding and comparison.

Users of financial statements

When interpreting financial statements it is important to ascertain who are the users of accounts and what information they need:

- shareholders and potential investors – primarily concerned with receiving an adequate return on their investment, but also with the stability/liquidity of the business

- suppliers and lenders – concerned with the security of their debt or loan

- management – concerned with the trend and level of profits, since this is the main measure of their success.

Other potential users include:

- financial institutions
- employees
- professional advisors to investors
- financial journalists and commentators.

3 Ratio analysis

Ratios use simple calculations based upon the interactions in sets of data. For example, changes in costs of sale are directly linked to changes in sales activity. Changes in sales activity also have an effect upon wages and salaries, receivables, inventory levels etc. Ratios allow us to see those interactions in a simple, concise format.

Ratios are of limited use on their own, thus, the following points should serve as a useful checklist if you need to analyse data and comment on it:

- What does the ratio literally mean?
- What does a change in the ratio mean?
- What is the norm?
- What are the limitations of the ratio?

4 Profitability ratios

Gross profit margin

On a unit basis the gross profit represents the difference between the unit sales price and the direct cost per unit. The margin works this out on an average basis across all sales for the year.

Gross profit margin is calculated as follows:

$$\frac{\text{Gross profit}}{\text{Sales revenue}} \times 100\%$$

Changes in this ratio may be attributable to:

- selling prices
- product mix
- purchase costs
- production costs
- inventory valuations

Gross profit margin

Comparing gross profit margin over time

If gross profit has not increased in line with sales revenue, you need to establish why not. Is the discrepancy due to:

- increased 'purchase' costs: if so, are the costs under the company's control (i.e. does the company manufacture the goods sold)?
- inventory write-offs (likely where the company operates in a volatile marketplace, such as fashion retail)? or
- other costs being allocated to cost of sales – for example, research and development (R&D) expenditure?

Inter-company comparison of gross profit margin

Inter-company comparison of margins can be very useful but it is especially important to look at businesses within the same sector. For example, food retailing is able to support low margins because of the high volume of sales. Jewellers would usually need higher margins to offset lower sales volumes.

Low margins usually suggest poor performance but may be due to expansion costs (launching a new product) or trying to increase market share. Lower margins than usual suggest scope for improvement.

Above-average margins are usually a sign of good management although unusually high margins may make the competition keen to join in and enjoy the 'rich pickings'.

Operating profit margin (net profit)

The **operating profit margin** or net profit margin is calculated as:

$$\frac{\text{PBIT}}{\text{Sales revenue}} \times 100\%$$

The operating margin is an expansion of the gross margin and includes all of the items that come after gross profit but before finance charges and taxation, such as selling and distribution costs and administration costs.

If the gross margin is a measure of how profitably a company can produce and sell its products and services the operating margin also measures how effectively the business manages/administers that process.

Therefore, if the gross margin has remained static but the operating margin has changed consider the following possibilities (these represent suggestions; it is not a comprehensive list):

*   changes in employment patterns (recruitment, redundancy etc)

*   changes to depreciation due to large acquisitions or disposals

*   significant write-offs of irrecoverable debt

*   changes in rental agreements

*   significant investments in advertising

*   rapidly changing fuel costs.

Operating profit margin

This is affected by more factors than the gross profit margin but it is equally useful to users and if the company does not disclose cost of sales it may be used on its own in lieu of the gross profit percentage.

One of the many factors affecting the trading profit margin is depreciation, which is open to considerable subjective judgement. Inter-company comparisons should be made after suitable adjustments to align accounting policies.

By the time you have reached operating (net) profit, there are many more factors to consider. If you are provided with a breakdown of expenses you can use this for further line-by-line comparisons. Bear in mind that:

- some costs are fixed or semi-fixed (e.g. property costs) and therefore not expected to change in line with revenue

- other costs are variable (e.g. packing and distribution, and commission).

ROCE

This is an important analysis tool as it allows users to assess how much profit the business generates from the capital invested in it. Profit margins of different companies are not necessarily comparable due to different sizes and business structures. You could have one company that makes large profits but based on huge levels of investment. Shareholders may decide they can make similar returns in different companies without such a high initial investment required.

In simple terms ROCE measures how much operating profit is generated for every $1 capital invested in the business.

$$\text{ROCE} = \frac{\text{Operating profit}}{\text{Capital employed}} \times 100\%$$

Capital employed can be measured in either of the two following ways:

- equity, plus interest-bearing finance, i.e. non-current loans plus share capital and reserves. or

- total assets less current liabilities

Note that either method will provide the same end answer to calculate capital employed.

ROCE

Once calculated, ROCE should be compared with:

- previous years' figures – provided there have been no changes in accounting policies, or suitable adjustments have been made to facilitate comparison (note, however that the effect of not replacing non-current assets is that their value will decrease and ROCE will increase)

- the company's target ROCE – where the company's management has determined a target return as part of its budget procedure, consistent failure by a part of the business to meet the target may make it a target for disposal

- other companies in same industry – care is required in interpretation, because of the possibility, noted above, of different accounting policies, ages of plant, etc.

The ratio also shows how efficiently a business is using its resources. If the return is very low, the business may be better off realising its assets and investing the proceeds in a high interest bank account! (This may sound extreme, but should be considered particularly for a small, unprofitable business with valuable assets such as property.) Furthermore, a low return can easily become a loss if the business suffers a downturn.

5 Net asset turnover

Net asset turnover

The **net asset turnover** is:

$$\frac{\text{Sales revenue}}{\text{Capital employed (net assets)}} = \text{times pa}$$

It measures management's efficiency in generating revenue from the net assets at its disposal. This is similar to ROCE but in this case we measure the amount of sales revenue generated for every $1 capital invested in the business. Generally speaking, the higher the ratio the more efficient the business is.

Further explanation of net asset turnover

Note that this can be further subdivided into:

- non-current asset turnover (by making non-current assets the denominator) and
- working capital turnover (by making net current assets the denominator).

Be aware that both ROCE and asset turnover can be significantly affected by a change in the business structure. For example, imagine that a manufacturing company buys a significant amount of property and plant in a year with the aim to increasing production and therefore sales. The short term affect is that ROCE and asset turnover will initially fall but this does not mean the business is actually performing any worse. It may even be an indication of future gains.

The reason is that the capital balance (net assets) will increase in comparison to the steady sales figures of the business. It cannot be expected that a business can buy new assets and simply grow immediately. It would take a number of years for a business to grow into their new assets and increase production until they operated at 100% capacity. Even if they could instantly use 100% of the new facilities it is unlikely that they will simply be able to sell all the new goods they produce instantly. They will have to find new customers, perhaps in new markets to sell them to. Of course, this does not take into account competitor responses!

In summary, the increase in capital would be both significant and instant. The consequent improvement in performance would take longer to achieve and would most likely be spread over a number of years. Both ROCE and asset turnover would fall instantly and then start to improve each year as revenues start to grow.

Relationship between ratios

ROCE can be subdivided into operating profit margin and asset turnover.

| Operating margin | × | asset turnover | = | ROCE |

$$\frac{\text{Operating profit}}{\text{Sales revenue}} \times \frac{\text{Sales revenue}}{\text{Capital employed}} = \frac{\text{Operating profit}}{\text{Capital employed}}$$

Further explanation of the relationship

Profit margin is often seen as an indication of the quality of products or services supplied (top-of-range products usually have higher margins).

Asset turnover is often seen as a measure of how intensively the assets are worked or how efficiently they are used to generate revenue.

A trade-off often exists between margin and asset turnover that means different businesses can actually achieve the same ROCE:

- Low-margin businesses (e.g. food retailers) often have intensive asset usage (i.e. they produce a high volume of goods to sell but sell them at low prices).

- Higher margin businesses (e.g. luxury jewellery items) produce less goods but sell them at a high price. Many of these businesses still use very labour intensive, rather than machine intensive, methods of production. Such crafts are highly valued and consumers are willing to pay a premium for them.

6 Liquidity and Efficiency ratios

These ratios assess the liquidity/solvency of a business (i.e. the ability to meet debt obligations) and how efficiently the company manages its working capital resources.

Current ratio

Current or working capital ratio:

$$\frac{\text{Current assets}}{\text{Current liabilities}} : 1$$

The current ratio measures the adequacy of current assets to meet liabilities as they fall due.

A high or increasing figure may appear safe but should be regarded with suspicion as it may be due to:

- high levels of inventory and receivables (this could mean inventory is unsaleable or that credit control is weak)

- high cash levels which could be put to better use (e.g. by investing in non-current assets).

Current ratio

The current ratio measures the adequacy of current assets to meet the company's short-term liabilities. It reflects whether the company is in a position to meet its liabilities as they fall due.

Traditionally, a current ratio of 2:1 or higher was regarded as appropriate for most businesses to maintain creditworthiness. However, more recently a figure of 1.5:1 is regarded as the norm.

The current ratio should be, however, looked at in the light of what is normal for the business. For example, supermarkets tend to have low current ratios because:

- there are few trade receivables

- there is a high level of trade payables

- there is usually very tight cash control, to fund investment in developing new sites and improving sites.

It is also worth considering:

- availability of further finance, e.g. is the overdraft at the limit? – very often this information is highly relevant but is not disclosed in the accounts

- seasonal nature of the business – one way of doing this is to compare the interest charges in the statement of profit or loss with the overdraft and other loans in the statement of financial position; if the interest rate appears abnormally high, this is probably because the company has had higher levels of borrowings during the year

- long-term liabilities, when they fall due and how will they be financed

- nature of the inventory – where inventories are slow moving, the quick ratio probably provides a better indicator of short-term liquidity.

Quick ratio

Quick ratio (also known as the liquidity and acid test) ratio:

$$\text{Quick ratio} = \frac{\text{Current assets} - \text{Inventory}}{\text{Current liabilities}} : 1$$

The quick ratio is also known as the acid test ratio because by eliminating inventory from current assets it provides the acid test of whether the company has sufficient liquid resources (receivables and cash) to settle its liabilities.

Quick ratio

Normal levels for the quick ratio range from 1:1 to 0.7:1.

Like the current ratio it is relevant to consider the nature of the business (again supermarkets have very low quick ratios).

Sometimes the **quick ratio** is calculated on the basis of a six-week time-frame (i.e. the quick assets are those which will turn into cash in six weeks; quick liabilities are those which fall due for payment within six weeks). This basis would usually include the following in **quick assets:**

*   bank, cash and short-term investments
*   trade receivables.

thus excluding prepayments and inventory.

Quick liabilities would usually include:

*   bank overdraft which is repayable on demand
*   trade payables, tax and social security
*   dividends.

Income tax liabilities may be excluded.

When interpreting the quick ratio, care should be taken over the status of the **bank overdraft**. A company with a low quick ratio may actually have no problem in paying its amounts due if sufficient overall overdraft facilities are available.

Inventory turnover period

Inventory turnover period is defined as:

$$\frac{\text{Inventory}}{\text{COS}} \times 365 \text{ days}$$

This simply measures how efficiently management uses its inventory to produce and sell goods.

An increasing number of days implies that management are holding onto inventory for longer. This could indicate lack of demand or poor inventory control.

Alternatively, the increase in inventory holding could be due to:

- buying bulk to take advantage of trade discounts
- reducing the risk of 'stockouts', or
- an expected increase in orders.

Either way, the consequence is that the costs of storing, handling and insuring inventory levels will also increase. There is also an increased risk of inventory damage and obsolescence.

Alternative

An alternative is to express the inventory turnover period as a number of times:

$$\frac{\text{Cost of sales}}{\text{Inventory}} = \text{times pa}$$

A high turnover indicates that management generally hold quite a low level of inventory in comparison to overall sales. This means their costs of holding inventory are reduced, although they may need more frequent deliveries. A just in time system would reflect this sort of strategy. A low inventory turnover indicates that management hold on to a high level of inventory in comparison to overall sales levels.

Inventory days – A word of caution

Year-end inventory is normally used in the calculation of inventory turnover. An average (based on the average of year-start and year-end inventories) may be used to have a smoothing effect, although this may dampen the effect of a major change in the period.

Inventory turnover ratios vary enormously with the nature of the business. For example, a fishmonger selling fresh fish would have an inventory turnover period of 1–2 days, whereas a building contractor may have an inventory turnover period of 200 days. Manufacturing companies may have an inventory turnover ratio of 60–100 days; this period is likely to increase as the goods made become larger and more complex.

For large and complex items (e.g. rolling stock or aircraft) there may be sharp fluctuations in inventory turnover according to whether delivery took place just before or just after the year end.

A manufacturer should take into consideration:

- reliability of suppliers: if the supplier is unreliable it is prudent to hold more raw materials

- demand: if demand is erratic it is prudent to hold more finished goods.

Receivables collection period

This is normally expressed as a number of days:

$$\frac{\text{Trade receivables}}{\text{Credit sales}} \times 365 \text{ days}$$

The ratio shows, on average, how long it takes to collect cash from credit customers once they have purchased goods. The collection period should be compared with:

- the stated credit policy
- previous period figures.

Increasing accounts receivables collection period is usually a bad sign suggesting lack of proper credit control which may lead to irrecoverable debts.

It may, however, be due to:

- a deliberate policy to attract more trade, or
- a major new customer being allowed different terms.

Falling receivables days is usually a good sign, though it could indicate that the company is suffering a cash shortage.

Receivables days

The trade receivables used may be a year-end figure or the average for the year. Where an average is used to calculate the number of days, the ratio is the average number of days' credit taken by customers.

For many businesses total sales revenue can safely be used, because cash sales will be insignificant. But cash-based businesses like supermarkets make the substantial majority of their sales for cash, so the receivables period should be calculated by reference to credit sales only.

The result should be compared with the stated **credit policy**. A period of 30 days or 'at the end of the month following delivery' are common credit terms.

The receivables days ratio can be distorted by:

- using year-end figures which do not represent average receivables
- factoring of accounts receivables which results in very low trade receivables
- sales on unusually long credit terms to some customers.

Payables payment period

This is usually expressed as:

$$\frac{\text{Trade payables}}{\text{Credit purchases}} \times 365 \text{ days}$$

This represents the credit period taken by the company from its suppliers.

The ratio is always compared to previous years:

- A long credit period may be good as it represents a source of free finance.
- A long credit period may indicate that the company is unable to pay more quickly because of liquidity problems.

If the credit period is long:

- the company may develop a poor reputation as a slow payer and may not be able to find new suppliers

- existing suppliers may decide to discontinue supplies

- the company may be losing out on worthwhile cash discounts.

In most sets of financial statements (in practice and in examinations) the figure for purchases will not be available therefore cost of sales is normally used as an approximation in the calculation of the accounts payable payment period.

Cash cycle

We can also consider the cash cycle as part of management of working capital. In effect, it may be regarded as the interaction of the inventory turnover, receivables collection period and payables payment period. The cash cycle is important to a business to ensure that it has adequate cash resources to meet the needs of the business. This may include ensuring that there are sufficient cash resources to do the following:

- to pay current liabilities as they fall due

- to meet any financing commitments that the business may have, such as repayment of loans and finance charges

- to meet regular weekly and/or monthly payroll costs

- to meet any capital commitments that a business may have

- to meet any sales and business tax commitments that a business may have.

The cash conversion cycle ('CCC') can be used to determine how many days cash is tied up on the working capital cycle as follows:

CCC = inventory holding period + receivables collection period
– creditors payment period.

Ideally, businesses would like to have cash tied up in working capital for the minimum number of days possible. In the case of cash retail business, such as a supermarket, the cash conversion cycle will be very short. In the case of a manufacturing business which also sells on credit, the cash conversion cycle will be considerably longer and therefore increase the working capital requirements of the business.

By way of illustration, suppose that two businesses provide you with the following information relating to working capital management:

	Business 1	Business 2
Inventory holding period	10 days	30 days
Receivables collection period	0 days	40 days
Payables payment period	40 days	35 days
	(30 days)	35 days

Business 1 holds inventory for a relatively short period of time and sales are made for cash, so there is no receivables collection period, whilst it also takes 40 days credit from suppliers. Cash is therefore collected in quicker than it is paid out. By contrast, Business 2 holds inventory for 30 days before it is sold, when credit customers then take, on average, forty days credit. This total of seventy days is then offset to the extent that the business takes credit from suppliers, 35 days, leaving a net cash conversion cycle of 35 days.

7 Financial position

When assessing the financial position of a business the main focus is its stability and exposure to risk. This is typically assessed by considering the way the business is structured and financed. This is referred to as **gearing**.

In simple terms gearing is a measure of the level of external debt a company has (e.g. outstanding loans) in comparison to equity finance (i.e. share capital and reserves).

Measuring gearing

There are two methods commonly used to express gearing as follows.

Debt/equity ratio:

$$\frac{\text{Long term debt}}{\text{Equity}}$$

Percentage of capital employed represented by borrowings:

$$\frac{\text{Long term debt}}{\text{Equity + long term debt}}$$

Long term debt includes non-current loan and redeemable preference share liabilities.

Equity includes share capital (and premium) balances plus reserves (revaluation reserve, retained earnings).

Note: Redeemable preference shares are treated as liabilities because they must be repaid and are therefore debts of the company. Irredeemable preference shares do not have to be repaid and are therefore treated the same as ordinary shares and included in equity.

High and low gearing

Risk

External debt finance is considered to be risky because there are mandatory, fixed repayment obligations. Failure to repay these amounts could lead to insolvency proceedings against the company.

Equity finance is less risky because there are no mandatory repayment obligations to shareholders. Failure to pay a dividend would not lead to insolvency proceedings.

Servicing of finance

The costs of servicing equity finance are generally considered to be higher than servicing external debt. This is because equity holders expect a greater return than they could achieve offering a fixed loan to a company. Remember lenders received fixed, mandatory repayments. They also take out security on the assets of a company. Equity holders do not have this comfort blanket; they get no guaranteed returns and they take on considerable risks. They would therefore expect greater returns on their investments; if they could not achieve this they would surely not accept the risk of buying shares and lend their money instead.

Therefore highly geared companies (high level of debt to equity) are considered to be riskier but comparatively cheaper to service than lower geared companies (and vice versa).

Low-geared businesses also tend to provide scope to increase borrowings when potentially profitable projects are available as they are generally perceived to be less risky by banks and can therefore borrow more easily.

Interest cover

$$\text{Interest cover} = \frac{\text{PBIT}}{\text{Interest payable}}$$

Interest cover indicates the ability of a company to pay interest out of profits generated:

- low interest cover indicates to shareholders that their dividends are at risk (because most profits are eaten up by interest payments) and

- the company may have difficulty financing its debts if its profits fall

- interest cover of less than two is usually considered unsatisfactory.

Interest cover

A business must have a sufficient level of long-term capital to finance its long-term investment in non-current assets. Part of the investment in current assets would usually be financed by relatively permanent capital with the balance being provided by credit from suppliers and other short-term borrowings. Any expansion in activity will normally require a broadening of the long-term capital base, without which 'overtrading' may develop (see below).

Suitability of finance is also a key factor. A permanent expansion of a company's activities should not be financed by temporary, short-term borrowings. On the other hand, a short-term increase in activity such as the 'January sales' in a retail trading company could ideally be financed by overdraft.

A major addition to non-current assets such as the construction of a new factory would not normally be financed on a long-term basis by overdraft. It might be found, however, that the expenditure was temporarily financed by short-term loans until construction was completed, when the overdraft would be 'funded' by a long-term borrowing secured on the completed building.

Test your understanding 1

Neville is a company that manufactures and retails office products. Their summarised financial statements for the years ended 30 June 20X4 and 20X5 are given below:

Statements of profit or loss for the year ended 30 June

	20X4	20X5
	$000	$000
Revenue	1,159,850	1,391,820
Cost of sales	(753,450)	(1,050,825)
Gross profit	406,400	340,995
Operating expenses	(170,950)	(161,450)
Profit from operations	235,450	179,545
Finance costs	(14,000)	(10,000)
Profits before tax	221,450	169,545
Tax	(66,300)	(50,800)
Net profit	155,150	118,745

Statements of Financial Position as at 30 June

	20X4		20X5	
	$000	$000	$000	$000
Non-current assets		341,400		509,590
Current Assets				
Inventory	88,760		109,400	
Receivables	206,550		419,455	
Bank	95,400		–	
		390,710		528,855
		732,110		1,038,445

Equity and reserves

Share capital	100,000	100,000
Share premium	20,000	20,000
Revaluation reserve	–	50,000
Retained earnings	287,420	376,165
	407,420	546,165

Non-current liabilities

Loans	83,100	61,600

Current liabilities

Payables	179,590	345,480
Overdraft	–	30,200
Tax	62,000	55,000
	241,590	430,680
	732,110	1,038,445

The directors concluded that their revenue for the year ended 30 June 20X4 fell below budget and introduced measures in the year end 30 June 20X5 to improve the situation. These included:

- cutting prices

- extending credit facilities to customers

- leasing additional machinery in order to be able to manufacture more products.

The directors' are now reviewing the results for the year ended 30 June 20X5.

Calculate the ratios for and comment upon the profitability, liquidity/efficiency and financial position of Neville for 20X4 and 20X5.

Chapter summary

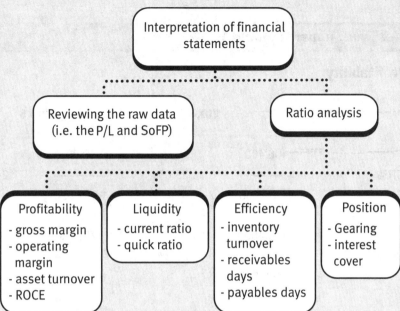

Test your understanding answers

Test your understanding 1

Profitability

	20X4		20X5	
GP%	$\dfrac{406,400}{1,159,850}$	35.0%	$\dfrac{340,995}{1,391,820}$	24.5%
OP%	$\dfrac{235,450}{1,159,850}$	20.3%	$\dfrac{179,545}{1,391,765}$	12.9%
ROCE	$\dfrac{235,450}{490,520}$	48.0%	$\dfrac{179,545}{607,765}$	29.5%
Asset turnover	$\dfrac{1,159,850}{490,520}$	2.36	$\dfrac{1,391,820}{607,765}$	2.29

The revenue of the entity has increased by 20% on last year. It would therefore appear that the strategy of cutting prices and extending credit facilities has attracted customers and generated an increase in revenue.

Despite this increase, the operating profit margin has declined from 20.3% to 12.9%.

There are several possible reasons behind this deterioration:

- the reduction in sales prices
- increased leasing costs
- increased depreciation due to the revaluation and additional purchases of non-current assets
- increased irrecoverable debt due to the extended credit facilities.

The return on capital employed has dropped significantly from 48% to 29.5%. The possible reasons for this decline include:

- the reduction in operating profit margins
- the revaluation of non-current assets, which would increase capital employed.

Liquidity/efficiency

	20X4		20X5	
Inventory days	$\dfrac{88{,}760 \times 365}{753{,}480}$	43 days	$\dfrac{109{,}400 \times 365}{1{,}050{,}825}$	38 days
Receivables days	$\dfrac{206{,}550 \times 365}{1{,}159{,}850}$	65 days	$\dfrac{419{,}455 \times 365}{1{,}391{,}820}$	110 days
Payables days	$\dfrac{179{,}590 \times 365}{753{,}450}$	87 days	$\dfrac{345{,}480 \times 365}{1{,}050{,}825}$	120 days
Current ratio	$\dfrac{390{,}710}{241{,}590}$	1.6:1	$\dfrac{528{,}855}{430{,}680}$	1.2:1
Quick ratio	$\dfrac{301{,}950}{241{,}590}$	1.2:1	$\dfrac{419{,}455}{430{,}680}$	1:1

The company's results show a deteriorating liquidity position; both the current and quick ratios have worsened. The main reasons for this appear to be:

- the reduction in cash and consequent increase in overdrafts
- the increase in trade payables

The overall cause could be the extension of credit facilities to customers. Credit customers are taking an extra 45 days to pay on average. As a result, Neville appear to have less cash to pay their suppliers and they are having to use up their cash resources and overdraft facilities.

Receivables days have increased from an appropriate level of 65 days to 110 days. Although the benefits of this strategy have been shown by the increase in revenue, it would seem that Neville have now allowed customers too much credit. It would be recommended that receivables days should be reduced to closer to 90 days.

The large increase in payables days could lead to problems, unless suppliers have specifically agreed to offer Neville extended repayment deadlines. If not, then they may refuse to sell goods to Neville on a credit basis.

Financial position

	20X4		20X5	
Interest cover	$\dfrac{235,450}{14,000}$	16.8	$\dfrac{179,545}{10,000}$	17.9
Gearing*	$\dfrac{83,100}{490,520}$	16.9%	$\dfrac{61,600}{607,765}$	10.1%

* Gearing has been calculated using the 'debt/debt + equity' formula.

Both the gearing level and the interest cover have fallen. The key reason appears to be the reduction in loans during the year.

It appears as though Neville have used cash to repay their loan finance. This does not appear to be a sensible decision because the reduction in cash within the business has led to an increase in expensive overdrafts and an increase in payables days, which may upset suppliers.

Both the gearing and the interest cover were strong in 20X4 (i.e. the interest cover was more than adequate and the gearing level appeared to be low). This indicated that Neville could afford to sustain its loans without significant penalty. It is now using an overdraft facility which will carry a much higher interest charge than long-term loans.

To improve its position Neville could seek further long terms loans. It is not a risky business from a gearing position and it has plenty of assets to use as security for any lenders.

21

Consolidated statement of financial position

Chapter learning objectives

Upon completion of this chapter you will be able to:

- define and describe the following in the context of group accounting
    - (i)   parent
    - (ii) subsidiary
    - (iii) control
    - (iv) consolidated or group financial statements
    - (v)   non-controlling interest
    - (vi) trade/simple investment
- describe the components of and prepare a consolidated statement of financial position or extracts thereof, including the following adjustments:
    - (i)   fair values
    - (ii) intra-group trading
    - (iii) unrealised profits
    - (iv) acquisition part-way through the year
- calculate goodwill using the full goodwill method.

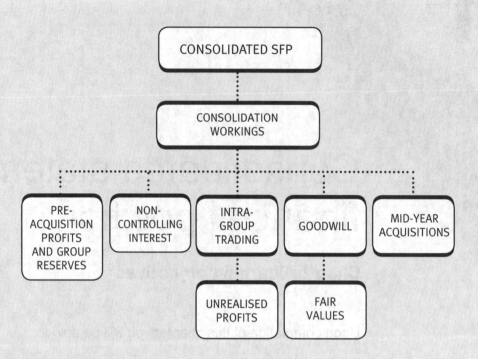

1 What is a group?

A group exists where one entity, the **parent**, has **control** over another entity, the **subsidiary**.

In accordance with IFRS 10 Consolidated Financial Statements control consists of three components:

(1) Power over the investee, which is normally exercised through the majority of voting rights (i.e. owning more than 50% of the equity shares).

(2) Exposure or rights to variable returns from involvement (e.g. a dividend).

(3) The ability to use power over the investee to affect the amount of investor returns. This is regarded as a crucial determinant in deciding whether or not control is exercised.

An **investor** is an entity which owns a shareholding in another entity.

An **investee** is an entity in which another entity has a shareholding.

2 Requirement to prepare consolidated financial statements

If one company controls another then IFRS 10 requires that a single set of consolidated financial statements be prepared to reflect the financial performance and position of the group as one combined entity. This reflects the fact that the investment of the parents' shareholders is now tied up in more than one entity. Their returns and the stability of their investment now reflect the performance and position of both entities.

In order to make informed decisions about their investment, shareholders would need to read and interpret the financial statements of both companies. If there were more than one subsidiary company this could become quite complex for shareholders. To this end one set of financial statements is prepared where the revenues, expenses, assets and liabilities of the parent and subsidiary are combined for ease of understanding and analysis.

3 The basic method of preparing a consolidated statement of financial position

(1) The assets and liabilities of the parent and the subsidiary are added together on a line-by-line basis.

(2) The investment in the subsidiary included in the parent's SoFP is replaced by a goodwill asset in the consolidated SoFP.

(3) The share capital and share premium balances of the parent and subsidiary are not added together; only the parent entity balances for share capital and share premium are included in the consolidated SoFP. This reflects the fact that the consolidated SoFP includes all of the assets and liabilities under the control of the parent entity.

(4) The amount attributable to non-controlling interests is calculated and shown separately on the face of the consolidated SoFP.

(5) The group share of the subsidiary's post-acquisition retained earnings is calculated and included as part of group retained earnings.

Non-controlling interests

Often when a parent entity controls a subsidiary it is due to the fact that it control voting rights (i.e. it owns more than 50% of the voting share capital). It is possible that it does not own all the shares, which means there are other, minority, shareholders. These are known as non-controlling interests.

For example: if the parent owns 80% of the ordinary share capital it is likely to have control due to the majority of voting rights they control (unless proven otherwise). The other 20% of shareholders are the non-controlling interests.

4 The mechanics of consolidation

You must be familiar with the following standard workings.

(W1) Establish the group structure

This is where you establish whether there is a parent-subsidiary relationship (i.e. does the parent have control?). You will need to identify the percentage shareholding of the parent and the non-controlling interest and the date the shares were acquired.

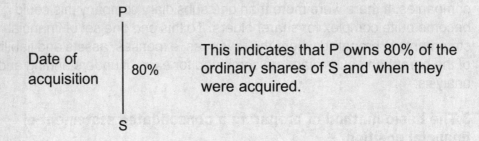

P

Date of acquisition | 80%

This indicates that P owns 80% of the ordinary shares of S and when they were acquired.

S

(W2) Net assets of subsidiary

	At date of acquisition	At the reporting date
	$	$
Share capital	X	X
Share premium	X	X
Revaluation surplus	X	X
Retained earnings	X	X
	—	—
	X	X
	—	—

The total of share capital and share premium from the subsidiary SoFP should be unchanged at both the date of acquisition and the reporting date.

(W3) Goodwill

	$
Fair value (FV) of consideration paid	X
FV of non-controlling interest (NCI) at acquisition	X
	—
	X
Less:	
FV of net assets at acquisition (W2)	(X)
	—
Goodwill on acquisition	X

(W4) **Non-controlling interest**

FV of NCI at acquisition (as in W3)	X
NCI share of post-acquisition reserves (W2)	X
	X

(W5) **Group retained earnings**

	$
P's retained earnings (100%)	X
P's % of sub's post-acquisition retained earnings	X
	X

5 Goodwill

The value of an entity will normally exceed the value of its net assets. The difference is **goodwill**. This represents assets not included in the statement of financial position of the acquired entity such as the reputation of the business, brand and the experience of employees.

Goodwill arises because the investor would rather buy a ready-made and established business than buy the individual components and set up the business themselves from nothing.

Illustration 1 – H Group

In order to illustrate the basic principles involved in a consolidated statement of financial position we will use the following example of H group, performing each calculation in turn and finally compiling the consolidated statement of financial position. Note that, in this illustration, H owns all of the shares issued by S and therefore there is no non-controlling interest to account for.

The statements of financial position of H and S as at 31 December 20X8 were as follows.

	H $	S $
Non-current assets:		
Property, plant & equipment	85,000	18,000
Investments:		
Shares in S	60,000	
	145,000	
Current assets	160,000	84,000
	305,000	102,000
Equity:		
Ordinary $1 shares	65,000	20,000
Share premium	35,000	10,000
Retained earnings	70,000	25,000
	170,000	55,000
Current liabilities	135,000	47,000
	305,000	102,000

H acquired a 100% holding in S on 1 January 20X8. At that date S's retained earnings were $15,000.

Prepare the consolidated statement of financial position for the H group as at 31 December 20X8.

Solution to Illustration 1

Group statement of financial position of H group as at 31 December 20X8.

		$
Non-current assets:		
Goodwill on acquisition (W3)		15,000
Property, plant & equipment	($85,000 + $18,000)	103,000
		118,000
Current assets	($160,000 + $84,000)	244,000
		362,000

Equity:		
Ordinary $1 shares (H only)		65,000
Share premium (H only)		35,000
Group retained earnings (W5)		80,000
		180,000
Current liabilities	($135,000 + $47,000)	182,000
		362,000

(W1) Group structure

H

| 100% owned

S

(W2) Net assets of S

	At date of acquisition	At reporting date
	$	$
Share capital	20,000	20,000
Share premium	10,000	10,000
Retained earnings	15,000	25,000
Net assets	45,000	55,000

(W3) Goodwill

	$
FV of consideration paid	60,000
FV of NCI at acquisition	N/A
	60,000
Less:	
FV of net assets at acquisition (W2)	(45,000)
Goodwill on acquisition (to SoFP)	**15,000**

(W4) **Non-controlling interest** – not applicable as H owns 100% of the issued share capital of S.

(W5) **Group retained earnings**

	$
H retained earnings per SoFP	70,000
Group share of S post-acquisition retained earnings (100% × ($25,000 – $15,000))	10,000
Group retained earnings at reporting date (to SOFP)	**80,000**

Fair value

When calculating goodwill and non-controlling interests the fair value method is used. This means that amounts are not calculated merely at their reported carrying amount.

Goodwill is the difference between the amount paid to acquire a controlling shareholding in another entity and the fair value of the assets acquired. However, the amount paid is rarely a simple cash transaction. With large entities, shares are often purchased for cash plus an additional payment that is deferred until some future date. Often the deferred payments are contingent upon achieving certain performance targets. Alternatively shares are exchanged, i.e. an entity purchases shares in a subsidiary in exchange for shares in itself. All of these elements of the 'consideration' must be valued in today's monetary terms as at the date of acquisition.

The value of the shareholding must also be considered. The net assets are usually calculated by totalling the assets reported on the SoFP and deducting liabilities. However, we have seen already that the book or carrying amounts often do not reflect their true market value. This is most common with property, plant and equipment. Property often appreciates in value, whereas in the financial statements of some entities it is stated at historic depreciated cost. Therefore the fair value of all assets and liabilities must be determined.

Fair value adjustments are explained in greater detail later in this chapter.

Illustration 2 – D Group

In order to illustrate the various workings involved in a consolidated statement of financial position we will use the example of D group, performing each calculation in turn and finally compiling the consolidated statement of financial position.

The statements of financial position of D and J as at 31 December 20X8.

	D $	J $
Non-current assets:		
Property, plant & equipment	85,000	18,000
Investments:		
Shares in J	60,000	
	145,000	
Current assets	160,000	84,000
	305,000	102,000
Equity:		
Ordinary $1 shares	65,000	20,000
Share premium	35,000	10,000
Retained earnings	70,000	25,000
	170,000	55,000
Current liabilities	135,000	47,000
	305,000	102,000

D acquired an 80% holding in J on 1 January 20X8. At this date J's retained earnings stood at $20,000. On this date, the fair value of the 20% non-controlling shareholding in J was $12,500.

Calculate the goodwill arising on the acquisition of J.

Solution to Illustration 2

(W1) Group structure

D

1 Jan X8 | 80%

J

(W2) Net assets of J

	At date of acquisition	At reporting date
	$	$
Share capital	20,000	20,000
Share premium	10,000	10,000
Retained earnings	20,000	25,000
Net assets	50,000	55,000

(W3) Goodwill

	$
FV of consideration paid	60,000
FV of NCI at acquisition	12,500
	72,500
Less:	
FV of net assets at acquisition (W2)	(50,000)
Goodwill on acquisition (to SoFP)	**22,500**

Test your understanding 1

Daniel acquired 80% of the ordinary share capital of Craig on 31 December 20X6 for $78,000. At this date the fair value of the net assets of Craig were $85,000. NCI is valued using the fair value method and the fair value of the NCI at the acquisition date was $19,000.

What goodwill arises on the acquisition?

6 Accounting treatment of non-controlling interests

Don't forget that where a group exists the parent controls the subsidiary, so the accounts of those two entities are consolidated. The non-controlling interests represent the 'other' shareholders of the subsidiary, where the parent owns less than 100% of the ordinary shares.

In the consolidated statement of financial position all of the assets and liabilities of the parent and subsidiary are added together at the reporting date. They are **NOT APPORTIONED.** On the lower part of the consolidated SoFP an amount is recognised that allocates a portion (i.e. their share) of the net assets to the non-controlling interests. This effectively recognises their share of the value of the business.

Illustration 3 – Non-controlling interest

Using the information for D Group from Illustration 2, calculate the non-controlling interest to include in the statement of financial position at 31 December 20X8.

Solution to Illustration 3

(W4) **Non-controlling interests**

FV of NCI at acquisition (as in W3)	12,500
NCI share of post-acquisition reserves (W2)	1,000
(20% × (55,000 – 50,000))	
	———
	13,500
	———

7 Group retained earnings and other components of equity

Pre-acquisition profits are the retained earnings of the subsidiary which exist at the date when it is acquired. These profits belong to the previous shareholders as they were earned during their period of ownership. The new parent cannot lay claim to these profits so they are excluded from group retained earnings.

Post-acquisition profits are those profits recognised in retained earnings by the subsidiary at the year-end but earned since the new parent purchased its shareholding. As these were earned during the ownership of the new parent an appropriate percentage (based upon the parent's % ownership) can be recognised in group retained earnings.

In the same way that retained earnings are allocated between pre- and post-acquisition elements, the same also applies to revaluation surplus if it is part of the subsidiary's statement of financial position. Normally. you will be provided with the revaluation surplus value at the date of acquisition, with any amount in excess of this regarded as a post-acquisition movement.

The mechanics of accounting for the post-acquisition increase in revaluation surplus are similar to accounting for the increase in retained earnings. If there has been no change in the revaluation surplus balance between the date of acquisition and the reporting date of the statement of financial position you are dealing with, it is treated as a pre-acquisition balance.

If the balance on revaluation surplus has increased between the date of acquisition and the reporting date of the statement of financial position you are dealing with, the increase is treated in a similar manner to the increase in retained earnings. The group share of the increase is included in the consolidated statement of financial position as a separate component of equity (don't include it as part of group retained earnings). The non-controlling interest share of the increase is allocated to the non-controlling interest shareholders within (W4) of the standard consolidation workings.

Illustration 4 – Retained earnings

Using the information for D Group from Illustration 2, calculate the group retained earnings to include in the group statement of financial position at 31 December 20X8.

Solution to Illustration 4

(W5) **Group retained earnings**

100% D's retained earnings	70,000
80% J post-acquisition retained earnings (80% × $(55,000 – 50,000 (W2))	4,000
	74,000

Illustration 5 – The consolidated SoFP

Using the information from Illustration 2 and the consequent calculations performed, prepare the consolidated statement of financial position of D Group as at 31 December 20X8.

Solution to Illustration 5

D consolidated statement of financial position as at 31 December 20X8

	$
Non-current assets	
Goodwill (W3)	22,500
PPE	
(85,000 + 18,000)	103,000
Current assets	
(160,000 + 84,000)	244,000
	———
	369,500
	———
Equity	
Share capital	65,000
Share premium	35,000
Group retained earnings (W5)	74,000
Non-controlling interest (W4)	13,500
	———
	187,500
Current liabilities	
(135,000 + 47,000)	182,000
	———
	369,500
	———

8 Fair values

Fair value of consideration and net assets

To ensure that an accurate figure is calculated for goodwill:

- the consideration paid for a subsidiary must be accounted for at fair value

- the subsidiary's identifiable assets and liabilities acquired must be accounted for at their fair values.

IFRS 13 para 9 defines fair value as:

"The price that would be received to sell an asset or paid to transfer a liability in an orderly transaction between market participants at the measurement date." i.e. it is an exit price.

The need to account on a fair value basis reflects the fact that the statement of financial position often values items (mainly non-current assets) at their historic cost less depreciation. This could mean the book value of assets (or carrying amount) is significantly different to their current market values, particularly in the case of assets that tend to appreciate in value, such as land and buildings.

Fair values

The subsidiary's identifiable assets and liabilities are included in the consolidated accounts at their fair values for the following reasons.

- Consolidated accounts are prepared from the perspective of the group, rather than from the perspectives of the individual entities. The book values of the subsidiary's assets and liabilities are largely irrelevant, because the consolidated accounts must reflect their cost to the group (i.e. to the parent), not their original cost to the subsidiary. The cost to the group is their fair value at the date of acquisition.

- Purchased goodwill is the difference between the value of an acquired entity and the aggregate of the fair values of that entity's identifiable assets and liabilities. If fair values are not used, the value of goodwill will be meaningless.

How to include fair values in consolidation workings

(1) Adjust both columns of W2 to bring the net assets to fair value at acquisition and reporting date. This will ensure that the fair value of net assets is carried through to the goodwill and non-controlling interest calculations.

	At acquisition $000	At reporting date $000
Ordinary share capital	X	X
Share premium	X	X
Revaluation surplus	X	X
Retained earnings	X	X
Fair value adjustments	X	X
	X	X

The fair value adjustment represents the amount required to adjust the relevant item from its current carrying amount in the SoFP to its identified fair value.

Note that the total of issued share capital and share premium balances of the subsidiary will be the same at the date of acquisition and at the reporting date.

If you have different values for issued share capital at these dates, either or both figures will be wrong. Similarly, if the subsidiary has a share premium account, the share premium carrying amount should be the same at both dates.

(2) At the reporting date make the adjustment on the face of the SoFP when adding across assets and liabilities.

Illustration 6 – Fair value adjustments

Hazelnut acquired 80% of the share capital of Peppermint on 1 January 20X3 for cash consideration of $1 million. At the date of acquisition, Peppermint had retained earnings of $125,000 and a revaluation surplus of $100,000.

Below are the statements of financial position of Hazelnut and Peppermint as at 31 December 20X4:

	Hazelnut	Peppermint
	$000	$000
Investment in Peppermint at cost	1,000	
Property, plant & equipment	5,500	1,500
Current assets:		
Inventory	550	100
Receivables	400	200
Cash	200	50
	———	———
	7,650	1,850
	———	———
Share capital	1,800	400
Revaluation surplus	200	100
Retained earnings	1,400	300
	———	———
	3,400	800
Non-current liabilities	3,000	400
Current liabilities	1,250	650
	———	———
	7,650	1,850
	———	———

> At acquisition the fair value of Peppermint's plant exceeded its carrying amount by $200,000. At the date of acquisition, the fair value of the 20% non-controlling interest in Peppermint was $380,000.
>
> **Calculate the fair value of the net assets of Peppermint at the date of acquisition and at the reporting date (i.e. Working 2).**

Solution to Illustration 6

(W2) **Net assets of Peppermint**

	At date of acquisition $000	At reporting date $000
Share capital	400	400
Revaluation surplus	100	100
Retained earnings	125	300
Plant fair value adjustment	200	200
	825	1,000

Test your understanding 2

Prepare the consolidated statement of financial position of Hazelnut Group as at 31 December 20X4. Include all relevant workings.

9 Intra-group trading

Types of intra-group trading

P and S may well trade with each leading to the following potential issues to be dealt with:

- receivables and payables in P and S that effectively cancel each other out

- dividends paid by the subsidiary recognised as income by the parent. Similarly, if a dividend is paid by one entity and received by the other, the net effect of this to the group is zero.

- unrealised profits on sales of inventory between the parent and the subsidiary. So that you can understand this concept consider the following question: can you make a profit if your right hand sells goods to your left hand? Obviously not and for the same reason a group cannot make profit when one part of the group sells goods to another part.

Current accounts

If P and S trade with each other then this will probably be done on credit leading to:

- a receivables (current) account in one entity's SoFP
- a payables (current) account in the other entity's SoFP.

These amounts should not be consolidated because the group would end up with a receivable to itself and a payable to itself - receivables and payables would consequently be overstated in the group SoFP.

They are therefore cancelled (contra'd) against each other on consolidation.

Illustration 7

Statements of financial position of P and S as at 30 June 20X8 are given below:

	P $	S $
Non-current assets:		
Land	4,500	2,500
Plant & equipment	2,400	1,750
Investments	8,000	–
	14,900	4,250
Current assets		
Inventory	3,200	900
Receivables	1,400	650
Bank	600	150
	5,200	1,700
	20,100	5,950

	$	$
Ordinary share capital of 50c each	5,000	1,000
Retained earnings	8,300	3,150
	13,300	4,150
Non-current liabilities	4,000	500
Current liabilities	2,800	1,300
	20,100	5,950

P acquired 75% of S on 1 July 20X5 when the balance on S's retained earnings was $1,150. P paid $3,500 for its investment in the share capital of S.

At the reporting date P recorded a payable to S of $400. This agreed to the corresponding amount in S's financial statements.

At the date of acquisition it was determined that S's land, carried at cost of $2,500, had a fair value of $3,750. At that date, S's plant was determined to have a fair value of $500 in excess of its carrying amount. The fair values had not been recorded by S.

The P group uses the fair value method to value the non-controlling interest which was $1,100 at the date of acquisition.

Calculate the consolidated receivables and payables figures of P group as at 30 June 20X8.

Solution to Illustration 7

Receivables = $1,400 + $650 – **$400** = $1,650

Payables = $2,800 + $1,300 – **$400** = $3,700

Test your understanding 3

Prepare the consolidated statement of financial position of P group, based on the preceding illustration, as at 30 June 20X8.

10 Unrealised profit

Profits made by members of a group on transactions with other group members are:

- recognised in the accounts of the individual entities concerned, but
- in terms of the group as a whole, such profits are unrealised and must be eliminated from the consolidated accounts (remember you cannot make profits if your right hand sells goods to your left!).

Such unrealised profits arise when one group entity sells good to another group entity and those goods have not been sold on externally by the end of the year. They are therefore known as unrealised profits held in inventory.

Intra-group trading and unrealised profit in inventory

When one group entity sells goods to another a number of adjustments may be needed.

- Current accounts must be cancelled (see earlier in this chapter).
- Where goods are still held by one entity at the reporting date, any unrealised profit must be cancelled.
- Inventory must be included at original cost to the group.

Adjustments for unrealised profit in inventory

(1) Determine the value of closing inventory still held within the group at the reporting date that are the result of intra-group trading.

(2) Use either the profit mark-up or sales margin to calculate how much of that value represents profit earned by the selling entity. The question will identify whether goods have been sold subject to either a mark-up or margin as appropriate.

(3) Make one of the following adjustments:

If the seller is the parent, the profit element is included in that entity's accounts and relates entirely to the controlling group.

Adjustment required:

Dr Group retained earnings (deduct the profit in W5)

Cr Group inventory

If the seller is the subsidiary, the profit element is included in the subsidiary's accounts and relates partly to the group, partly to non-controlling interests (if any).

Adjustment required:

Dr Subsidiary retained earnings (deduct the profit in W2 – at reporting date)

Cr Group inventory

Unrealised profit adjustment alternative

The simple adjustment when the seller is the subsidiary is to adjust the subsidiary's retained earnings in working 2. However if you are not preparing all the workings an alternative method is as follows:

Dr Group retained earnings (group %) – W5

Dr Non-controlling interests (NCI %) – W4

Cr Group inventory (100%)

Illustration 8

H acquired 90% of the ordinary share capital of S on 1 January 20X2 when the retained earnings of S were $5,000. Statements of financial position at 31 December 20X3 were as follows:

	H		S	
	$000	$000	$000	$000
Non-current assets:				
Property, plant & equipment		100		30
Investment in S at cost		34		
		134		30
Current assets:				
Inventory	90		20	
Receivables	110		25	
Bank	10		5	
		210		50
		344		80

KAPLAN PUBLISHING

Equity:	$000	$000
Share capital of $1 each	15	5
Retained earnings	159	31
	174	36
Non-current liabilities	120	28
Current liabilities	50	16
	344	80

S sold goods to H at a transfer price of $18,000, including a mark-up of 50%. Two-thirds of those goods remained in inventory at the year-end. The current accounts in H and S stood at $22,000 on that day.

The H group uses the fair value method to value the non-controlling interest. The fair value of the non-controlling interest at acquisition was $4,000.

Calculate the unrealised profit adjustment required for the consolidated statement of financial position of H Group. Show the relevant correcting journal.

Solution to Illustration 8

Provision for unrealised profit or 'PURP'

Sales	$18,000	150%
COS		100%
Gross profit	$6,000	50%

$\frac{50}{150} \times 18000 = 6000.$

The total profit made on the transaction was $6,000. If two-thirds of the goods remain in inventory at the end of the year, that means 4,000 of unrealised profit remains within the group ($6,000 × 2/3).

Double entry adjustment when the subsidiary sells to the parent:

Dr S's retained earnings (W2) $4,000

Cr Group inventory $4,000

Note that this method still needs to account for the allocation of the adjustment for unrealised profit between the parent and subsidiary. This will be achieved when accounting for the respective group and non-controlling interest share of the movement in net assets i.e. when compiling workings (4) and (5) for a group statement of financial position. This is normally the approach to adopt when answering a long form question.

Alternative:

Dr Group retained earnings (90%) $3,600

Dr Non-controlling interests (10%) $400

Cr Group inventory $4,000

Note that the alternative has allocated part of the adjustment for unrealised profit to the non-controlling interest, based upon their shareholding. This is usually the approach to adopt when answering multiple-choice or objective test questions.

Test your understanding 4

Prepare the consolidated statement of financial position for the H Group, based on the preceding illustration, as at 31 December 20X3.

11 Mid-year acquisitions

Calculation of reserves at date of acquisition

If a parent entity acquires a subsidiary mid-year, the net assets must be calculated at the date of acquisition.

The net assets at acquisition can be calculated as the net assets at the start of the subsidiary's financial year plus the retained for part of the year up to the date of acquisition, together with any fair value adjustments at the date of acquisition.

To calculate this, it is normally assumed that S's profit after tax has accrued evenly throughout the year.

Illustration 9

Consolidated Statement of Financial Position

On 1 May 20X7 K acquired 60% of S, paying $76,000 cash. The summarised statements of financial position of the two entities at 30 November 20X7 were:

	K $	S $
Non-current assets:		
Property, plant & equipment	138,000	115,000
Investments	98,000	–
Current assets:		
Inventory	15,000	17,000
Receivables	19,000	20,000
Cash	2,000	–
	272,000	152,000
Share capital of $1 each	50,000	40,000
Retained earnings	189,000	69,000
	239,000	109,000
Current liabilities:	33,000	43,000
	272,000	152,000

The following information is relevant:

(1) At 30 November 20X7, the inventory of S included goods purchased at a cost of $8,000 from K at cost plus 25%. None of the goods had been sold on by S by the reporting date.

(2) The K Group values the non-controlling interest using the fair value method. At the date of acquisition the fair value of the 40% non-controlling interest was $50,000.

(3) S earned a profit after tax for the year of $9,000 in the year ended 30 November 20X7.

Calculate group retained earnings of K Group as at 30 November 20X7.

Solution to Illustration 9

Net assets

	Acquisition date $	Reporting date $
Share capital of $1 shares	40,000	40,000
Retained earnings	63,750	69,000
	103,750	109,000

RE @ acq'n (balance) (ß)	63,750
Post-acq profit (7/12 × 9,000)	5,250
RE @ reporting date	69,000

PURP – Inventory

Profit in inventory (25/125 × $8,000) = $1,600

Group retained earnings

	$
100% K	189,000
PURP	(1,600)
60% S post-acq profit	
(60% × (109,000 – 103,750 (W2)))	3,150
	190,550

Test your understanding 5

Prepare the consolidated statement of financial position of K Group, based upon the preceding illustration, as at 30 November 20X7.

Test your understanding 6

The following statements of financial position were extracted from the books of two companies at 31 December 20X9.

	Derek $	Clive $
Non-current assets:		
Property, plant & equipment	75,000	11,000
Investments (shares in Clive)	27,000	
	102,000	
Current assets	214,000	33,000
	316,000	44,000
Equity:		
Share capital	80,000	4,000
Share premium	20,000	6,000
Retained earnings	40,000	9,000
	140,000	19,000
Current liabilities	176,000	25,000
	316,000	44,000

Derek acquired all of the share capital of Clive on 1 January 20X9. The retained earnings of Clive were $2,000 at the date of acquisition.

Prepare the consolidated statement of financial position of Derek as at 31 December 20X9.

Chapter summary

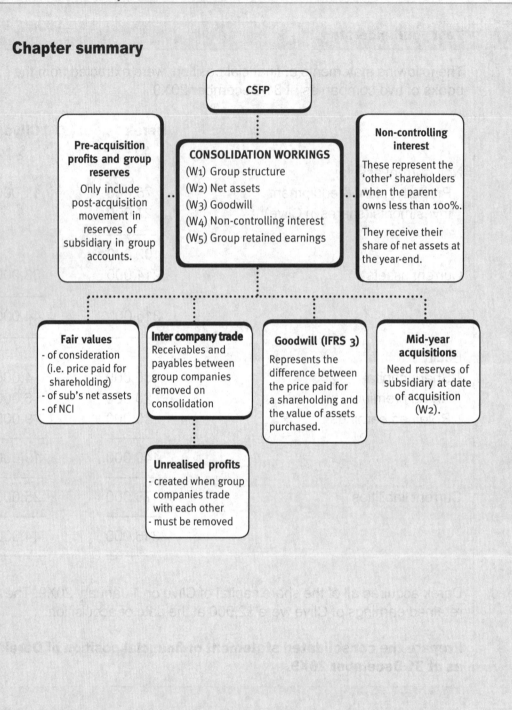

CSFP

Pre-acquisition profits and group reserves

Only include post-acquisition movement in reserves of subsidiary in group accounts.

CONSOLIDATION WORKINGS

(W1) Group structure
(W2) Net assets
(W3) Goodwill
(W4) Non-controlling interest
(W5) Group retained earnings

Non-controlling interest

These represent the 'other' shareholders when the parent owns less than 100%.

They receive their share of net assets at the year-end.

Fair values

- of consideration (i.e. price paid for shareholding)
- of sub's net assets
- of NCI

Inter company trade

Receivables and payables between group companies removed on consolidation

Goodwill (IFRS 3)

Represents the difference between the price paid for a shareholding and the value of assets purchased.

Mid-year acquisitions

Need reserves of subsidiary at date of acquisition (W2).

Unrealised profits

- created when group companies trade with each other
- must be removed

Test your understanding answers

Test your understanding 1

	$
Fair value of consideration	78,000
FV of NCI at acquisition	19,000
	97,000
Less:	
Fair value of net assets at acquisition	(85,000)
Goodwill on acquisition	12,000

Test your understanding 2

Hazelnut consolidated statement of financial position at 31 December 20X4

	$000
Goodwill (W3)	555
Property, plant & equipment (5,500 + 1,500 + 200)	7,200
Current assets:	
Inventory (550 + 100)	650
Receivables (400 + 200)	600
Cash (200 + 50)	250
	9,255

	$000
Share capital	1,800
Revaluation surplus	200
Retained earnings (W5)	1,540
	3,540
Non-controlling interest (W4)	415
	3,955
Non-current liabilities (3,000 + 400)	3,400
Current liabilities (1,250 + 650)	1,900
	9,255

Note that the revaluation surplus of the subsidiary is a pre-acquisition balance and is therefore not part of group revaluation surplus at the reporting date.

Workings

(W1) Group structure

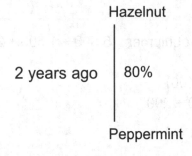

Hazelnut

2 years ago | 80%

Peppermint

(W2) Net assets of Peppermint

	At date of acquisition $000	At reporting date $000
Share capital	400	400
Revaluation surplus	100	100
Retained earnings	125	300
Fair value adjustment: plant	200	200
	825	1,000

Note that, as there is no movement in revaluation surplus balance, all of the movement in net assets relates to retained earnings.

(W3) Goodwill

	$000
Fair value of consideration	
Cash paid	1,000
FV of NCI at acquisition	380
	1,380
Less:	
Fair value of net assets at acquisition (W2)	(825)
Goodwill on acquisition	555

(W4) Non-controlling interest

	$000
FV of NCI at acquisition (as in W3)	380
NCI share of post-acquisition reserves	35
(20% × (1,000 – 825) (W2))	
	415

(W5) Group retained earnings

	$000
Hazelnut retained earnings	1,400
Peppermint (80% × (1,000 – 825))	140
	1,540

Test your understanding 3

Consolidated statement of financial position as at 30 June 20X8

	$
Non-current assets	
Goodwill (W3)	700
Land (4,500 + 2,500 + 1,250 (W2))	8,250
Plant & equipment (2,400 + 1,750 + 500 (W2))	4,650
Investments (8,000 – 3,500 (cost of investment in S))	4,500
	18,100
Current Assets	
Inventory (3,200 + 900)	4,100
Receivables (1,400 + 650 – 400 (inter-co))	1,650
Bank (600 + 150)	750
	24,600
Equity	
Share capital of 50c each	5,000
Retained earnings (W5)	9,800
Non-controlling Interest (W4)	1,600
	16,400
Non-current liabilities (4,000 + 500)	4,500
Current liabilities (2,800 + 1,300 – 400 (inter-co))	3,700
	24,600

Workings

(W1) Group structure

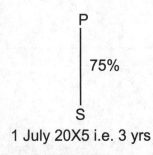

P

75%

S

1 July 20X5 i.e. 3 yrs

(W2) **Net assets**

	Acquisition date	Reporting date
	$	$
Share capital	1,000	1,000
Retained earnings	1,150	3,150
FV Adj Land (3,750 – 2,500)	1,250	1,250
FV Adj Plant	500	500
	3,900	5,900

(W3) **Goodwill**

	$
Fair value of consideration	3,500
FV of NCI at acquisition	1,100
	4,600
Less:	
Fair value of net assets at acquisition (W2)	(3,900)
Goodwill on acquisition	700

(W4) **Non-controlling interest**

	$
FV of NCI at acquisition (as in W3)	1,100
NCI share of post-acquisition reserves (W2)	500
(25% × (5,900 – 3,900))	
	1,600

(W5) **Group retained earnings**

	$
100% P	8,300
75% of S post-acq retained earnings	
(75% × (5,900 – 3,900))	1,500
	9,800

Test your understanding 4

H - Consolidated statement of financial position as at 31 December 20X3

Non-current assets		$000
Goodwill (W3)		28.0
Property, plant & equipment (100 + 30)		130.0
		158.0
Current Assets		
Inventory (90 + 20 – 4 (W6))	106.0	
Receivables (110 + 25 – 22 intra-co receivable)	113.0	
Bank (10 + 5)	15.0	
		234.0
		392.0

Equity		$000
Share capital of $1		15.0
Group retained earnings (W5)		178.8
NCI (W4)		6.2
		200.0
Non-current liabilities (120 + 28)		148.0
Current liabilities (50 + 16 – 22 intra-co payable)		44.0
		392.0

Workings

(W1) Group structure

```
H
|   90%    01/01/X2
S
```

(W2) Net assets

	Acquisition date $000	Reporting date $000
Share capital	5.0	5.0
Retained earnings	5.0	31.0
PURP (W6)		(4.0)
	10.0	32.0

(W3) Goodwill

	$000
Fair value of consideration	34.0
FV of NCI at acquisition	4.0
	38.0
Less:	
Fair value of net assets at acquisition (W2)	(10.0)
Goodwill on acquisition	28.0

(W4) Non-controlling interest

	$000
FV of NCI at acquisition (as in W3)	4.0
NCI share of post-acquisition reserves (W2)	2.2
$(10\% \times (32 - 10))$	
	6.2

(W5) Group reserves

	$000
100% H	159.0
90% S post-acq	
$(90\% \times (\$32 - \$10 \text{ (W2)}))$	19.8
	178.8

(W6) PURP

	$000	Percentage
Sales	18	150
COS		100
Gross profit	6	50

× 2 / 3
PURP = $4,000

Test your understanding 5

Consolidated statement of financial position as at 30 November 20X7

	$
Non-current assets	
Goodwill (W3)	22,250
PPE (138,000 + 115,000)	253,000
Investments (98,000 – 76,000)	22,000
	297,250
Current Assets	
Inventory (15,000 + 17,000 – 1,600 (W6))	30,400
Receivables (19,000 + 20,000)	39,000
Cash	2,000
	368,650
Share capital	50,000
Group retained earnings (W5)	190,550
Non-controlling Interest (W4)	52,100
	292,650
Current liabilities (33,000 + 43,000)	76,000
	368,650

Workings

(W1) Group structure

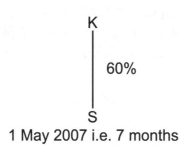

K

60%

S

1 May 2007 i.e. 7 months

(W2) Net assets

	Acquisition date	Reporting date
	$	$
Share capital	40,000	40,000
Retained earnings	63,750	69,000
	103,750	109,000
RE @ acq'n (balance) (ß)		63,750
Post-acq profit (7/12 × 9,000)		5,250
RE @ reporting date		69,000

(W3) Goodwill

	$
Fair value of consideration	76,000
FV of NCI at acquisition	50,000
	126,000
Less:	
Fair value of net assets at acquisition (W2)	(103,750)
Goodwill on acquisition	22,250

(W4) Non-controlling interest

	$
FV of NCI at acquisition (as in W3)	50,000
NCI share of post-acquisition reserves (W2)	2,100
(40% × (109,000 – 103,750))	
	52,100

(W5) Group retained earnings

	$
100% K	189,000
PURP (W6)	(1,600)
60% S post-acq profit	
(60% × (109,000 – 103,750 (W2)))	3,150
	190,550

(W6) PURP – Inventory

Profit in inventory (25/125 × $8,000) $1,600

Test your understanding 6

Consolidated statement of financial position of Derek Group as at 31 December 20X9

	$
Non-current assets:	
Goodwill (W3)	15,000
PPE (75,000 + 11,000)	86,000
Current assets (214,000 + 33,000)	247,000
	348,000
Share capital (Derek only)	80,000
Share premium (Derek only)	20,000
Group retained earnings (W5)	47,000
	147,000
Current liabilities (176,000 + 25,000)	201,000
	348,000

(W1) Establish the group structure

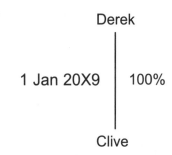

Derek

1 Jan 20X9 | 100%

Clive

(W2) Net assets of Clive

	At date of acquisition	At the reporting date
	$	$
Share capital	4,000	4,000
Reserves:		
Share premium	6,000	6,000
Retained earnings	2,000	9,000
	12,000	19,000

(W3) Goodwill

	$
Fair value of consideration	27,000
Less:	
Fair value of net assets at acquisition (W2)	(12,000)
Goodwill on acquisition	15,000

(W4) NCI

Not applicable to this example as Clive is 100% owned.

(W5) Group retained earnings

	$
Derek retained earnings (100%)	40,000
Clive – group share of post-acquisition retained earnings 100% × (19,000 – 12,000 (W2))	7,000
	47,000

Consolidated statement of profit or loss and associates

Chapter learning objectives

Upon completion of this chapter you will be able to

- describe the components of and prepare a consolidated statement of profit or loss or extracts thereof, including the following adjustments:
  - (i) intra-group trading
  - (ii) unrealised profit
  - (iii) mid-year acquisitions
- define and identify an associate
- describe the principle of equity accounting.

1 Overview

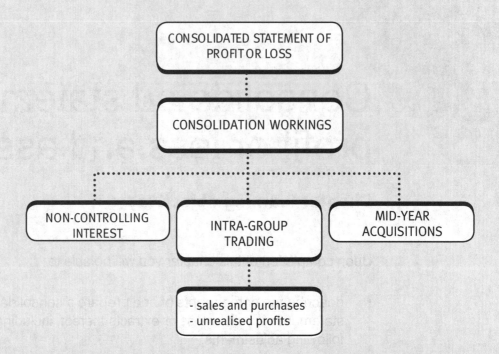

2 Introduction

The consolidated statement of profit or loss presents the financial performance of all group entities (i.e. parent and subsidiaries under common control) in one statement.

3 The basic principles

The consolidated statement of profit or loss follows the same basic principles as the consolidated statement of financial position. There are fewer adjustments, and they often reflect the profit or loss perspective of adjustments already dealt with for the consolidated statement of financial position. The steps for consolidating the statements of profit or loss are as follows:

(1) Add together the revenues and expenses of the parent and the subsidiary.

   If the subsidiary is acquired part-way through the year all the revenues and expenses of the subsidiary must be time apportioned during the consolidation process.

(2) Eliminate intra-group sales and purchases.

(3) Eliminate unrealised profit held in closing inventory relating to intra-group trading.

(4) Calculate the profits attributable to the non-controlling interests.

After profit for the year show split of profit between amounts attributable to the parent's shareholders and the non-controlling interest (to reflect ownership).

4 Non-controlling interest

This is calculated as:

NCI % × subsidiary's profit after tax	X
Less:	
NCI % × PURP (when the sub is the seller only)	(X)
	X

Depreciation on fair value adjustments and impairment of goodwill is not examinable for this syllabus.

Illustration 1

The statements of profit or loss for P and S for the year ended 31 August 20X4 are shown below. P acquired 75% of the ordinary share capital of S several years ago.

	P	S
	$000	$000
Revenue	1,200	400
Cost of sales	(1,080)	(360)
Gross profit	120	40
Administrative expenses	(75)	(30)
Profit before tax	45	10
Tax	(15)	(6)
Profit for the year	30	4

Prepare the consolidated statement of profit or loss for the year.

Solution to Illustration 1

Consolidated statement of profit or loss of P group for the year ended 31 August 20X4

	$000
Revenue (1,200 + 400)	1,600
Cost of sales (1,080 + 360)	(1,440)
	——
Gross profit	160
Administrative expenses (75 + 30)	(105)
	——
Profit before tax	55
Tax (15 + 6)	(21)
	——
Profit for the year	34
	——
Attributable to:	
Group (bal fig)	33
Non-controlling interest (W1)	1
	——
	34
	——

(W1) Non-controlling interest

NCI share of subsidiary profit for the year (NCI% × sub's profit for the year)

25% × $4,000 = $1,000

5 Intra-group trading

Sales and purchases

The effect of intra-group trading must be eliminated from the consolidated statement of profit or loss. Such trading will be included in the sales revenue of one group entity and the purchases of the other.

- Consolidated sales revenue = P's revenue + S's revenue – intra-group sales.

- Consolidated cost of sales = P's COS + S's COS – intra-group purchases.

6 Provision for unrealised profits

Inventory

If any goods traded between the parent and the subsidiary are included in closing inventory, their value must be adjusted to the lower of cost and net realisable value (NRV) to the group (as in the CSFP).

The adjustment for unrealised profit should be shown as an increase to cost of sales (return inventory back to true cost to group and eliminate unrealised profit).

Illustration 2 – PURP

On 1 January 20X9 P acquired 60% of the ordinary shares of S.

The following statements of profit or loss have been produced by P and S for the year ended 31 December 20X9.

	P	S
	$000	$000
Revenue	630	260
Cost of sales	(210)	(105)
Gross profit	420	155
Distribution costs	(90)	(30)
Administration expenses	(60)	(45)
Profit from operations	270	80
Investment income from S	18	
Profit before taxation	288	80
Tax	(65)	(13)
Profit for the year	223	67

During the year ended 31 December 20X9 P had sold $42,000 worth of goods to S. These goods had cost P $28,000. On 31 December 20X9 S still had half of these goods in inventories at the year end.

Calculate group revenues and costs of sale for the year ended 31 December 20X9.

Solution to Illustration 2

Unrealised profit in inventory

	$000
Selling price	42
Cost of goods	(28)
Total profit	14
Provision for unrealised profit: ½ × $14	**7**

(handwritten: 42 – 28)

Group revenue

This equals P's revenue + S's revenue – intragroup sales:

630 + 260 – 42 = **848**

Group cost of sales

This equals P's COS + S's COS – intragroup purchases + unrealised profits (this is added so that it increases costs and reduces overall group profits).

210 + 105 – 42 + 7 = **280**

Test your understanding 1

Prepare the consolidated statement of profit or loss of P Group for the year ended 31 December 20X9, based upon the preceding illustration.

7 Mid-year acquisitions

Mid-year acquisition procedure

If a subsidiary was acquired part way through the year, then the subsidiary's results should only be consolidated from the date of acquisition, i.e. the date on which control was acquired.

In practice this will require time apportionment of the results of S in the year of acquisition. For this purpose, unless indicated otherwise, assume that revenue and expenses accrue evenly. After time-apportioning S's results, deduct post-acquisition intra-group items as normal.

Note, however, that accounting for items of other comprehensive the group statement of profit or loss and other comprehensive inc excluded from the syllabus. Therefore, only items affecting the gro statement of profit or loss are examinable.

e.g

Illustration 3 – Mid-year acquisitions

The following statements of profit or loss have been produced by P and S for the year ended 31 March 20X9.

	P	S
	$000	$000
Revenue	151,800	108,850
Cost of sales	(71,900)	(51,100)
Gross profit	79,900	57,750
Operating expenses	(35,600)	(25,650)
Profit from operations	44,300	32,100
Investment income	1,400	600
Profit before taxation	45,700	32,700
Tax	(23,100)	(16,300)
Profit for the year	22,600	16,400

- On 30 November 20X8 P acquired 75% of the issued ordinary share capital of S. No dividends were paid by either entity during the year. The investment income is from listed investments and has been correctly accounted for.

- The profits of both entities are deemed to accrue evenly over the year.

Prepare the consolidated statement of profit or loss of P Group for the year ended 31 March 20X9.

Solution to Illustration 3

P consolidated statement of profit or loss for the year ended 31 March 20X9

	$000
Revenue	188,083
(151,800 + (108,850 × 4/12))	
Cost of sales	(88,933)
(71,900 + (51,100 × 4/12))	
Gross profit	99,150
Operating expenses	(44,150)
(35,600 + (25,650 × 4/12))	
Profit from operations	55,000
Investment income	1,600
(1,400 + (600 × 4/12))	
Profit before taxation	56,600
Tax	(28,533)
(23,100 + (16,300 × 4/12))	
Profit for the year	28,067
Amount attributable to:	
Equity holders of the parent	26,700
Non-controlling interest	1,367
(25% × (16,400 × 4/12))	
	28,067

Note:

P acquired 75% of the issued ordinary share capital of S on 30 November 20X8. This is the date on which control passed and hence the date from which the results of S should be reflected in the consolidated statement of profit or loss.

All reserves earned by S in the four months since that date are post-acquisition reserves.

The previous eight months' profit from 1 April 20X8 to 30 November 20X9 are all pre-acquisition.

Test your understanding 2

Set out below are the draft statements of profit or loss of P and its subsidiary S for the year ended 31 December 20X7.

On 1 January 20X6 P purchased 75% of the ordinary shares in S.

	P	S
	$000	$000
Revenue	300	150
Cost of sales	(180)	(70)
	———	———
Gross profit	120	80
Operating expenses	(47)	(23)
	———	———
Profit from operations	73	57
Finance costs		(2)
	———	———
Profit before taxation	73	55
Tax	(25)	(16)
	———	———
Profit for the year	48	39
	———	———

- During the year S sold goods to P for $20,000, making a mark-up of one third. Only 20% of these goods had been sold before the end of the year, the remainder is still in inventory.

Prepare the consolidated statement of profit or loss for the year ended 31 December 20X7.

8 IAS 28 Accounting for investments in associates and joint ventures

Definition of an associate

IAS 28 defines an **associate** as:

An entity over which the investor has significant influence and that is neither a subsidiary nor an interest in a joint venture.

Please note that joint ventures are not part the syllabus for this paper.

Significant influence is the power to participate in the financial and operating policy decisions of the investee but is not control or joint control over those policies.

An **investor** is an entity which owns a shareholding in another entity. An **investee** is an entity in which another entity has a shareholding.

An investor is presumed to have significant influence over another entity when it has a shareholding in that other entity between 20% and 50%.

Principles of equity accounting and reasoning behind it

Equity accounting is a method of accounting whereby the investment is initially recorded at cost and adjusted thereafter for the post-acquisition change in the investor's share of net assets of the associate.

The effect of this is that the consolidated statement of financial position includes:

- 100% of the assets and liabilities of the parent and subsidiary entity on a line-by-line basis

- a single 'investments in associates' line within non-current assets which includes the group share of the assets and liabilities of any associate.

The consolidated statement of profit or loss includes:

- 100% of the income and expenses of the parent and subsidiary entity on a line-by-line basis

- a single 'share of profit of associates' line which includes the group share of any associate's profit after tax.

Note: In order to equity account, the parent entity must already be producing consolidated financial statements (i.e. it must already have at least one subsidiary).

IAS 28 Investments in Associates

Accounting for associates according to IAS 28

The equity method of accounting is normally used to account for associates in the consolidated financial statements.

The equity method should not be used if:

- the investment is classified as held-for-sale in accordance with IFRS 5, or

- the parent is exempted from having to prepare consolidated accounts on the grounds that it is, itself, a wholly or partially owned subsidiary of another entity (IFRS 10).

9 Associates in the consolidated statement of financial position

Preparing the CSFP including an associate

The CSFP is prepared on a normal line-by-line basis following the acquisition method for the parent and subsidiary.

The associate is included as a non-current asset investment calculated as:

	$000
Cost of investment	X
Share of post-acquisition profits	X
Less: impairment losses	(X)
Less: group share of PURP (P = seller)	(X)
	——
	X
	——

The group share of the associate's post-acquisition profits or losses and any impairment of the investment in the associate will also be included in the group retained earnings calculation.

10 Associates in the consolidated statement of profit or loss

Equity accounting

The equity method of accounting requires that the consolidated statement of profit or loss:

- does not include dividends from the associate

- instead, it includes the group share of the **associate's profit after tax** less any impairment of the associate in the year (included after group profit from operations in arriving at the **group profit before tax** in the consolidated statement of profit or loss).

Trading with the associate

Generally the associate is considered to be outside the group as the investor is only able to exercise significant influence, rather than control.

Therefore any sales or purchases between group companies and the associate are not normally eliminated and will remain part of the consolidated figures in the statement of profit or loss.

Instead it is normal practice to adjust only for the group share of any unrealised profit in inventory.

Simple investments

When an entity invests in the shares of another entity but acquires neither control, nor significant influence, this is referred to as a 'simple' or 'trade' investment. In this case the investment is carried as an non-current asset in the statement of financial position and any dividends received from the investee are included in the statement of profit or loss.

11 Chapter summary

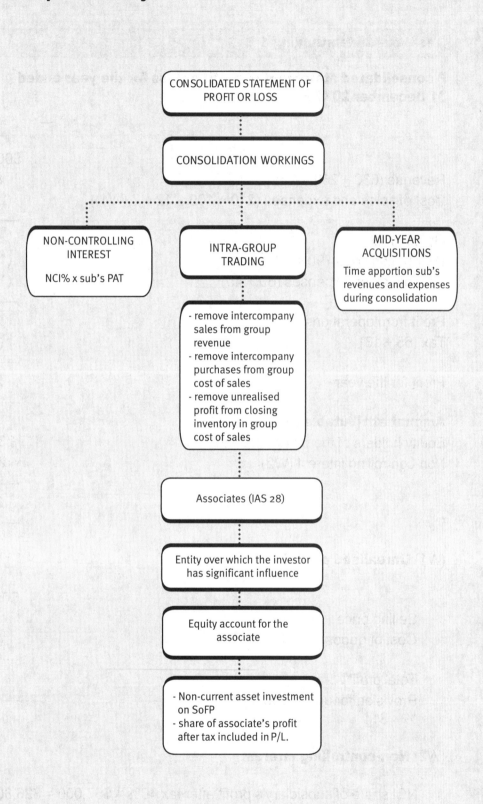

CONSOLIDATED STATEMENT OF PROFIT OR LOSS

CONSOLIDATION WORKINGS

NON-CONTROLLING INTEREST

NCI% x sub's PAT

INTRA-GROUP TRADING

MID-YEAR ACQUISITIONS

Time apportion sub's revenues and expenses during consolidation

- remove intercompany sales from group revenue
- remove intercompany purchases from group cost of sales
- remove unrealised profit from closing inventory in group cost of sales

Associates (IAS 28)

Entity over which the investor has significant influence

Equity account for the associate

- Non-current asset investment on SoFP
- share of associate's profit after tax included in P/L.

Test your understanding answers

Test your understanding 1

P consolidated statement of profit or loss for the year ended 31 December 20X9

	P $000
Revenue (630 + 260 – 42)	848
Cost of sales and expenses (210 + 105 – 42 + 7 (W1))	(280)
Gross profit	568
Distribution costs (90 + 30)	(120)
Administration expenses (60 + 45)	(105)
Profit from operations	343
Tax (65 + 13)	(78)
Profit for the year	265
Amount attributable to:	
Equity holders of the parent (bal fig)	238.2
Non-controlling interest (W2)	26.8
	265

(W1) Unrealised profit in inventory

	$000
Selling price	42
Cost of goods	(28)
Total profit	14
Provision for unrealised profit	7
½ × $14	

(W2) Non-controlling interest

NCI share of subsidiary's profit after tax 40% × $67,000 = $26,800

P consolidated statement of profit or loss for the year ended 31 December 20X7

	P
	$000
Revenue (300 + 150 – 20)	430
Cost of sales and expenses (180 + 70 – 20 + 4 (W1))	(234)
	———
Gross profit	196
Operating expenses (47 + 23)	(70)
	———
Profit from operations	126
Finance costs	(2)
	———
Profit before taxation	124
Tax (25 + 16)	(41)
	———
Profit for the year	83
	———

Profit for the year – amount attributable to:

Equity holders of the parent	74.25
Non-controlling interest (W2)	8.75
	———
	83.00
	———

(W1) Unrealised profit in inventory

	$000
Selling price	20.00
Cost (100/133% × $20)	(15.00)
	———
Total profit	5.00
Provision for unrealised profit 80% × $5	4.00

(W2) Profit for the year – non-controlling interest

	$000
NCI share of subsidiary's profit after tax (25% × $39)	9.75
Less NCI share of PURP (25% × $4 (W1))	(1.00)
	———
	8.75
	———

PRACTICE QUESTIONS

Section A: Multiple Choice Questions

All questions are worth two marks.

The regulatory and conceptual framework

(1) **When preparing financial statements under historic cost accounting in periods of inflation, directors:**

A   must reduce asset values

B   must increase asset values

C   must reduce dividends

D   need make no adjustments

(2) **If the owner of a business takes goods from inventory for his own personal use, the accounting concept to be considered is the:**

A   relevance concept

B   capitalisation concept

C   money measurement concept

D   separate entity concept

(3) **A 'true and fair view' is one which:**

A   presents the accounts in such a way as to exclude errors which would affect the actions of those reading them

B   occurs when the accounts have been audited

C   shows the accounts of an organisation in an understandable format

D   shows the assets on the statement of financial position at their current market price

(4) **Which concept is followed when a business records the cost of a non-current asset even though it does not legally own it?**

A   substance over form

B   prudence

C   accruals

D   going concern

(5) The IASB Conceptual Framework for Financial Reporting gives various qualitative characteristics that make financial information useful.

   Which of the following only contains qualitative characteristics of useful information contained in the Framework?

   A   prudence, consistency, understandability, faithful representation, substance over form

   B   accruals basis, going concern concept, consistency, prudence, true and fair view

   C   faithful representation, neutrality, substance over form, completeness, consistency, faithful and free from material error

   D   relevance, faithful representation, timeliness, comparability, verifiability.

(6) **The accounting concept or convention which, in times of rising prices, tends to understate asset values and overstate profits, is the:**

   A   going concern concept

   B   prudence concept

   C   realisation concept

   D   historical cost concept

Double entry bookkeeping

(7) **Which of the following is correct?**

   A   A debit entry will increase non-current assets

      A debit entry will increase drawings

      A debit entry will increase profit

   B   A credit entry will increase a bank overdraft

      A debit entry will increase payables

      A credit entry will increase receivables

C   A debit entry will increase profit

A debit entry will increase receivables

A debit entry will decrease payables

D   A debit entry will increase receivables

A credit entry will decrease non-current assets

A credit entry will increase profit

(8) **A credit balance on a ledger account indicates:**
A   an asset or an expense
B   a liability or an expense
C   an amount owing to the organisation
D   a liability or revenue

(9) **The double entry system of bookkeeping normally results in which of the following balances on the ledger accounts?**

	Debit balances	**Credit balances**
A	Assets and revenues	Liabilities, capital and expenses
B	Revenues, capital and liabilities	Assets and expenses
C	Assets and expenses	Liabilities, capital and revenues
D	Assets, expenses and capital	Liabilities and revenues

(10) **The main aim of accounting is to:**
A   maintain ledger accounts for every asset and liability
B   provide financial information to users of such information
C   produce a trial balance
D   record every financial transaction individually

(11) **A credit entry could lead to:**
A   an increase in assets or increase in liabilities
B   an increase in expense or an increase in share capital
C   an increase in liabilities or an increase in share capital
D   an increase in liabilities and a decrease in sales

Sales tax

(12) All the sales of Gail, a retailer, were made at a price inclusive of sales tax at the standard rate of 17.5% and all purchases and expenses bore sales tax at the standard rate. For the three months ended 31 March 2005 gross sales were $23,500, purchases were $12,000 (net) and expenses $800 (net).

How much is due to the tax authority for the quarter?

A $1,260

B $1,400

C $1,594

D $1,873

(13) **The revenue account is:**

A   credited with the total of sales made, including sales tax

B   credited with the total of sales made, excluding sales tax

C   debited with the total of sales made, including sales tax

D   debited with the total of sales made, excluding sales tax

(14) **If sales (including sales tax) amounted to $27,612.50 and purchases (excluding sales tax) amounted to $18,000, the balance on the sales tax account, assuming all items are subject to sales tax at 17.5%, would be:**

A $962.50 debit

B $962.50 credit

C $1,682.10 debit

D $1,682.10 credit

(15) A new entity was formed with an initial issue of 1,000 shares sold for $1 cash. Inventory costing $800 net of sales tax at 17.5% was purchased on credit. Half of this inventory was then sold for $1,000 plus sales tax, the customer paying promptly in cash.

The accounting equation after these transactions would show:

A   assets $1,775 less liabilities $175 equals capital $1,600

B   assets $2,775 less liabilities $975 equals capital $1,200

C   assets $2,575 less liabilities $800 equals capital $1,775

D   assets $2,575 less liabilities $975 equals capital $1,600

Inventory

(16) Tracey's business sells three products – A, B and C. The following information was available at the year-end:

	A	B	C
	$	$	$
	per unit	per unit	per unit
Original cost	7	10	19
Estimated selling price	15	13	20
Selling and distribution costs	2	5	6
Units of inventory	20	25	15

The value of inventory at the year-end should be:

A $675

B $670

C $795

D $550

(17) An inventory record card shows the following details:

January   1   50 units in inventory at a cost of $10 per unit

            4   90 units purchased at a cost of $15 per unit

         10   65 units sold

         20   30 units purchased at a cost of $20 per unit

         26   40 units sold

What was the value of inventory at 31 January using the FIFO method?

A $1,125

B $725

C $975

D $1,000

(18) **What would be the effect on a business' profit, which has been calculated including inventory at cost, of discovering that one of its inventory items which cost $7,500 has a net realisable value of $8,500?**

    A   an increase of $8,500

    B   an increase of $1,000

    C   no effect at all

    D   a decrease of $1,000

(19) **According to IAS 2 Inventories, which of the following costs should be included in valuing the inventories of a manufacturing business?**

    (1) Carriage outwards

    (2) Depreciation of factory plant

    (3) Carriage inwards

    (4) General administrative overheads

    A   All four items

    B   1, 3 and 4 only

    C   1 and 2 only

    D   2 and 3 only

(20) The closing inventory of X amounted to $116,400 excluding the following two inventory lines:

    –   400 items which had cost $4 each. All were sold after the statement of financial position date for $3 each, with selling expenses of $200 for the batch.

    –   200 different items which had cost $30 each. These items were found to be defective at the statement of financial position date. Rectification work after the statement of financial position amounted to $1,200, after which they were sold for $35 each, with selling expenses totalling $300.

Which of the following total figures should appear in the statement of financial position of X for inventory?

    A $122,300

    B $121,900

    C $122,900

    D $123,300

Non-current assets

(21) At 1 January 2005, Mary had motor vehicles which cost $15,000. On 31 August 2005 she sold a motor vehicle for $5,000 which had originally cost $8,000 and which had a carrying amount of $4,000 at the date of disposal. She purchased a new motor vehicle which cost $10,000 on 30 November 2005.

Mary's policy is to depreciate motor vehicles at a rate of 25% pa on the straight-line basis, based on the number of months' ownership.

What was the depreciation charge for the year ended 31 December 2005?

$..........

(22) **Which of the following best explains what is meant by 'capital expenditure'?**

A expenditure on non-current assets, including repairs and maintenance

B expenditure on expensive assets

C expenditure relating to the issue of share capital

D expenditure relating to the acquisition or improvement of noncurrent assets

(23) A non-current asset was purchased at the beginning of Year 1 for $2,400 and depreciated by 20% pa by the reducing-balance method. At the beginning of Year 4 it was sold for $1,200.

The result of this was:

A a loss on disposal of $240.00

B a loss on disposal of $28.80

C a profit on disposal of $28.80

D a profit on disposal of $240.00

(24) Giles bought a new machine from abroad. The machine cost $100,000 and delivery and installation costs were $7,000. Testing it amounted to $5,000. Training employees on how to use the machine cost of $1,000.

What amount should be capitalised as the cost of the machine in the statement of financial position?

$..........

(25) Joseph's machinery cost account showed a balance of $5,000 at 1 January 2005. During the year he had the following transactions:

28 February	Disposed of machine costing $300
31 March	Acquired machine costing $1,000
1 November	Disposed of machine costing $600

Joseph depreciates machines at a rate of 10% pa on the straight-line basis based on the number of months' ownership.

What is the depreciation charge in respect of machinery for the year ended 31 December 2005?

A $545

B $540

C $510

D $630

(26) B acquired a lorry on 1 May 20X0 at a cost of $30,000. The lorry has an estimated useful life of four years, and an estimated resale value at the end of that time of $6,000. B charges depreciation on the straight-line basis, with a proportionate charge in the period of acquisition.

What will the depreciation charge for the lorry be in B's ten-month accounting period to 30 September 20X0?

A $3,000

B $2,500

C $2,000

D $5,000

Accruals and prepayments

(27) The electricity account for the year ended 30 April 2005 was as follows:

	$
Electricity accrued at 1 May 2004	250
Payments made during the year in relation to:	
Quarter ending 30 June 2004	400
Quarter ending 30 September 2004	350
Quarter ending 31 December 2004	425
Quarter ending 31 March 2005	450

Which of the following is the appropriate entry for electricity?

	Accrued at 30 April 2005	**Charge to statement of profit or loss for year ended 30 April 2005**
A	$Nil	$1,375
B	$150	$1,525
C	$300	$1,675
D	$450	$1,825

(28) The year end of Lansdown is 31 December. The entity pays for its electricity by a standing order of $100 per month. On 1 January 2005 the statement from the electricity supplier showed that Lansdown had overpaid by $25. Lansdown received electricity bills for the four quarters starting on 1 January 2005 and ending on 31 December 2005 for $350, $375, $275 and $300 respectively.

Which of the following is the correct entry for electricity in Lansdown's statement of profit or loss and statement of financial position for the year ending 31 December 2005?

	P/L	**SFP**
A	$1,300	$75 accrual
B	$1,300	$75 prepayment
C	$1,200	$125 accrual
D	$1,200	$125 prepayment

(29) At 1 January 2005, Michael had a prepayment of $200 in respect of rent. He paid $1,200 on 1 March 2005 in respect of the year ended 28 February 2006

What was the charge to the statement of profit or loss in respect of rent for the year ended 31 December 2005?

A $1,400

B $1,200

C $1,100

D $1,300

(30) At 31 December 2003, Tony had accrued $240 in respect of light and heat for the quarter ending 31 December 2003. In January 2004 he discovered that he had under-accrued by $10.

The bills for the next four quarters were as follows (q.e. = quarter ended):

Amount	Relating to	Data paid
$260	q.e. 31 March 2004	15 April 2004
$220	q.e. 30 June 2004	17 July 2004
$210	q.e. 30 September 2004	14 October 2004
$230	q.e. 31 December 2004	19 January 2005

Tony always accrues for expenses based on the last bill.

What was the charge to the statement of profit or loss in respect of light and heat for the 15-month accounting period ended 31 March 2005?

A $1,160

B $1,150

C $930

D $920

(31) Stationery paid for during the year amounted to $1,350. At the beginning of the year there was an inventory of stationery on hand of $165 and an outstanding stationery invoice for $80. At the end of the year there was an inventory of stationery on hand of $140 and an outstanding stationery invoice for $70.

The stationery figure to be shown in the statement of profit or loss for the year was:

A $1,195

B $1,335

C $1,365

D $1,505

Irrecoverable debts and allowances for receivables

(32) At 30 April 20X5, Gareth had a receivables balance of $50,000 and an allowance for receivables of $800. Following a review of receivables, Gareth wishes to write off an irrecoverable debt of $1,000 and increase the allowance for receivables by $1,650.

What will be the net balance included in the statement of financial position for receivables at 30 April 20X5?

$..........

(33) As at 31 March, Phil had receivables of $82,500. Following a review of receivables, Phil has decided to write off the following irrecoverable debts:

John	$1,000
Beatrice	$500
Peter	$3,250

Phil would like to adjust the allowance for receivables to $1,250. The current balance on the allowance for receivables account is $2,000. Phil also received $300 from a debt that had been written off at an earlier date.

What was the charge to the statement of profit or loss in respect of irrecoverable debt expense and the entry on the statement of financial position for net receivables at 31 March?

	Statement of profit or loss expense	Statement of financial position
A	$4,250	$75,950
B	$4,450	$77,750
C	$4,450	$75,950
D	$4,250	$77,750

(34) At the start of the year Joe had an allowance of $700 against receivables. During the year, of this amount, $450 went bad and $150 was received; the balance remained unpaid at the year end. Subsequently, a further debt of $170 went bad. At the year-end Joe decided to increase the allowance for receivables by $240.

What was the total irrecoverable debt expense for the year?

$..........

(35) Doris currently has a receivables balance of $47,800 and an allowance for receivables of $1,250. She has just received $150 in respect of half of a debt that she had made an allowance against. She now believes the other half of the debt to be bad and wants to write it off. She also wants to increase the allowance for receivables to $1,500.

What is the total charge to the statement of profit or loss in respect of these items?

$..........

(36) At the year end, Harold had a receivables balance of $100,000 and an allowance for receivables of $5,000. He has not yet accounted for a receipt of $500 in respect of a debt which he had previously provided against or a receipt of $1,000 in respect of a debt which had been written off in the previous year. Harold wishes to reduce the allowance for receivables by $1,965.

What balances will be shown in his statement of financial position at the year-end for receivables and the allowance for receivables?

	Receivables	Allowance
A	$98,500	$2,535
B	$99,500	$3,535
C	$98,500	$3,035
D	$99,500	$3,035

(37) James has been advised that one of his customers has ceased trading and that it is almost certain that he will not recover the balance of $720 owed by this customer.

What entry should James make in his general ledger?

A	Dr	Receivables	$720
	Cr	Irrecoverable debts	$720
	Being write off of irrecoverable debt		
B	Dr	Irrecoverable debts	$720
	Cr	Receivables	$720
	Being write off of irrecoverable debt		
C	Dr	Receivables	$720
	Cr	Bank	$720
	Being write off of irrecoverable debt		
D	Dr	Bank	$720
	Cr	Receivables	$720
	Being write off of irrecoverable debt.		

(38) Gordon's receivables owe a total of $80,000 at the year end. These include $900 of long-overdue debts that might still be recoverable, but for which Gordon has created an allowance for receivables. During the year, Gordon also wrote off an amount of $1,582.

Which of the following statements best describes Gordon's position regarding receivables as at the year end?

    A   Trade receivables of $80,000, a specific allowance of $900 and a bad debt of $1,582

    B   Trade receivables of $78,418, a specific allowance of $1,582 and a bad debt of $900

    C   Trade receivables of $80,000 and a specific allowance of $2,482

    D   Trade receivables of $78,418 and a specific allowance of $682

Books of prime entry and control accounts

(39) **Which of the following is not the purpose of a receivables ledger control account?**

    A   A receivables ledger control account provides a check on the arithmetic accuracy of the personal ledger

    B   A receivables ledger control account helps to locate errors in the trial balance

    C   A receivables ledger control account ensures that there are no errors in the personal ledger

    D   Control accounts deter fraud

(40) **Which one of the following is a book of prime entry and not part of the double-entry system?**

    A   the sales ledger

    B   the petty cash book

    C   the sales ledger control account

    D   the purchase ledger

(41) **On 1 January 2005 the balance of receivables was $22,000. Calculate the closing receivables after taking the following into consideration:**

	$
Sales	120,000
Bank receipts	115,000
Discount allowed	1,000
Discount received	3,000
Dishonoured cheque	9,000
Contra – Set off	5,000

- A $30,000
- B $23,000
- C $12,000
- D $28,000

Control account reconciliations

(42) A receivables ledger control account had a closing balance of $8,500. It contained a contra to the purchase ledger of $400, but this had been entered on the wrong side of the control account.

The correct balance on the receivables ledger control account should be:

- A $7,700 debit
- B $8,100 debit
- C $8,400 debit
- D $8,900 debit

(43) The receivables ledger control account at 1 May had balances of $32,750 debit and $1,275 credit. During May sales of $125,000 were made on credit. Receipts from receivables amounted to $122,500 and cash discounts of $550 were allowed. Refunds of $1,300 were made to customers. The closing credit balance is $2,000.

The closing debit balances at 31 May should be:

- A $35,175
- B $35,675
- C $36,725
- D $34,725

(44) A supplier sends you a statement showing a balance outstanding of $14,350. Your own records show a balance outstanding of $14,500.

The reason for this difference could be that:

A   The supplier sent an invoice for $150 which you have not yet received

B   The supplier has allowed you $150 cash discount which you had omitted to enter in your ledgers

C   You have paid the supplier $150 which he has not yet accounted for

D   You have returned goods worth $150 which the supplier has not yet accounted for

(45) **A credit balance of $917 brought forward on Y's account in the books of X means that:**

A   X owes Y $917

B   Y owes X $917

C   X has paid Y $917

D   X is owed $917 by Y

(46) **In a receivables ledger control account, which of the following lists is composed only of items which would appear on the credit side of the account?**

A   Cash received from customers, sales returns, irrecoverable debts written off, contras against amounts due to suppliers in the accounts payable ledger

B   Sales, cash refunds to customers, irrecoverable debts written off, discounts allowed

C   Cash received from customers, discounts allowed, interest charged on overdue accounts, irrecoverable debts written off

D   Sales, cash refunds to customers, interest charged on overdue accounts, contras against amounts due to suppliers in the accounts payable ledger

Bank reconciliations

(47) The following information relates to a bank reconciliation.

    (i)   The bank balance in the cash book before taking the items below into account was $5,670 overdrawn.

    (ii) Bank charges of $250 on the bank statement have not been entered in the cash book.

    (iii) The bank has credited the account in error with $40 which belongs to another customer.

    (iv) Cheque payments totalling $325 have been correctly entered in the cash book but have not been presented for payment.

    (v) Cheques totalling $545 have been correctly entered on the debit side of the cash book but have not been paid in at the bank.

What was the balance as shown by the bank statement before taking the items above into account?

A $5,670 overdrawn

B $5,600 overdrawn

C $5,740 overdrawn

D $6,100 overdrawn

(48) At 31 August 2005 the balance on an entity's cash book was $3,600 credit. Examination of the bank statements revealed the following:

    –   Standing orders amounting to $180 had not been recorded in the cash book.

    –   Cheques paid to suppliers of $1,420 did not appear on the bank statements.

What was the balance on the bank statement at 31 August 2005?

A $5,200 overdrawn

B $5,020 overdrawn

C $2,360 overdrawn

D $3,780 overdrawn

(49) An organisation's cash book has an operating balance of $485 credit. The following transactions then took place:

- cash sales $1,450 including sales tax of $150

- receipts from customers of debts of $2,400

- payments to payables of debts of $1,800 less 5% cash discount

- dishonoured cheques from customers amounting to $250.

The resulting balance in the bank column of the cash book should be:

A $1,255 debit

B $1,405 debit

C $1,905 credit

D $2,375 credit

(50) The cash book shows a bank balance of $5,675 overdrawn at 31 March 2005. It is subsequently discovered that a standing order for $125 had been entered twice and that a dishonoured cheque for $450 had been debited in the cash book instead of credited.

The correct bank balance should be:

A $5,100 overdrawn

B $6,000 overdrawn

C $6,250 overdrawn

D $6,450 overdrawn

(51) A bank reconciliation was prepared for Q as follows:

	$
Overdraft per bank statement	38,600
Add: deposits not credited	41,200
	────
	79,800
Less: outstanding cheques	3,300
	────
Overdraft per cash book	76,500
	────

Assuming the bank statement balance of $38,600 to be correct, what should the cash book balance be?

A $76,500 overdrawn, as stated

B $5,900 overdrawn

C $700 overdrawn

D $5,900 cash at bank

(52) **After checking a business cash book against the bank statement, which of the following items could require an entry in the cash book?**

(1) Bank charges

(2) A cheque from a customer which was dishonoured

(3) Cheque not presented

(4) Deposits not credited

(5) Credit transfer entered in bank statement

(6) Standing order entered in bank statement.

A 1, 2, 5 and 6

B 3 and 4

C 1, 3, 4 and 6

D 3, 4, 5 and 6

Correction of errors and suspense accounts

(53) Faulty goods costing $210 were returned to a supplier but this was recorded as $120 in the ledger accounts.

What is the journal entry necessary to correct the error?

	Dr		Cr	
A	Suspense	90	Purchases returns	90
B	Purchases	90	Payables	90
C	Payables	90	Suspense	90
D	Payables	90	Purchases returns	90

(54) A suspense account was opened when a trial balance failed to agree. The following errors were later discovered:

 – a gas bill of $420 had been recorded in the gas account as $240

 – discount of $50 given to a customer had been credited to discounts received

 – interest received of $70 had been entered in the bank account only.

The original balance on the suspense account was:

A debit $210

B credit $210

C debit $160

D credit $160

(55) Molly starts up in business as a florist on 1 April 2004. For the first six months, she has a draft profit of $12,355.

On investigation you discover the following:

 – Rent paid for the 12 months ending 31 March 2005 of $800 has not been recorded in the accounts.

 – Closing inventory in the accounts at a cost of $1,000 has a net realisable value of $800.

What is the adjusted profit for the period?

A $11,355

B $11,755

C $12,155

D $12,555

(56) **In an accounting system where individual receivables and payables ledger accounts are maintained as an integral part of the double entry system, which of the following errors will not be identified by a trial balance?**

A overcasting of the sales day book

B undercasting of the analysed cash book

C failure to transfer a non-current asset to the disposal account when sold

D transposition error in an individual receivables account

(57) A trial balance has been extracted and a suspense account opened. One error relates to the misposting of an amount of $400, being discount received from suppliers, which was posted to the wrong side of the discount received account

What is the correcting journal entry?

		Dr	Cr
A	Discount received	$400	
	Suspense		$400
B	Suspense	$400	
	Discount received		$400
C	Discount received	$800	
	Suspense		$800
D	Suspense	$800	
	Discount received		$800

(58) An entity, Y, purchased some plant on 1 January 20X0 for $38,000. The payment for the plant was correctly entered in the cash book but was entered on the debit side of plant repairs account. Y charges depreciation using the straight-line basis at 20% pa, with a proportionate charge in the year of acquisition and assuming no scrap value at the end of the life of the asset.

How will Y's profit for the year ended 31 March 20X0 be affected by the error?

A   Understated by $30,400

B   Understated by $36,100

C   Understated by $38,000

D   Overstated by $1,900

(59) The trial balance of Z failed to agree, the totals being:

Debit $836,200

Credit $819,700

A suspense account was opened for the amount of the difference and the following errors were found and corrected:

(1) The totals of the cash discount columns in the cash book had not been posted to the discount accounts. The figures were discount allowed $3,900 and discount received $5,100.

(2) A cheque for $19,000 received from a customer was correctly entered in the cash book but was posted to the customer's account as $9,100.

What will the remaining balance on the suspense account be after the correction of these errors?

A $25,300 credit

B $7,700 credit

C $27,700 credit

D $5,400 credit

(60) The trial balance of C did not agree, and a suspense account was opened for the difference. Checking in the bookkeeping system revealed a number of errors.

(1) $4,600 paid for motor van repairs was correctly treated in the cash book but was credited to motor vehicles asset account.

(2) $360 received from B, a customer, was credited in error to the account of BB.

(3) $9,500 paid for rent was debited to the rent account as $5,900.

(4) The total of the discount allowed column in the cash book had been debited in error to the discounts received account.

(5) No entries had been made to record a cash sale of $100.

Which of the errors above would require an entry to the suspense account as part of the process of correcting them?

A   3 and 4

B   1 and 3

C   2 and 5

D   2 and 3

Statement of financial position and statement of profit or loss

(61) **Which of the following is the accounting equation**

    A   Assets – Liabilities + Share Capital = Retained Earnings

    B   Assets = Liabilities – Capital + Retained Earnings

    C   Assets – Liabilities – Capital = Retained Earnings

    D   Assets + Liabilities = Capital + Retained Earnings

(62) **With respect to the statement of profit or loss which of the following statements is true?**

    A   It illustrates a business' financial position.

    B   It includes dividends paid

    C   It illustrates the business' financial performance

    D   It has to show the results for one year

(63) **What is included in the statement of financial position of an entity?**

    A   Share capital, retained earnings, assets and liabilities

    B   Share capital, dividends paid, revenue and assets

    C   Assets, liabilities, profit on disposals of non-current assets and share capital

    D   Dividends paid, assets, discounts and liabilities

(64) **Which of the following is incorrect?**

    A   The statement of financial position and statement of profit or loss form part of the financial statements of a business

    B   The statement of financial position illustrates the accounting equation

    C   The statement of profit or loss illustrates the accounting equation

    D   The statement of financial position and statement of profit or loss illustrate the financial position and performance of the business

(65) **Which statement is not true?**

    A   Inventory is shown on the statement of profit or loss and in the statement of financial position

    B   Expenses should be included on the statement of profit or loss

    C   Inventory should be included on the statement of financial position only

    D   Receivables are included in current assets on the statement of financial position

From trial balance to financial statements

The following is the extract of Jessie's trial balance as at 31 December 2005:

	Dr $	Cr $
Buildings	580,000	
Buildings accumulated depreciation		116,000
Plant and machinery	50,000	
Plant and machinery accumulated depreciation		12,500
Receivables	25,800	
Allowance for receivables		1,900
Rent	34,000	
Insurance	30,000	
Irrecoverable debts	1,800	

The following notes are provided:

(i) Buildings are depreciated at 2% pa on a straight-line basis.

(ii) Plant and machinery is depreciated at 25% pa on a reducing balance basis.

(iii) Additional irrecoverable debts of $3,200 were discovered at the year end. It has been decided to make an allowance for receivables of 5% on the adjusted receivables at the year end.

(iv) The monthly rental charge is $3,000.

(v) The insurance charge for the year is $24,000.

Using the above information attempt the following questions.

(66) **The depreciation charge for buildings for the year and the net book value (CV) at the year-end will be:**

	Depreciation charge $	CV $
A	11,600	568,400
B	9,280	464,000
C	11,600	452,400
D	11,600	464,000

(67) The depreciation charge for plant and machinery for the year and the CV at the year-end will be:

	Depreciation charge	CV
	$	$
A	9,375	37,500
B	12,500	25,000
C	9,375	40,625
D	9,375	28,125

(68) The total irrecoverable debt expense for the year and the closing net receivable balance will be:

	Irrecoverable debt expense	Receivables
	$	$
A	4,230	21,470
B	5,000	21,470
C	5,770	21,830
D	2,430	19,670

(69) What is the charge for rent and insurance for the year and the closing accrual and prepayment?

		Charge for the year		Closing accrual/prepayment	
			$		$
A	Rent		30,000	Rent accrual	3,000
	Insurance		24,000	Insurance prepayment	6,000
B	Rent		36,000	Rent accrual	2,000
	Insurance		24,000	Insurance prepayment	6,000
C	Rent		36,000	Rent accrual	3,000
	Insurance		24,000	Insurance prepayment	6,000
D	Rent		30,000	Rent accrual	3,000
	Insurance		30,000	Insurance prepayment	6,000

Company accounts

(70) Geese's trial balance shows an overprovision in respect of income tax for the year ended 31 December 2004 of $5,000. Geese estimates that tax liability in respect of the year ended 31 December 2005 will be $23,000.

What is the tax charge in Geese's statement of profit or loss and the statement of financial position entry for the year ended 31 December 2005?

	Charge in statement of profit or loss	Statement of financial position
A	$5,000	$18,000
B	$23,000	$18,000
C	$18,000	$23,000
D	$28,000	$23,000

(71) **The correct journal entry to record the issue of 100,000 50c shares (fully paid) at an issue price of $2.50 a share is:**

			$	$
A	Dr	Bank	250,000	
	Cr	Share capital		100,000
	Cr	Share premium		150,000
B	Dr	Bank	250,000	
	Cr	Share capital		50,000
	Cr	Share premium		200,000
C	Dr	Bank	50,000	
	Cr	Share premium		50,000
D	Dr	Share capital	100,000	
	Dr	Share premium	150,000	
	Cr	Bank		250,000

(72) A company has the following share capital:

	Authorised $000	Issued $000
25c ordinary shares	8,000	4,000
6% 50c preference shares	2,000	1,000

In addition to providing for the year's preference dividend, an ordinary dividend of 2c per share is to be paid before the year end.

What are total dividends for the year?

A $140,000

B $380,000

C $440,000

D $760,000

(73) **Retained earnings are:**

A accumulated and undistributed profits of a company

B amounts which cannot be distributed as dividends

C amounts set aside out of profits to replace revenue items

D amounts set aside out of profits for a specific purpose

(74) On 1 April 2004 the balance on B's retained earnings was $50,000 credit. The balance on 31 March 2005 was $100,000 credit. On 10 March 2005 dividends of $50,000 were declared in respect of the year ended 31 March 2005, payable on 31 May 2005.

Based on this information, profit after tax (but before dividends) for the year ended 31 March 2005 was:

A Nil

B $50,000

C $100,000

D $150,000

Accounting standards

(75) Jackson's year end is 31 December 2005. In February 2006 a major credit customer went into liquidation and the directors believe that they will not be able to recover the $450,000 owed to them.

How should this item be treated in the financial statements of Jackson for the year ended 31 December 2005?

A   The irrecoverable debt should be disclosed by note

B   The financial statements are not affected

C   The debt should be provided against

D   The financial statements should be adjusted to reflect the irrecoverable debt

(76) A former employee is claiming compensation of $50,000 from Harriot, a limited liability company. The company's solicitors have stated that they believe that the claim is unlikely to succeed. The legal costs relating to the claim are likely to be in the region of $5,000 and will be incurred regardless of whether or not the claim is successful.

How should these items be treated in the financial statements of Harriot Ltd?

A   Provision should be made for $55,000

B   Provision should be made for $50,000 and the legal costs should be disclosed by note

C   Provision should be made for $5,000 and the compensation of $50,000 should be disclosed by note

D   No provisions should be made but both items should be disclosed by note

(77) Cowper has spent $20,000 researching new cleaning chemicals in the year ended 31 December 2005. It has also spent $40,000 developing a new cleaning product which will not go into commercial production until next year. The development project meets the criteria laid down in IAS 38.

How should these costs be treated in the financial statements of Cowper for the year ended 31 December 2005?

A $60,000 should be capitalised as an intangible asset on the statement of financial position

B $40,000 should be capitalised as an intangible asset and should be amortised; $20,000 should be written off to the statement of profit or loss

C $40,000 should be capitalised as an intangible asset and should not be amortised; $20,000 should be written off to the statement of profit or loss

D $60,000 should be written off to the statement of profit or loss

(78) The directors of ABC estimated that inventory which had cost $50,000 had a net realisable value of $40,000 at 30 June 2005 and recorded it in the financial statements for the year ended 30 June 2005 at this lower value in accordance with IAS 2. They have since found out that the net realisable value of the inventory is only likely to be $30,000.

What adjustments, if any, should be made in the financial statements in respect of this inventory?

A   No adjustments required

B   Increase the value of inventory by $10,000

C   Decrease the value of inventory by $10,000

D   Decrease the value of inventory by $20,000

(79) **Which of the following items are non-adjusting items per IAS 10?**

(a) the issue of new share or loan capital

(b) financial consequences of losses of non-current assets or inventory as a result of fires or floods

(c) information regarding the value of inventory sold at less than cost thus resulting in a reduction in the value of inventory

(d) mergers and acquisitions

(e) bankruptcy of a credit customer.

A (a), (b) and (d)

B (c) and (e)

C (a), (d) and (e)

D (b), (c) and (e)

(80) **Which of the following correctly describes how research and development expenditure should be treated in accordance with IAS 38?**

A Research and development expenditure must be written off to the statement of profit or loss as incurred

B Research and development expenditure should be capitalised as an intangible asset on the statement of financial position

C Research expenditure should be written off to the statement of profit or loss; development expenditure must be capitalised as an intangible asset provided that certain criteria are met

D Research expenditure should be capitalised as an intangible asset provided that certain criteria are met; development expenditure should be written off to the statement of profit or loss

(81) **Who issues International Financial Reporting Standards?**

A The Auditing Practices Board

B The Stock Exchange

C The International Accounting Standards Board

D The government

(82) **Which of the following statements concerning the accounting treatment of research and development expenditure are true, according to IAS 38 Intangible Assets?**

(1) If certain criteria are met, research expenditure may be recognised as an asset.

(2) Research expenditure, other than capital expenditure on research facilities, should be recognised as an expense as incurred.

(3) In deciding whether development expenditure qualifies to be recognised as an asset, it is necessary to consider whether there will be adequate finance available to complete the project.

(4) Development expenditure recognised as an asset must be amortised over a period not exceeding five years.

(5) The financial statements should disclose the total amount of research and development expenditure recognised as an expense during the period.

A   1, 4 and 5

B   2, 4 and 5

C   2, 3 and 4

D   2, 3 and 5

(83) IAS 10 Events after the Reporting Period regulates the extent to which events after the reporting period date should be reflected in financial statements.

Which of the following lists of such events consists only of items that, according to IAS 10 should normally be classified as non-adjusting?

A   Insolvency of a receivable whose account receivable was outstanding at the statement of financial position date, issue of shares or loan notes, a major merger with another company

B   Issue of shares or loan notes, changes in foreign exchange rates, major purchases of non-current assets

C   A major merger with another company, destruction of a major non-current asset by fire, discovery of fraud or error which shows that the financial statements were incorrect

D   Sale of inventory giving evidence about its value at the statement of financial position date, issue of shares or loan notes, destruction of a major non-current asset by fire

Incomplete records

(84) Ashley started a company on 1 January 2005. He purchased the entire share capital of the company for $7,600 cash. With the cash the company acquired the following assets:

Van	$2,000
Inventory	$1,000
Receivables	$500
Prepaid insurance for inventory	$100

At the end of the first year of trading, the company had the following:

Van	$1,800
Fixtures	$500
Inventory	$840
Receivables	$600
Payables	$400
Cash	$3,400

What was Ashley's profit or loss for the year?

A $860 profit

B $860 loss

C $140 profit

D $140 loss

(85) A company started has opening net assets of $10,000. At the end of the year's trading the company had earned a profit of $5,000 and had the following assets and liabilities:

Non-current assets	$20,000
Current assets	$15,000
Current liabilities	$8,000

During the year the company paid dividends of $2,000.

How much share capital was issued during in the year?

A $20,000

B $24,000

C $10,000

D $14,000

(86) **If Harry's mark-up on cost of sales is 15%, what is his gross profit margin?**

A   12.5%

B   13.04%

C   15%

D   17.65%

(87) A company had opening net assets of $10,000 and closing net assets of $4,500. During the period the company issued $4,000 new share capital and paid dividends of $8,000.

The profit or loss during the period was:

A $9,500 loss

B $1,500 loss

C $7,500 profit

D $17,500 profit

(88) **From the following information, calculate the value of purchases:**

	$
Opening payables	142,600
Cash paid	542,300
Discounts received	13,200
Goods returned	27,500
Closing payables	137,800

A $302,600

B $506,400

C $523,200

D $578,200

(89) Carol owns a shop. The only information available for the year ended 31 December 2005 is as follows:

Inventory at 1 January 2005	$3,500
Inventory at 31 December 2005	$1,350
Sales	$17,000
Gross profit margin	25%

What were the purchases of the shop for the year?

A $11,450

B $12,750

C $14,900

D $10,600

(90) The following information is relevant to the calculation of the sales figure for Alpha, a sole trader who does not keep proper accounting records:

	$
Opening receivables	29,100
Cash received from credit customers and paid into the bank	381,600
Expenses paid out of cash received from credit customers before banking	6,800
Irrecoverable debts written off	7,200
Refunds to credit customers	2,100
Discounts allowed to credit customers	9,400
Cash sales	112,900
Closing receivables	38,600

The figure which should appear in Alpha's statement of profit or loss for sales is:

A $525,300

B $511,700

C $529,500

D $510,900

(91) A sole trader who does not keep full accounting records wishes to calculate her sales revenue for the year.

The information available is:

(1)	Opening inventory	$17,000
(2)	Closing inventory	$24,000
(3)	Purchases	$91,000
(4)	Standard gross profit percentage	40% on sales revenue

Which of the following is the sales revenue figure for the year calculated from these figures?

A $117,600

B $108,000

C $210,000

D $140,000

(92) A business compiling its accounts for the year to 31 January each year pays rent quarterly in advance on 1 January, 1 April, 1 July and 1 October each year. After remaining unchanged for some years, the rent was increased from $24,000 per year to $30,000 per year as from 1 July 20X0.

Which of the following figures is the rent expense which should appear in the statement of profit or loss for the year ended 31 January 20X1?

A $27,500

B $29,500

C $28,000

D $29,000

(93) On 31 December 20X0 the inventory of V was completely destroyed by fire. The following information is available:

(1) Inventory at 1 December 20X0 at cost $28,400.

(2) Purchases for December 20X0 $49,600.

(3) Sales for December 20X0 $64,800.

(4) Standard gross profit percentage on sales revenue 30%.

Based on this information, which of the following is the amount of inventory destroyed?

A $45,360

B $32,640

C $40,971

D $19,440

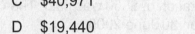

Statement of cash flows

(94) In the year ended 31 December 2005, Lamb bought new vehicles from Warwick Motors with a list price of $100,000 for $70,000 cash and an allowance against old motor vehicles of $30,000. The value of the vehicles taken in part exchange was $27,000.

Lamb sold other vehicles with a carrying amount of $12,000 for $15,000 cash.

In Lamb's statement of cash flows for the year ended 31 December 2005, how would the above transactions be presented under the heading 'Investing activities'?

	Cash inflow	Cash outflow
A	–	$76,000
B	$45,000	$100,000
C	$15,000	$70,000
D	$15,000	$100,000

(95) Baldrick had the following balances in its statement of financial position as at 30 June 2004 and 30 June 2005:

	30 June 2005	30 June 2004
	$	$
Current liabilities		
Taxation payable	600	400
Dividends	3,300	2,500
(declared before the year-end)		
Non-current liabilities		
8% Loan notes	50,000	40,000
Capital and reserves		
Accumulated profits	65,500	45,500

In the year ended 30 June 2005 taxation of $550 was paid. The additional loan notes were issued on 30 June 2005.

What was the profit before tax of Baldrick for the year ended 30 June 2005?

$..........

(96) At 31 December 2004, Topaz had provided $50,000 in respect of income tax. At 31 December 2005, the company estimated that its income tax bill in respect of the year would be $57,000. The amount charged in the statement of profit or loss for the year ended 31 December 2005 in respect of income tax was $60,000.

How much will appear in the statement of cash flows for the year ended 31 December 2005 in respect of income tax?

A $50,000

B $53,000

C $57,000

D $60,000

(97) Evans had the following balances in its statement of financial positions as at 30 June 2004 and 2005:

	2004	2005
10% Loan notes	$150,000	$130,000
Share capital	$100,000	$120,000
Share premium	$35,000	$45,000

How much will appear in the statement of cash flows for the year ended 30 June 2005 under the heading of 'Financing activities'?

$..........

The following information relates to Questions 98 and 99.

Scents had the following balances in its statements of financial position as at 30 September 2004 and 2005:

	2004	2005
Loan interest accrual	$5,000	$3,000
Approved ordinary dividends	$20,000	$25,000
10% Loan notes	$100,000	$100,000
Ordinary share capital	$150,000	$150,000
8% Preference share capital	$50,000	$50,000

(98) **How much will appear in the statement of cash flows for the year ended 30 September 2005 for the loan interest and preference dividend paid?**

A $10,000

B $12,000

C $16,000

D $32,000

(99) **How much will appear in the statement of cash flows for the year ended 30 September 2005 for the ordinary dividend paid?**

A $20,000

B $24,000

C $25,000

D $29,000

(100) IAS 7 Statement of Cash Flows requires the statement of cash flows prepared using the indirect method to include the calculation of net cash from operating activities.

Which of the following lists consists only of items which could appear in such a calculation?

A   Depreciation, increase in receivables, decrease in payables, proceeds of sale of plant

B   Increase in payables, decrease in inventories, profit on sale of plant, depreciation

C   Increase in payables, depreciation, decrease in receivables, proceeds of sale of plant

D   Depreciation, interest paid, equity dividends paid, purchase of plant

Interpretation of financial statements

The following information relates to Questions 101 and 102.

	20X6 $m	20X5 $m
Statement of profit or loss (extracts)		
Operating profit	550	360
Profit before tax	550	360
Statement of financial position (extracts)		
Capital and reserves	2,000	1,500
10% loan notes	500	500

(101) **What is the return on capital employed for the years 20X5 and 20X6?**

	20X6	20X5
A	22.0%	18%
B	20.8%	15.5%
C	20.8%	18%
D	22.0%	15.5%

(102) **What is the total gearing for the years 20X5 and 20X6? Use the debt as a percentage of total capital employed method.**

	20X6	20X5
A	20%	33.3%
B	25%	25%
C	80%	75%
D	20%	25%

(103) **From the following information regarding the year to 31 August 20X6, what is the payables payment period?**

	$
Sales	50,000
Cost of sales	40,000
Opening inventory	6,000
Closing inventory	3,800
Payables at 31 August 20X6	4,750

A   41 days

B   48 days

C   54 days

D   46 days

(104) **From the following information regarding the year to 31 March 20X6, what are the current and quick ratios?**

	$
Inventory	5,320
Receivables	10,420
Cash at bank	3,200
Payables	4,100
Overdraft	3,121

	Current ratio	Quick ratio
A	2.62	1.89
B	2.62	3.84
C	3.86	2.56
D	4.62	3.32

(105) Sale are $260,000. Purchases are $150,000. Opening inventory is $22,000. Closing inventory is $26,000.

What is the inventory turnover?

A   5.6 times

B   10 times

C   7 times

D   10.8 times

Consolidated statement of financial position

(106) At the 1 January 20X2 Y acquired 75% of the share capital of Z for $400,000. At that date the share capital of Z consisted of 600,000 ordinary shares of 50c each and its reserves were $50,000.

The fair value of NCI at the date of acquisition was $100,000.

In the consolidated statement of financial position of Y and its subsidiary Z at 31 December 20X6, what amount should appear for goodwill?

A $150,000

B $137,500

C $55,000

D $110,000

(107) Skinny acquired 75% of the share capital Coltart for $35,000 on the 1 January 20X4. Details of the share capital and reserves of Skinny and Coltart at 31 December 20X6 are as follows:

	Skinny	Coltart
	$	$
Share capital	50,000	20,000
Reserves	40,000	15,000

At the date of acquisition Coltart had reserves of $10,000.

What figure should appear in the consolidated statement of financial position of Skinny and its subsidiary Coltart for reserves as at 31 December 20X6?

A $41,250

B $42,750

C $43,250

D $43,750

(108)Austen acquired 60% of the share capital of Dicken for $300,000 on 1 January 20X5. Details of the share capital and reserves of Austen and Dickens at 31 December 20X6 are as follows:

	Austen	Dickens
	$	$
Share capital	300,000	200,000
Reserves	200,000	75,000

At the date of acquisition Dickens had reserves of $60,000. The fair value of NCI at acquisition was $80,000.

What figure should appear in the consolidated statement of financial position of Austen and its subsidiary Dickens for reserves as at 31 December 20X6?

A $180,200

B $209,000

C $290,200

D $290,200

(109)At the 1 January 20X5 Purves acquired 80% of the share capital of Trollope for $100,000. At that date the share capital of Trollope consisted of 50,000 $1 shares and reserves of $30,000. At the 31 December 20X6 the reserves of Purves and Trollope were as follows:

	Purves	Trollope
	$	$
Reserves	400,000	50,000

The fair value of NCI at acquisition was $75,000.

What figure should appear in the consolidated statement of financial position of Purves and its subsidiary Trollope, for non-controlling interest?

A $16,000

B $20,000

C $79,000

D $80,000

(110) At the 1 January 20X3 Y acquired 80% of the share capital of Z for $750,000. At that date the share capital of Z consisted of 600,000 ordinary shares of $1 each and its reserves were $50,000.

The fair value of non-controlling interest was valued at $150,000.

In the consolidated statement of financial position of Y and its subsidiary Z at 31 December 20X6, what amount should appear for goodwill?

A $250,000

B $184,000

C $138,000

D $138,000

Consolidated statement of profit or loss

(111) X owns 60% of the equity share capital of Y and 40% of the equity share capital of Z. The statement of profit or loss of the three entities showed the following revenue for the year ended 31 August 20X7:

	$m
X	16
Y	8
Z	7

During the year X sold goods to Y and Z for $2 million and $1 million respectively. All goods were sold on to third parties by Y and Z by the end of the year.

How much will be included in the consolidated statement of profit or loss of the X group for revenue for the year ended 31 August 20X7?

A $24m

B $21m

C $22m

D $28m

(112)Sat is the sole subsidiary of Shindo. The cost of sales figures for 20X1 for Sat and Shindo were $11 million and $10 million respectively. During 20X1 Shindo sold goods which had cost $2 million to Sat for $3 million. Sat has not yet sold any of these goods.

What is the consolidated cost of sales figure for 20X1?

A $16 million

B $18 million

C $19 million

D $20 million

(113)Crunchy Co acquired 70% of the ordinary share capital of Nut Co six years ago. The following information relates to Nut Co for the year ended 30 June 20X3:

	$
Sales revenue	600,000
Cost of sales	338,000
Distribution costs	113,000
Taxation	38,000

What is the profit attributable to the non-controlling interest in the consolidated statement of profit or loss?

A $33,300

B $78,750

C $45,000

D $77,700

(114) K Co acquired 60% of the ordinary share capital of Special Co five years ago. The following information relates to Special Co for the year ended 30 September 20X3:

	$
Sales revenue	960,000
Cost of sales	540,000
Administration expenses	180,000
Taxation	60,000

What is the profit attributable to the non-controlling interest in the consolidated statement of profit or loss?

A $108,000

B $72,000

C $168,000

D $77,700

(115) P Ltd acquired 60% of the ordinary shares of S Ltd several years ago when the reserves of S stood at $980. In the year ended 31 July 20X7 P sold goods to S costing $500 for $600.(20% mark-up on cost). At the year-end half of these goods still remained in inventory.

What will be the provision for unrealised profit adjustment for the year ended 31 July 20X7, for the P group?

A   Deduct $500 from the cost of sales

B   Deduct $50 from the cost of sales

C   Add $50 to the cost of sales

D   Add $100 to the cost of sales

(116) **Which of the following statements regarding the method of consolidation is true?**

(1) Subsidiaries are equity accounted

(2) Associates are consolidated in full

A   Neither statement

B   Statement 1 only

C   Both statements

D   Statement 2 only

(117)Which of the following statements are true?

(1) An associated undertaking is when a parent has control over the associate

(2) Associates are equity accounted

(3) Subsidiaries are consolidated in full

(4) An associate is a non-controlling interest

A   all of the above

B   Statement 2 and 3 only

C   None of the above

D   Statement 1 only

Section B: Accounts Preparation

(1) Symmetry

Symmetry is a limited liability company. Financial statements need to be produced for the year ended 31 December 20X1. An initial trial balance is presented below:

	Dr $	Cr $
Revenue		405,000
Purchases	140,000	
Administrative expenses	105,000	
Distribution expenses	55,000	
Plant and machinery – cost	120,000	
Plant and machinery – accumulated depreciation at 1 January 20X1		35,000
Trade receivables	30,500	
Allowance for receivables – 1 January 20X1		3,000
Inventory – 1 January 20X1	16,000	
Share capital		3,000
Trade payables		24,000
Retained earnings – 1 January 20X1		7,000
6% Loan		100,000
Cash	110,500	

The following notes are relevant to the preparation of the financial statements for the year ended 31 December 20X1:

(i)   The current year tax bill has been estimated at $5,000.

(ii) Trade receivables include $2,000 which is now considered irrecoverable. The allowance for receivables needs to be increased to $5,000.

(iii) The cost of inventory as at 31 December 20X1 is $14,000. This includes a damaged item which cost $100. It can be sold for $130 if repaired. These repairs will cost $40.

(iv) No interest has been accrued on the loan, which was taken out on 1 July 20X1.

(v)   Plant and machinery is depreciated on a reducing balance basis at a rate of 10%. Depreciation is charged to cost of sales.

Prepare a statement of profit or loss for the year ended 31 December 20X1 and a statement of financial position as at 31 December 20X1.

(15 marks)

Statement of profit or loss for year ended 31 December 20X1

	$
Revenue	
Cost of sales	
Gross profit	
Administrative expenses	
Distribution expenses	
Operating profit	
Finance costs	
Profit before taxation	
Income tax expense	
Profit after taxation	

Statement of financial position as at 31 December 20X1

$

Assets
Non-current assets
Property, plant and equipment

Current assets
Inventories
Trade and other receivables
Cash and cash equivalents

Total assets

Equity and liabilities
Share capital
Retained earnings
Loan
Trade and other payables
Interest accrual
Tax payable

Total equity and liabilities

(2) **Zbox**

Zbox, a limited liability company, is preparing its financial statements for the year ended 31 December 20X1. An initial trial balance is presented below:

	Dr $	Cr $
Revenue		760,000
Purchases	320,000	
Administrative expenses	145,000	
Distribution expenses	59,000	
Vehicles – cost	900,000	
Vehicles – accumulated depreciation at 1 January 20X1		350,000
Trade and other receivables	65,000	
Allowance for receivables – 1 January 20X1		1,000
Inventory – 1 January 20X1	43,000	
Share capital ($1 each)		10,000
Trade and other payables		42,000
Retained earnings – 1 January 20X1		428,000
Cash	59,000	

The following notes are relevant to the preparation of the financial statements for the year ended 31 December 20X1:

(i) The current year tax bill has been estimated at $25,000.

(ii) No entries have been made in respect of a dishonoured cheque for $6,000.

(iii) Vehicles are depreciated at a rate of 20% per year on a straight line basis. This should be charged to distribution expenses.

(iv) Closing inventory has been valued correctly at $51,000.

(v) An interim dividend of 20c per ordinary share was paid during the year. This has been charged to administrative expenses.

(vi) The accountant of Zbox believes that there are no doubtful debts and therefore that the allowance for receivables is no longer required.

(vii) It has been determined that the purchase day book was undercast by $4,000. Zbox is not registered for sales tax.

Prepare a statement of profit or loss for the year ended 31 December 20X1 and a statement of financial position as at 31 December 20X1.

(15 marks)

Statement of profit or loss for year ended 31 December 20X1

$

Revenue	
Cost of sales	
Gross profit	
Administrative expenses	
Distribution expenses	
Profit before tax	
Income tax expense	
Profit after tax	

Statement of financial position as at 31 December 20X1

$

Assets

Non-current assets

Property, plant and equipment	

Current assets

Inventories	
Trade and other receivables	
Cash and cash equivalents	

Total assets	

Equity and liabilities

Share capital	
Retained earnings	
Trade and other payables	
Tax payable	

Total equity and liabilities	

(3) **P and S**

The statements of profit or loss for two companies, P and S, for the year ended 31 December 20X1 are presented below:

	P	S
	$000	$000
Revenue	950	423
Cost of sales	(400)	(150)
Gross profit	550	273
Administrative expenses	(200)	(120)
Operating profit	350	153
Investment income	60	20
Finance costs	–	(5)
Profit before tax	410	168
Taxation	(100)	(33)
Profit for the year	310	135

The following notes are relevant to the preparation of the consolidated financial statements:

(i) P bought 80% of the ordinary shares in S on 1 January 20X0.

(ii) During the year ended 31 December 20X1, S sold goods to P for $50,000 making a gross profit margin of 20%. All of these goods remained in the inventory of P at the year end.

(a) **Using the individual company financial statements, calculate the following ratios for P and S for the year ended 31 December 20X1:**

    (i) **Gross profit margin**

    (ii) **Operating profit margin**

    (iii) **Receivables collection period**

    Assume that P has receivables of $200,000 and that S has receivables of $150,000. All answers should be rounded to one decimal place.

    (6 marks)

(b) **Prepare a consolidated statement of profit or loss for the year ended 31 December 20X1.**

    (9 marks)

(a)

	P	S
Gross profit margin (%)		
Operating profit margin (%)		
Receivables collection period (days)		

(b)

Consolidated statement of profit or loss for the year ended 31 December 20X1

	$000
Revenue	
Cost of sales	
Gross profit	
Administrative expenses	
Operating profit	
Investment income	
Finance costs	
Profit before taxation	
Income tax expense	
Profit after taxation	
Profit attributable to:	
Owners of P	
Non-controlling interest	

(4) ABC and XYZ

The statements of financial position for ABC and XYZ as at 31 December 20X1 are presented below.

	ABC $	XYZ $
Assets		
Non-current assets		
Property, plant and equipment	240,000	297,000
Investment	200,000	–
Current assets		
Inventories	75,000	56,000
Trade and other receivables	120,000	94,000
Cash and cash equivalents	5,000	52,000
Total assets	640,000	499,000
Equity and liabilities		
Equity		
Share capital	100,000	50,000
Retained earnings	342,000	334,000
Non-current liabilities		
Loans	100,000	50,000
Current liabilities		
Trade and other payables	98,000	65,000
Trade equity and liabilities	640,000	499,000

The following notes are relevant to the preparation of the consolidated financial statements:

– ABC acquired 75% of the ordinary shares of XYZ for $200,000 several years ago. At the acquisition date, the retained earnings of XYZ were $100,000. The fair value of the non-controlling interest at acquisition was $50,000.

– The carrying amount of the net assets of XYZ approximated their fair values, with the exception of some land. This land held in the accounts of XYZ at its cost of $60,000 but was estimated to have a fair value of $100,000. This land is still held at 31 December 20X1.

– During the year, ABC sold goods on credit to XYZ for $20,000 making a profit on the sale of $6,000. All of these goods are still included in the inventories of XYZ and the invoice has not yet been settled.

(a) **Using the individual financial statements, calculate the following ratios for ABC and XYZ for the year ended 31 December 20X1:**

   (i) **The quick ratio (x:1)**

   (ii) **Gearing (in terms of the percentage of capital employed represented by borrowings)**

All ratios should be calculated to one decimal place.

(4 marks)

(b) **Prepare the consolidated statement of financial position for the ABC group as at 31 December 20X1.**

(11 marks)

(a)

	ABC	XYZ
Quick ratio (X:1)		
Gearing (%)		

(b)

Consolidated statement of financial position
as at 31 December 20X1

$

Assets
Non-current assets
Property, plants and equipment
Goodwill
Current assets
Inventories
Trade and other receivables
Cash and cash equivalents

Total Assets

Equity and liabilities
Equity
Share capital
Retained earnings
Non-controlling interest
Non-current liabilities
Loans
Current liabilities
Trade and other payables

Total equity and liabilities

PRACTICE ANSWERS

Section A: Multiple Choice Questions

The regulatory and conceptual framework

(1) **D**

(2) **D**

(3) **A**

(4) **A**

(5) **D**

The other three contain items which are not considered to contribute towards reliability.

(6) **D**

Double entry bookkeeping

(7) **D**

(8) **D**

(9) **C**

(10) **B**

(11) **C**

Sales tax

(12) **A**

Sales tax

	$		$
Purchases	2,100	Sales	3,500
(17.5 % × 12,000)		23,500 × 17.5/117.5	
Expenses	140		
(17.5% × 800)			
Bal c/f	1,260		
	3,500		3,500
		Bal b/f	1,260

(13) **B**

(14) **B**

Sales tax

	$		$
Purchases	3,150.00	Sales	4,112.50
(17.5 % × 18,000)		27,612.50 × 17.5/117.5	
Bal c/f	962.50		
	4,112.50		4,112.50
		Bal b/f	962.50

(15) **D**

		$	$
Assets	Cash (1,000 + 1,175)		2,175
	Inventory		400
			2,575
Liabilities	Payables (800 × 1.175)	940	
	Sales tax (175 – 140)	35	
			(975)
			1,600
Capital	Share capital		1,000
	Profit (1,000 – 400)		600
			1,600

Inventory

(16) **D**

	A	B	C	Total
	$	$	$	$
Cost	7	10	19	
NRV	13	8	14	
Lower of cost or NRV	7	8	14	
× Number of units	20	25	15	
Valuation	140	200	210	550

(17) **A**

(35 × $15) + (30 × $20) = $1,125

(18) **C**

(19) **D**

(20) **C**

400 items		$
Cost	400 × $4	1,600
NRV	(400 × $3) – $200	1,000
Therefore use NRV.		
200 items		$
Cost	200 × $30	6,000
NRV	(200 × $35) – $1,200 – $300	5,500
Therefore use NRV.		

Total inventory figure = $116,400 + $1,000 + $5,500 = $122,900.

Non-current assets

(21) **$3,291**

	$
Assets held all year ($15,000 – 8,000) × 25%	1,750
Asset disposed of $8,000 × 25% × 8/12	1,333
Asset acquired $10,000 × 25% × 1/12	208
	———
Total depreciation	3,291
	———

(22) **D**

(23) **B**

	$
Proceeds of sale	1,200.00
CV at disposal (2,400 – 480 – 384 – 307.20)	(1,228.80)
	—————
Loss on disposal	(28.80)
	—————

Depreciation to disposal

Yr 1: $2,400 × 20% = $480

Yr 2: $(2,400 – 480) × 20% = $384

Yr 3: $(2,400 – 480 – 384) × 20% = $307.20

(24) **$112,000**

$100,000 + $7,000 + $5,000 = $112,000

(25) **B**

	$
Assets held all year (5,000 – 300 – 600) × 10%	410
Disposals	
$300 × 10% × 2/12	5
$600 × 10% × 10/12	50
Acquisition $1,000 × 10% × 9/12	75
	———
Total depreciation	540
	———

(26) **B**

$$\frac{\$30,000 - \$6,000}{4} \times \frac{5}{12} = \$2,500$$

Accruals and prepayments

(27) **B**

Electricity

	$		$
Bank	400	Bal b/f	250
Bank	350		
Bank	425	Profit or loss (balancing figure)	1,525
Bank	450		
Bal c/f (ß)	150		
	1,775		1,775

Accrual ⅓ × 450 = 150 for 1 month

(28) **A**

Electricity

	$		$
Bal b/f	25		
Bank (12 × 100)	1,200		
		Profit or loss (350 + 375 + 275 + 300)	1,300
Bal c/f (ß)	75		
	1,300		1,300
		Bal b/f	75

(29) **B**

Rent

	$		$
Bal b/f	200		
Bank	1,200	Profit or loss (ß)	1,200
		Bal c/f	200
	1,400		1,400
Bal b/f (2/12 × 1,200)	200		

(30) **A**

Light and heat

	$		$
Bank (240 + 10)	250	Bal b/f	240
Bank	260		
Bank	220		
Bank	210	Profit or loss (ß)	1,160
Bank	230		
Bank c/f	230		
	1,400		1,400
		Bal b/f	230
		(last quarter's bill)	

(31) **C**

Stationery payable

	$		$
		Bal b/f	80
Bank	1,350	Purchases of stationery (ß)	1,340
Bal c/f	70		
	1,420		1,420
		Bal b/f	70

Opening inventory + Purchases – Closing inventory = $165 + $1,340 – $140 = $1,365

Irrecoverable debts and allowances for receivables

(32) **$46,550**

$50,000 - $1,000 - $2,450 = $46,550

(33) **A**

Receivables

	$		$
Bal b/f	82,500	Irrecoverable debts	4,750
		Bal c/f	77,750
	82,500		82,500
Bal b/f	77,750		

Irrecoverable debts expense

	$		$
Receivables	4,750	Decrease in allowance	750
(1000 + 500 + 3250)		Cash receipt from debt previously written off	300
		Profit or loss account	3,700
	4,750		4,750

	$
Allowance required at 31 March	1,250
Opening allowance	2,000
Movement in allowance balance	750 decrease

Net receivables = $77,750 – $1,250 = $76,500

(34) **$260**

Allowance for receivables

	$		$
		Bal b/f	700
Irrecoverable debts (ß)	360		
Bal c/f	340		
	———		———
	700		700
	———		———
		Bal b/f	340

Irrecoverable debts

	$		$
Receivables	450	Decrease in allowance	360
Receivables	170	Profit or loss account	260
	———		———
	620		620
	———		———

Allowance required at end of year = $700 – $450 – $150 + $240 = $340

(35) **$400**

Receivables

	$		$
Bal b/f	47,800	Bank	150
		Irrecoverable debts	150
		Bal c/f	47,500
	———		———
	47,800		47,800
	———		———
Bal b/f	47,500		

Irrecoverable debt expense

	$		$
Increase in allowance	250	Profit or loss expense	400
Receivables	150		
	400		400

(36) **D**

Receivables

	$		$
Bal b/f	100,000	Bank	500
		Bal c/f	99,500
	100,000		100,000
Bal b/f	99,500		

Allowance for receivables

	$		$
		Bal b/f	5,000
Profit or loss	1,965		
Bal c/f	3,035		
	5,000		5,000
		Bal b/f	3,035

(37) **B**

This is an example of an irrecoverable debt being written off. Credit the receivables account in order to clear the debt and debit the irrecoverable debts account with the amount of the debt written off.

(38) **A**

The bad debt of $1,582 already been removed from receivables during the year. The specific allowance of $900 (it has not yet been written off as bad) will be offset against receivables in the year-end financial accounts.

Books of prime entry and control accounts

(39) **C**

(40) **B**

(41) **A**

Receivables

	$		$
Bal b/f	22,000	Bank	115,000
Sales	120,000		
		Discounts allowed	1,000
Dishonoured cheque	9,000	Contra	5,000
		Bal c/f	30,000
	151,000		151,000
Bal b/f	30,000		

Control account reconciliations

(42) **A**

$8,500 – ($400 × 2) = $7,700

(43) **C**

Receivables ledger control account

	$		$
Bal b/f	32,750	Bal b/f	1,275
Sales	125,000	Bank	122,500
Refunds	1,300	Discounts allowed	550
Bal c/f	2,000	Bal c/f	36,725
	161,050		161,050
Bal b/f	36,725	Bal b/f	2,000

(44) **B**

(45) **A**

(46) **A**

The other three lists all contain one item which should appear on the debit side of the account.

Bank reconciliations

(47) D

Bank – cash book

	$		$
		Bal b/f (i)	5,670
		Bank charges (ii)	250
Bal c/f	5,920		
	5,920		5,920
		Bal b/f	5,920

	$
Balance per bank statement (ß)	(6,100)
Add: Error (iii)	(40)
Add: Outstanding cheques (iv)	(325)
Less: Outstanding lodgements(v)	545
Balance per cash book	(5,920)

(48) C

	$	
Balance per bank statement (ß)	($2,360)	old
Add: Outstanding cheques	($1,420)	
Balance per cash book (3,600 + 180)	($3,780)	old

(49) B

Bank – cash book

	$		$
Sales	1,450	Bal b/f	485
Receivables	2,400	Payables (0.95 × 1,800)	1,710
		Dishonoured cheques	250
		Bal c/f	1,405
	3,850		3,850
Bal b/f	1,405		

(50) D

Bank – cash book

	$		$
Standing order	125	Bal b/f	5,675
		Dishonoured cheque ($450 × 2)	900
Bal c/f	6,450		
	6,575		6,575
		Bal b/f	6,450

(51) C

The bank reconciliation should have been calculated as follows:

	$
Overdraft per bank statement	(38,600)
Add deposits not yet credited	41,200
Less outstanding cheques	2,600
	(3,300)
Overdraft per cash book	(700)

(52) A

Items 3 and 4 relate to timing differences only and would appear in the bank reconciliation.

Correction of errors and suspense accounts

(53) **D**

(54) **A**

Suspense

	$		$
Bal b/f (ß)	210	Gas (420 – 240)	180
Interest receivable	70	Discounts (50 × 2)	100
	280		280

(55) **B**

Draft profit for the period	$12,355
Six months' rent 6/12 × 800	($400)
Closing Inventory adjustment (1,000 – 800)	($200)
	$11,755

(56) **C**

(57) **D**

(58) **B**

The profit will be understated by the following amount:

	$
Amount charged in error to the repairs account	38,000
Less depreciation chargeable on the plant (3/12 × 20% × $38,000)	(1,900)
	$36,100

(59) **D**

	$	
Opening balance on suspense account ($836,200 – $819,700)	16,500	Cr
Difference remaining after postings to the discount accounts ($5,100 – $3,900)	(1,200)	
Difference from cheque incorrectly posted ($19,000 – $9,100)	(9,900)	
	———	
	$5,400	Cr
	———	

(60) **B**

Items 1 and 3 would result in an imbalance in the trial balance and therefore require an entry to the suspense account. Items 2, 4 and 5 do not affect the balancing of the accounts.

Statement of financial position and statement of profit or loss

(61) **C**

(62) **C**

(63) **A**

(64) **C**

(65) **C**

From trial balance to financial statements

(66) **C**

Depreciation charge = $11,600 (2% × $580,000)

CV = $452,400 [$580,000 – ($116,000 + $11,600)]

(67) **D**

Depreciation charge = $9,375 [25% × $37,500 ($50,000 – $12,500)]

Carrying amount = $28,125 [$50,000 – ($12,500 + $9,375)]

(68) **A**

	$
Irrecoverable debts $1,800 + 3,200 =	5,000
Decrease in allowance for receivables	(770)
Total irrecoverable debt expense	**4,230**
Receivables ($25,800 – 3,200)	22,600
Less: Closing allowance for receivables	(1,130)
Net closing receivables	**21,470**

Closing allowance for receivables	
[5% × ($25,800 – 3,200)]	1,130
Opening allowance for receivables	1,900
Decrease in allowance for receivables	770

(69) **B**

	Charge for the year			Closing
	$			$
Rent	**36,000**	**Rent accrual**		**2,000**
	(12 × $3,000)	Due	36,000	
		Paid	34,000	
		Accrual	2,000	
Insurance	**24,000**	**Insurance prepayment**		**6,000**
		Paid	30,000	
		Due	24,000	
		Prepayment	6,000	

Company accounts

(70) **C**

	$
2005 estimate	23,000
Overprovision 2004	(5,000)
	18,000
Tax liability	23,000

(71) **B**

(72) **B**

		$
Preference dividends (6% × 1,000,000)	=	60,000
Ordinary dividends (16,000,000 × 0.02)	=	320,000
Total dividend	=	380,000

(73) **A**

(74) **C**

	$
Profit after tax (balancing figure)	100,000
Dividends	(50,000)
Profit for year	50,000
Accumulated profit b/f	50,000
Accumulated profit c/f	100,000

Accounting standards

(75) **D**

(76) **C**

(77) **C**

(78) **C**

(79) **A**

(80) **C**

(81) **C**

(82) **D**

Statements 2, 3 and 5 are correct

(83) **B**

The other lists contain adjusting items

Incomplete records

(84) **B**

Change in net assets = Change in share capital + Profits for the year

Opening net assets = $7,600 (i.e. all the assets purchased and the remaining cash)

Closing net assets = $6,740

There is no change in share capital after incorporation

($860) = 0 + Profit/loss for the year

Loss for year = $860

(85) **D**

Change in net assets = Change in share capital + profit for year – dividends paid

$27,000 – $10,000 =Change in share capital + $5,000 – $2,000

Share capital issued = $14,000

(86) **B**

	%
Sales	115
Cost of Sales	100
Gross profit	15

15/115 = 13.04%

(87) **B**

Closing net assets – opening net assets = share capital issued + profit for year – dividends

$4,500 – $10,000 = $4,000 + profit/(loss) – $8,000

Loss for year = $1,500

(88) **D**

Payables

	$		$
Bank	542,300	Bal b/f	142,600
Discounts received	13,200		
Returns outwards	27,500	Purchases (ß)	578,200
Bal c/f	137,800		
	720,800		720,800
		Bal b/f	137,800

(89) **D**

Cost of Sales = 75% × $17,000 = $12,750

Purchases = $12,750 + $1,350 – $3,500 = $10,600

(90) **A**

Credit sales can be calculated as a balancing figure on the Receivables ledger control account.

Receivables ledger control account

	$		$
Balance b/f	29,100	Bank takings	381,600
Bank – refunds	2,100	Expenses	6,800
Credit sales	412,400	Irrecoverable debts	7,200
(balance)		Discounts allowed	9,400
		Balance c/f	38,600
	443,600		443,600

Credit sales = $412,400, cash sales = $112,900,

Total sales = $525,300

(91) **D**

	$
Opening inventory	17,000
Purchases	91,000
Closing inventory	(24,000)
Cost of sales	84,000

Sales = $84,000 × 100/60 = $140,000

(92) **A**

The rent expense for the year should be:

(5/12 × $24,000) + (7/12 × $30,000) = $27,500

(93) B

Cost of sales = 70% × $64,800 =	$45,360
	$
Opening inventory	28,400
Purchases	49,600
Cost of sales	(45,360)
Loss of inventory	32,640

Statement of cash flows

(94) C

(95) $24,050

	$
Retained profit for the year $(65,500 – 45,500)	20,000
Dividends	3,300
Taxation $(600 + 550 – 400)	750
Profit before tax	24,050

(96) B

Income tax

	$		$
		Bal b/f	50,000
Bank (ß)	53,000		
		Profit or loss	60,000
Bal c/f	57,000		
	110,000		110,000
		Bal b/f	57,000

(97) **$10,000 inflow**

	$	
Issue of share capital $(20,000+10,000)	30,000	inflow
Repayment of loan notes	20,000	outflow
	_____	
	10,000	inflow
	_____	

(98) **C**

Loan interest payable

	$		$
		Bal b/f	5,000
Bank (ß)	12,000	Profit or loss	10,000
		(100,000 × 10%)	
Bal c/f	3,000		
	_____		_____
	15,000		15,000
	_____		_____
		Bal b/f	3,000

Preference dividends 8% × $50,000 = $4,000

Total payments = $12,000 + $4,000 = $16,000

(99) **A**

(100) **B**

All other lists contain one or more items that would not appear in the calculation of net cash from operating activities

Interpretation of financial statements

(101) **A**

20X6   550 / 2,500 = 22.0%

20X5   360 / 2,000 = 18%

(102) **D**

20X6   500 / 2,500 = 20%

20X5   500 / 2,000 = 25%

KAPLAN PUBLISHING

(103)**D**

Opening inventory + purchases – closing inventory = cost of sales

6,000 + purchases – 3,800 = 40,000

Purchases = 40,000 + 3,800 – 6,000 = 37,800

4,750 / 37,800 × 365 = 46 days

(104)**A**

Current ratio

18,940 / 7,221 = 2.62

Quick ratio

5,320 + 10,420 + 3,200 = 13,620 / 7,221 = 1.89

(105)**A**

Inventory turnover = cost of sales/closing inventory

Cost of sales = 22,000 + 150,000 – 26,000 = 146,000

Inventory turnover = 146,000 / 26,000 = 5.6 times

Consolidated statement of financial position

(106)**A**

	$
Cost of investment	400,000
Fv of NCI @ acquisition	100,000
Less NA @ acquisition	(350,000)
	150,000

(107)**D**

	$
Reserves 40,000 + (5,000 × 75%)	43,750
	43,750

(108)**B**

	$
Retained earnings (200,000 + (15,000 × 60%)	209,000
	209,000

(109)**C**

	$
FV of NCI @acquisition	75,000
Share of post-acquisition profits (20% × $20,000)	4,000
	79,000

(110)**A**

	$
Cost of investment	750,000
FV of NCI @ acquisition	150,000
Less NA @ acquisition	(650,000)
	250,000

Consolidated statement of profit or loss

(111)**C**

Revenue = X $16 + Y $8 – Intercompany transaction $2 = $22.

Y is a subsidiary and Z is an associate. Therefore Z's revenue will not be included and the inter-company sales with Z will not be eliminated.

(112)**C**

11 + 10 – 3 (intra group trading) + 1 (PURP) = 19

(113)A

Profit = (600 − 338 − 113 − 38) × 30% = 33,300

(114)B

Profit = (960 − 540 − 180 − 60) × 40% = 72,000

(115)C

Sales $600 − Cost $500 = Profit $100

Half of these goods are in inventory = PURP $100 × ½ = $50 which needs to be added back to cost of sales

(116)A

Subsidiaries are consolidated in full and associates are equity accounted.

(117)B

Section B: Accounts Preparation

(1) Symmetry

Statement of profit or loss for year ended 31 December 20X1

Revenue	405,000
Cost of sales (W1)	(150,510)
Gross profit	254,490
Administrative expenses (W2)	(109,000)
Distribution expenses	(55,000)
Operating profit	90,490
Finance costs ($100,000 × 6% × 6/12)	(3,000)
Profit before taxation	87,490
Income tax expenses	(5,000)
Profit after taxation	82,490

Statement of financial position as at 31 December 20X1

Property, plant and equipment (120,000 – 35,000 – 8,500 (W1))	76,500
Inventories (W2)	13,990
Trade and other receivables (W4)	23,500
Cash and cash equivalents	110,500
Total assets	224,490
Share capital	3,000
Retained earnings (7,000 + 82,490 (P/L))	89,490
Loan	100,000
Trade payables	24,000
Interest accrual	3,000
Tax payable	5,000
Total equity and liabilities	224,490

(W1) Cost of sales

Opening inventory	16,000
Purchases	140,000
Depreciation	8,500
((120,000 – 35,000) × 10%)	
Closing inventory	(13,990)
	150,510

(W2) Closing inventory

Damaged inventory:	
Cost:	100
NRV ($130 – $40)	90
Impairment	10

Closing inventory = 14,000 – 10 = $13,990

(W3) **Administrative expenses**

Per trial balance	105,000
Irrecoverable debt write off	2,000
Increase in allowance	2,000
	109,000

(W4) **Receivables**

Per trial balance	30,500
Irrecoverable debts	(2,000)
	28,500
Allowance (3,000 + 2,000)	(5,000)
	23,500

(2) **Zbox**

Statement of profit or loss for year ended 31 December 20X1

	$
Revenue	760,000
Cost of sales (W1)	(316,000)
Gross profit	444,000
Administrative expenses (W2)	(142,000)
Distribution expenses (W3)	(239,000)
Profit before tax	63,000
Income tax expense	(25,000)
Profit after tax	38,000

Statement of financial position as at 31 December 20X1

	$
Assets	
Non-current assets	
Property, plant and equipment	370,000
($900,000 – $350,000 – $180,000 (W3))	
Current assets	
Inventories	51,000
Trade and other receivables	71,000
($65,000 + $6,000 (W4))	
Cash and cash equivalents ($59,000 – $6,000 (W4))	53,000
Total assets	545,000
Equity and liabilities	
Share capital	10,000
Retained earnings	464,000
($428,000 + £38,000 (P/L) – $2,000 dividend (W2))	
Trade and other payables	46,000
($42,000 + $4,000 (W1))	
Tax payable	25,000
Total equity and liabilities	545,000

(W1) Cost of sales

Opening inventory	43,000
Purchases	320,000
Day book error	4,000
Closing inventory	(51,000)
	316,000

The day book has been undercast. Therefore the correcting entry is:

Dr Purchases	$4,000
Cr Payables	$4,000

(W2) Administrative expenses

Per trial balance	145,000
Decrease in allowance	(1,000)
Dividend error ($0.2 × 10,000)	(2,000)
	142,000

Remember, ordinary dividends are not an expense. They are charged through retained earnings.

(W3) Distribution costs

Per trial balance	59,000
Depreciation	180,000
($900,000 × 20%)	
	239,000

(W4) Dishonoured cheque

No entries have been made. Therefore the following adjustment is required.

Dr Trade and other receivables	$6,000
Cr Cash and cash equivalents	$6,000

(3) P and S

(a)

	P	S
Gross profit margin (%) P: (550/950) × 100 S: (273/423) × 100	57.9	64.5
Operating profit margin (%) P: (350/950) × 100 S: (153/423) × 100	36.8	36.2
Receivables collection period (days) P: (200/950) × 365 days S: (150/423) × 365 days	76.8	129.4

(b)

Consolidated statement of profit or loss for the year ended 31 December 20X1

	$000
Revenue (950 + 423 – 50)	1,323
Cost of sales (400 + 150 – 50 + 10 (W1))	(510)
Gross profit	813
Administrative expenses (200 + 120)	(320)
Operating profit	493
Investment income (60 + 20)	80
Finance costs (0 + 5)	(5)
Profit before taxation	568
Income tax expense (100 + 33)	(133)
Profit after tax	435
Profit attributable to:	
Owners of P (bal fig)	410
Non-controlling interest (W2)	25
	435

(W1) PURP

$50k/100 × 20 = $10k

The double entry to adjust for this is:

Dr Cost of sales (P/L)	$10k
Cr Inventory (SFP)	$10k

(W2) Non-controlling interest

	$000
NCI % of S's PAT (20% × $135k)	27
NCI % of PURP (20% × $10k (W1))	(2)
	25

(4) **ABC and XYZ**

(a)

	ABC	XYZ
Quick ratio (X:1) ABC: ($120k + $5k)/$98k XYZ: ($94k + $52k)/$65k	1.3	2.2
Gearing (%) ABC: ($100k/($100k + $342k +$100k)) XYZ: ($50k/(50k + $334k +$50k))	18.5	11.5

(b)

**Consolidated statement of financial position
as at 31 December 20X1**

	$
Assets	
Non-current assets	
Property, plants and equipment	577,000
($240,000 + $297,000 + $40,000 FV uplift)	
Goodwill (W3)	60,000
Current assets	
Inventories	125,000
($75,000 + $56,000 – $6,000 PURP)	
Trade and other receivables	194,000
($120,000 + $94,000 – $20,000)	
Cash and cash equivalents	57,000
($5,000 +$52,000)	
Total assets	1,013,000
Equity and liabilities	
Equity	
Share capital	100,000
Retained earnings (W5)	511,500
Non-controlling interest (W4)	108,500
Non-current liabilities	
Loans ($100,000 + $50,000)	150,000
Current liabilities	
Trade and other payables ($98,000 + $56,000	143,000
– $20,000)	
Total equity and liabilities	1,013,000

(W1) Group structure

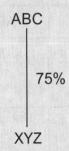

ABC

75%

XYZ

(W2) Net assets of XYZ

	$ Reporting date	$ Acquisition	$ Post-acquisition
Share capital	50,000	50,000	
Retained earnings	334,000	100,000	
FV (Uplift ($100,000 – $60,000)	40,000	40,000	
	424,000	190,000	234,000

(W3) Goodwill

	$000
Consideration	200,000
Less net assets at acquisition (W2)	(190,000)
Add NCI at acquisition	50,000
	60,000

(W4) Non-controlling interest

	$
NCI at acquisition	50,000
NCI % of XYZ post-acquisition retained earnings (25% × $234,000 (W2))	58,500
	108,500

(W5) **Retained earnings**

	$
100% of ABC	342,000
PURP	(6,000)
75% of XYZ post-acquisition retained earnings (75% × $234,000 (W2))	175,500
	511,500

Index

Index

KAPLAN PUBLISHING

Index

Index